T0384403

Routledge Revivals

We Too Can Prosper

First published in 1953, *We Too Can Prosper* is the outcome of a unique collaboration between Mr. Graham Hutton, the author, Mr. Geoffrey Crowther, his friend and fellow economist, and a panel of experts nominated by the employers' organisations and trade unions represented on the British Productivity Council. The Council invited the author and Mr. Crowther, as independent economists, to bring together the experience of the 66 Productivity Teams which visited America since 1949 and combine it with their own expert knowledge of economic conditions on both sides of the Atlantic, to throw light on Britain's industrial future.

The book covers an enormous range of subjects: from education to mechanisation, from consumers' habits to advertising, and from the rate of installing capital equipment to the roles of government, competition and 'bigness in business.' Painstakingly, simply and logically, the book shows that if the British people want to overcome recurrent economic crises and raise their standards of life, they can do so quickly, provided they organise to do so. This book will be of interest to students of economics, economic history and development.

We Too Can Prosper

The Promise of Productivity

Graham Hutton

Routledge
Taylor & Francis Group

First published in 1953
by George Allen & Unwin

This edition first published in 2022 by Routledge
4 Park Square, Milton Park, Abingdon, Oxon, OX14 4RN
and by Routledge
605 Third Avenue, New York, NY 10017

Routledge is an imprint of the Taylor & Francis Group, an informa business

© George Allen & Unwin, 1953

Publisher's Note
The publisher has gone to great lengths to ensure the quality of this reprint but points out that some imperfections in the original copies may be apparent.

Disclaimer
The publisher has made every effort to trace copyright holders and welcomes correspondence from those they have been unable to contact.

A Library of Congress record exists under LCCN: 53012088

ISBN: 978-1-032-26603-9 (hbk)
ISBN: 978-1-003-28911-1 (ebk)
ISBN: 978-1-032-26614-5 (pbk)

Book DOI 10.4324/9781003289111

We Too
Can Prosper

The Promise of Productivity

GRAHAM HUTTON

Published for the British Productivity Council
formerly the
Anglo-American Council on Productivity (U.K. Section)
by
George Allen and Unwin Ltd
RUSKIN HOUSE   MUSEUM STREET   LONDON

FIRST PUBLISHED IN MAY 1953
SECOND IMPRESSION JULY 1953

PRINTED IN GREAT BRITAIN
in 11 *point Times Roman*
BY UNWIN BROTHERS LIMITED
WOKING AND LONDON

Foreword

by the British Productivity Council

The Anglo-American Council on Productivity was responsible for organizing a unique form of international co-operation. Sixty-six teams, representing management, technicians and operatives, and drawn either from specific industries or from experts in certain techniques of service to industry generally, went to the U.S.A. from the U.K. under the Marshall Aid Plan to study the experience of America in raising productivity and to see which of the methods adopted there could be applied or adapted to the needs of British industry. All these teams have drawn up comprehensive reports and recommendations—in practically every case unanimous—and they are being closely studied in the various industries in the U.K., already with striking results.

Yet it appeared to the U.K. Section of the Council that there were many common threads running through the sixty-six reports, and if these could be drawn out and the conclusions skilfully analysed, not only industry as a whole but the general public too could learn much. Higher productivity is the brightest hope for every man, woman and child that the standard of living can be maintained and improved. Its importance and the universal concern in its achievement therefore cannot be exaggerated.

This assessment of the results of the experiment the U.K. Section thought could best be made by an independent observer who had not only studied the findings of the teams but was also personally acquainted with economic conditions in America and Great Britain. It was fortunate in persuading

Mr. Graham Hutton to undertake the task and in getting Mr. Geoffrey Crowther to agree to help him. A panel including representatives of the three constituent organizations forming the U.K. Section of the Council[1] was also established to offer its wide experience to the author.

That is the origin of the present book. The stimulating work which has resulted consists in the main of the author's own impressions, modified in the light of the advice of the Panel. The British Productivity Council—which has taken over responsibility for the work of the U.K. Section of the Anglo-American Council on Productivity—would wish to make clear that the members of the Council do not necessarily, either collectively or individually, subscribe to all the views expressed in it. Nevertheless the Council has no hesitation in warmly commending the book, with the challenge it sounds, to the attention of all who are interested in the improvement of the efficiency of British industry.

Chairman

Deputy Chairman

[1] The British Employers' Confederation, the Federation of British Industries and the Trades Union Congress.

Author's Preface

This book is about the implications for Britain today of the sixty-six A.A.C.P. Teams' experiences in comparing American and British industrial efficiency. Though these Teams had relatively little time in America, they brought much experience to bear on specialized segments of industry with which they had long been familiar in Britain. It is not surprising, therefore, that the implications for British industry which they emphasized were in many cases apparent to specialists in Britain and elsewhere before any Team ever landed in America.

Dr. L. Rostas, who made the classic statistical study of American and British productivity, said six years ago

by far the most important way of increasing the standard of living of the population is to increase productivity in manufacturing industry[1]

and he has since, and elsewhere, emphasized the more intensive use in America—and not only in manufacturing industry—of man-power and machinery.

I may be permitted to cite my own words of five years ago:

If, in fact, Britain—whatever her governments—fails to get a lot more new productive capital equipment installed during the next few years, and especially by the end of the E.R.P. and its annual subsidies in 1952, then the immediate post-war standards of living of Britons will come in jeopardy. No foreseeable change in the terms of foreign trading in our favour can offset such long-run unfavourable factors as the loss of our investment income from abroad, the end of E.R.P., the vast development of domestic manufacturing industries in foreign lands formerly our clients, and the increased and increasing export capacities of such countries as the U.S.A., Canada, Brazil, India, etc.—to which we must in all probability

[1] *Comparative Productivity in British and American Industry*, by L. Rostas, National Institute of Economic and Social Research Occasional Papers XIII, Cambridge University Press, 1948, p. 93.

add, in the next few years, Japan, Western Germany, Italy, Czecho-slovakia, Poland, and our near neighbours in Western Europe.[1]

Thus, the great value of the A.A.C.P. Teams' reports lies in the massive testimony they contain—by typical and responsible leaders from both sides of British industry, as well as from independent experts—in support of one conclusion: *British industrial productivity must be raised, and can be raised, comparatively quickly.* The testimony of 'theorists' and of 'practical businessmen'—of economists, trade unionists and managers—is thus, for once, unanimous. This book is an attempt to show what is involved in the raising of industrial productivity; what the evidence is for faith in it as an overriding national policy; and in what setting—of thought and action, values and beliefs—such a policy ought to be viewed if it is to succeed.

* * * * *

Productivity is perhaps best analysed under two main headings: first, the *internal factors* of productivity, i.e. the conditions of productivity which are internal to an industry or a company; and secondly the *external factors*, i.e. the conditions which are external to the *powers, authority, or control* of an industry or company. The external factors are therefore of wider scope—local, national, international. Naturally both sets of factors affecting productivity interact: a company will react to *external* factors in various *internal* ways. But on the whole the distinction, as a tool of analysis, is useful. Accordingly Chapters 2 to 5 inclusive are concerned with management, mainly with its internal factors of productivity; Chapters 6 and 7 with the human factors of productivity (labour, industrial relations, incentives, etc.) which can be both internal and external factors; and Chapters 8 and 9 with external factors proper.

* * * * *

The conception of this book is described in the Council's Foreword. It would not have been written without the help and counsel of my old friend and colleague, Mr. Geoffrey

---

[1] 'Without Capital for Survival,' by Graham Hutton, *The Nineteenth Century and After*, 1948, September, p. 121.

8

Crowther, to whose knowledge of economic conditions on both sides of the Atlantic I am deeply indebted. It has been brought to birth by a long process of discussion and deliberation, starting with a conference with the team leaders and a number of Trade Union representatives attended by Mr. Crowther and myself. The book also owes a great deal to the painstaking comments and suggestions of an advisory panel composed of:

Mr. Tom Williamson	General Secretary, National Union of General and Municipal Workers, and Member of the General Council of the Trades Union Congress.
Mr. E. M. Amphlett	Member of the Council of the British Employers' Confederation.
Mr. Edwin Fletcher	Secretary, Production Department, Trades Union Congress.
[1]Mr. Norman Pleming	Chairman and Managing Director, Associated Industrial Consultants Ltd.
[1]Mr. L. H. C. Tippett	An Assistant Director, The British Cotton Industry Research Association (Shirley Institute).
Mr. Bertram White	Technical Director, Federation of British Industries.

I gladly record especial gratitude to Mr. Sinclair Horne, the British Productivity Council's Information Officer, for his invaluable editorial aid. Only those who have had to struggle with drafts and re-drafts will appreciate what that means. And I wish to thank the tireless and long-suffering clerical staff of the B.P.C. for their highly efficient assistance.

Obviously, the book is not exactly what Mr. Crowther or I would have written on our own or what I did write in the first draft. It may be all the better for that. It has also the virtue that it represents an honest and co-operative attempt to secure the widest common ground for a statement of the problem of productivity, in which as far as possible the views of many economic groupings in the nation, often opposed on other than purely economic grounds, should be reconciled. So the book is neither the statement of one or two men's views, nor a mere official report drawn up by a 'neutral' rapporteur. It must

[1] Consultants to the Anglo-American Council on Productivity (U.K. Section).

stand or fall by the weight of its facts and arguments. And it must be commended or countered without regard to the personalities of its sponsors, counsellors or author. In this way it is perhaps something new in serious publications: something between the report of a special inquiry and the statement of a personal view.

The decisive factor in my own willingness to do the work was the serious eagerness with which very busy and responsible men from 'both sides of industry' were prepared to discuss the raw material of this book with such care for truth and such regard for national well-being. To me, as to them and to all members of the A.A.C.P. Teams, there appears no alternative to a raising of our industrial productivity but an accelerating, and ultimately catastrophic, fall in our standards of living.

The task may be harder, slower here than in other European countries. But nowhere is it more imperative. On its performance depend the defence of our country, the welfare of our people, and the future of our children.

Contents

1

Productivity and Progress

The Economics of Progress

At various times various catchwords prevail. These catchwords can be dangerous. The danger is not that they may be untrue. The danger lies in their becoming catchwords alone, mere substitutes for urgently essential thought and action. The danger today—particularly in Western Europe, particularly in Britain—is that 'productivity' will become merely a 'blessed word,' a catchword refuge, a word at which appropriate noises and gestures are made on all sides, but a word which becomes inoperative just when it should become operative.

What exactly does productivity mean?

Like 'efficiency,' 'rationalization' or 'scientific management,' it means almost the same thing as economics; something economical. It means avoidance of waste, lightening of work, producing more from the same ingredients while maintaining quality. It is impossible to think of it without thinking of progress. In terms of the social and economic betterment of humanity—Communist and non-Communist, agricultural and industrial, urban and rural—productivity is the indispensable condition of progress. Rising productivity means material progress. And in America, as in Britain, millions living at the highest material standards yet reached want still higher standards. Even more so do the bulk of humanity outside the West, not of white skin, who still live one poor meal away from starvation. Raising productivity is the condition of material progress.

But productivity of what?

Much misunderstanding arises here. Productivity is not production. Production is mere volume of output; it may be falling while productivity is rising; and vice versa. Productivity is the efficiency, the economy, the best organization of production. You can increase *production* easily by not counting the costs; by taking on more labour, buying more materials and fuel and power, and machines. But you only increase *productivity* if you turn out more output from the same quantity, or less, of the ingredients of production. If one hundred men in a factory produce the same number of the same goods over the same period as 125 men in another factory equal in all other respects, then although the *production* of both factories is the same the *productivity* of labour in the factory employing only one hundred men is obviously higher.

In America, where this 'blessed word' has naturally achieved pre-eminence, productivity generally means the fruitfulness of human work: physical output per man-hour or man-year. That is natural in a country where human skill has always been costly relative to other ingredients of production, and where machinery is therefore more plentiful and important. In Britain one could usefully talk about productivity per ton of fuel consumed; or productivity per machine-year (reckoned as the hours in a year a given machine was used as a percentage of the hours it *could* have been used); or productivity per unit of capital employed in the business for a month or year; and so on.

The main factors contributing to high industrial productivity or efficiency can be listed thus:

(1) Adequate buildings, plant and productive capital equipment, intensively used, and kept up-to-date by replacement;
(2) adequate skilled and unskilled labour, trained to use all the equipment fully;
(3) adequate and steady supplies of raw materials, fuel and power and transport and other services;
(4) managerial skills and technical knowledge, applied to the organization of production and lowering of costs;
(5) assured and potentially developable markets;
(6) a climate of opinion favourable to social order and political stability.

But in all industrial countries man-power is so much in demand and so costly and important that productivity has popularly come to be understood as the fruitfulness or efficiency of human work. Productivity is 'the relation of output to man-hours of effort expended,'[1] all other things remaining unchanged. This definition is as valid for mechanized industry as for our older manual crafts like bricklaying or carpentry and joinery.

There are two very important 'productivities' of human labour to be distinguished—first, that of 'operative' labour (generally, but not necessarily, wage-labour using the capital equipment directly); and secondly that of 'non-operative,' i.e. administrative, executive and clerical labour (generally, but not necessarily, salary-labour) which only directly uses building-space, furniture, office machinery, etc. If other things remained the same and a business were to expand its clerical staff by 50% and cut its operative staff by 50% chaos would ensue; costs per unit would soar. The opposite—doubling the operatives—could bring the same chaotic result. There is an art—and a by now fast-growing science—of so mixing the ingredients of production that the maximum of goods is produced per unit of human work, with the minimum of waste, and therefore at the minimum cost per unit. The art or science of good management cannot successfully be pursued without continuous attention to the productivity of *all* the ingredients in production. 'The best balance between (labour) productivity, machine utilization and costs must be struck.'[2] That continuous attention becomes good management.

Where that attention has been closest and most continuous in the last fifty years it has resulted in the widest and most rapid material progress: in the United States, in industrial Canada, in industrial Switzerland and Sweden, and—more sporadically, with severe interruptions, and in varying sectors of the industrial economy—in Britain, Belgium, France, Germany, Italy and other industrial countries of the West. The yardstick of good management, of good industrial relations, and of economic progress is the productivity of the ingredients of production.

In America at the end of last century Henry George called his famous book *Progress and Poverty*. He thought that increasing mechanization and industrialization must spell

---

[1] *Steel Founding* report, p. 1.   [2] *Cotton Spinning* report, p. xi.

increasing poverty. Though he was anti-Marxist, he shared Marxian analysis as far as that! But he would scarcely recognize the America—and the Americans' life—of today; and he would find little poverty which he could recognize in its nineteenth-century dress.

Material progress has made all this possible. In other countries, too, the terrible problems of nineteenth-century industrial—and agrarian—poverty have been overcome. Far from being the breeding-grounds of a sinking, impoverished, property-less proletariat, the cities and towns of Western lands have become centres of health, welfare and leisure, compared with those of but fifty years ago. Material progress alone can eliminate poverty. That is not to say that material progress is everything, or that material poverty is the worst of the evils that afflict mankind. Material progress is simply a great instrument for good. And the only way of achieving more material progress today—in Russia, America or Britain—is by lightening the load of human work, by increasing the load carried by machinery, and therefore by making the machinery and the non-human energy required to run it. That has been the only 'secret' of progress since the first sub-human hunter used his first tool—a weapon.

America and Productivity

Fifty years ago an American industrial worker turned out roughly the same amount in a day as his opposite number in Britain, Germany or France, and enjoyed broadly the same standard of living. Today, he turns out from two to five times as much; and eight hours' work buys for an American from one and a half to four times the quantity of goods that eight hours' work buys for a British or West European worker. After World War II consumption *per head* in America had risen more than 50% above its pre-war level. In Britain it remained at that level, even in 1951.

In 1951 the gross output of some two hundred million souls in Western Europe came to about $150,000 millions' worth of goods and services. In the same year, one hundred and fifty-two

16

million Americans turned out more than twice that value of goods and services.[1]

The productivity of labour in American industry has multiplied by three in the past fifty years, and is still rising by about one-half every ten to fifteen years. In Britain, it has moved erratically, largely due to the effects of two wars within forty years. Between those wars, recovery was effected and progress in the productivity of labour in industry went ahead fast after 1931. But the Second World War and its effects held up the advance; and not until 1947 was the productivity of 1939 reached. By 1951 it had risen some 15% above the 1939 figure, only to fall back again during 1952, owing to a recession in foreign trade and some disruption of industry due to rearmament. Industrial productivity in Britain today is broadly twice what it was fifty years ago. But it is still not rising as fast as the American,[2] and by comparison with it is a laggard.

Between 1950 and 1951 the mere *increase* in American output was more than the total output of Britain—yet America has only three times Britain's population, and has a smaller proportion of all her people at work in manufacturing industry. The U.S.A., with fewer than twenty-five millions engaged in manufacturing, produces one-third of all the world's goods, and one-half of its manufactures.

There are a few short qualifications to these comparisons. America has produced and installed eight horse-power behind every worker, whereas Western Europe has only produced and installed two and a half. America has been unscathed by direct warfare on her soil in the two World Wars, and has been in each of them for a shorter time. And America has not denuded her industries of capital to fight wars, and to recover from them. Yet when all that is said, no explanation has been furnished *why* America has so much capital equipment per worker, or so

[1] Figures cited by Mr. Paul Hoffman, then Administrator of the Marshall Plan, in 'Productivity for Freedom' article, London, *Sunday Times*, December 9, 1951.

[2] Indices of industrial productivity are subject to wide margins of error. For the above—and other—comparisons cited in this book the author has used the official and the London and Cambridge Economic Service's indices of industrial production, together with the official figures of employment, the national income, etc. See Appendix A.

much non-human energy to furnish the horse-power to it, or makes such intense use of machinery and replaces it so rapidly. These more illuminating explanations will emerge later. Here, we need only state the facts and proceed to apply their implications to Britain.

If British productivity were as high as American, many (indeed, most) of Britain's domestic economic problems would disappear. Problems caused for her by world conditions would, of course, remain—food supplies, shares of world trade, etc.— but the following advantages could be secured if British productivity were as high as American:

(a) an even larger defence burden could be shouldered with ease; but simultaneously

(b) import and payments deficits with the outside world could be managed without crises;

(c) the burden of taxation could be substantially lightened;

(d) consumers' standards of living could be substantially raised—either by increasing consumers' own spending-power, or by expanding State welfare services;

(e) hours of work could be reduced; and

(f) the savings of persons or businesses (or of both, in the nation as a whole) could be greatly increased, and invested in both technical progress at home and in the development of undeveloped (or under-developed) resources abroad.

It seems like a recipe for the millennium. Yet there is no particularly *American* secret about the recipe. The ingredients of that recipe are well known. In the past fifty years Americans may have performed what seem prodigies of production; yet when the sixty-six A.A.C.P. Teams between 1949 and 1952 made comprehensive inquiries in so many American industries (most of which they already knew by their own technical experience) not one could report that the U.S. prodigies of production were achieved by methods unknown, or technically impossible, in Britain. Moreover, it is noteworthy that over the whole range of manufacturing and mining industries in America, basic weekly hours of work (in contrast with hours actually worked) are not as many as in Britain, and that—as far as biologists, educationalists, psychologists, sociologists and the productivity teams themselves can tell—the skill and intelligence of the mass of American workers are not inherently superior to those of British and West European workers. Would any scientist expect them to become inherently superior in only two generations? If Americans can achieve these miracles of production it is by training, equipment and organization.

'Ah!' the European is inclined to object, 'but the American production set-up, taken as a whole, can afford to run with a vast amount of slack in the rope—idle plant, machinery not fully utilized, a bigger pool of temporarily unemployed labour, big stocks of raw materials always available. So a sudden spurt in total production, and in productivity, is always possible there. In Britain, or Europe, we have no slack anywhere: either in machinery, materials, man-power or reserves of capital.'

That may have been true in three periods of American economic development during the past fifty years: in and after the 1907 slump, the slump after World War I, and the Great Depression of 1929–35. But the spurt of American production and productivity has never been sudden. It has gone on steadily, cumulatively, for a century, and it has gone on even when there *was* slack in the rope. America entered the period of World War II with slack in her rope. It was the taking up of that slack which largely enabled her to fufil her own and her Allies' requirements without making her civilian consumers reduce their national standard of living. But our European objector forgets that America had also vastly to expand investment in productive capacity (largely by governmental saving and investment) after 1941, and that most Europeans and most Americans in 1945 expected wholesale unemployment of men and machines in America. Instead of that, the war-time slogan of Mr. Roosevelt which was reckoned a fantasy—'Sixty million jobs!'—has been realized, maintained, and exceeded. Both with and without rearmament, the production and the productivity of American industry have steadily mounted.

Take an example from peacetime, and during depression. In 1940 the average hourly wage in the American motor-car industry had been almost doubled compared with its level in 1934; yet the cost of the labour used for each car remained what it had been in 1934. Better machines, used better, under better management, had so raised the productivity of the labour that the wage rate could almost double in six years. 'It was a better automobile for the consumer's money. The wage rate was nearly doubled, and there were more people at work in the industry. The owners of the business were also getting a better return on their investments.'[1]

All this is not to say, of course, that a highly geared economy—the most highly capitalized, the most highly dependent on new investment in the world—is not highly delicate, highly vulnerable, highly volatile. It is. But the American economic system enjoys one vast advantage over others. It may be more volatile. It may put a crushing task and responsibility on the men who run it. They may fail, now and then, to measure up to both that task and that respon- sibility. But, after all counter-balancing items in the comparison with European economic systems have been cancelled, the American economy retains its striking advantage: it delivers the goods—more and more of them. That is because of its enormous and growing productive *potential*. That potential is overwhelmingly one of machines, of *non*-human energy, and of capital equipment of all kinds, coupled with the willingness of people to get the most out of the machines. So the overcoming of social and economic problems in America is, more than anywhere else on earth, not so much a matter of human work and sacrifice as of good organization, good management and good ideas applied in good work.

To have such vast and non-human productive potential without good organization, management and the will to make it all work, is wasteful and vexatious; but at any rate there is then the *chance* that people can be taught to become sensible and efficient, and therefore to make themselves highly prosper- ous. On the other hand, to have good organization, manage- ment and the will to work, but no productive equipment, is more wasteful and vexatious still: for then the *chance* of becoming highly prosperous can only be realized by much more human labour and sacrifice, spread over a long time in

1 'Productivity for Freedom' article by Paul Hoffman, London, *Sunday Times*, December 9, 1951.

which the necessary equipment has to be made and installed. The point is that more mechanical equipment means less physical labour, on the whole, but more and better human work to make the machines give of their best. If you want more capital equipment, to make human work lighter and more fruitful, you must first save to make the new equipment (or to buy it from abroad); and secondly, you must then train, reorganize and re-deploy human work so as to get the most from the new equipment.

Either way there is no doing away with human work. If it is less needed to produce the original goods, it will be more needed to make and maintain the machines which are now producing them. Human work—which is everywhere a kind of cost—cannot be stabilized or standardized in an industrial country. It must be itself in constant adaptation and development to match the constant adaptations and development of machines. Otherwise both industry and the people's standards of life will stagnate.

It is worth looking into all this more closely before we pull up the curtain on the main argument.

Labour and Capital

No two words are more misused and misconceived than these. To look at them closely, let us compare two superficially dissimilar systems: the American and the Russian.

The American prodigies of production today, as compared with their rough equality to West European performance fifty years ago, are due to a large number of technical excellences. Among them are more *non*-human energy per worker, more mechanical aids per worker, more intense use (and therefore more rapid obsolescence and replacement) of machinery and equipment, and more skilled management of these and other elements of production. All this boils down to one phrase, 'more capital, more used, and better organized.'

The Soviet Russian economic system seems at the opposite extreme from the American. Russia started as the laggard of all Western nations in the industrial handicap fifty years ago. She has still a surplus of human beings and a deficiency of capital

21

equipment of all kinds. The percentage of annual output forcibly 'saved' from consumption in Russia is perhaps double the *proportion* saved and invested in America. Yet even today—after the rigours of forced saving and forced labour for a generation—the *accumulation* of capital equipment in Russia, to help her human beings, is slow compared with that of America; and if you take it per head of population, even slower. The logical result in Russia has been to use human energy and toil inhumanely, intensively, for very long hours, even by forced and State-directed labour, in order to create machinery and get the best productivity out of it.

Conversely, America has had (apart from temporary and short periods) a long-run scarcity of human beings relative to all her other economic resources, from the time of Alexander Hamilton's famous *Report on Manufactures* in the closing years of the eighteenth century. The history of the American tariff is largely the history of the development of two things: the natural resources and the (originally) artificial industries of America, to a point at which no tariff protection is needed (though it still exists). The costly American labour, and the development of the country's rich resources by capital equipment—both behind tariff protection—resulted in a snowball process. That process was constantly accelerated between 1880 and 1929 by vast immigration, which settled mainly in the ever-growing industrial towns and cities.

After 1929 when large-scale immigration stopped, population went on expanding surprisingly, especially after 1945[1]; but American labour, even so, became *relatively* more scarce because of the far more rapid accumulation of capital equipment. (The process was only temporarily interrupted by the Great Depression of 1929–35.) So without straining sense one could say that in American industry the attitude of management and of organized labour has been to treat machinery as expendable, and to husband human labour; to shorten hours of work and to raise rates of pay. And in order to do this, the policy has been to utilize the ever-growing mechanical equipment to the fullest possible extent. This has led, logically, to the policy

[1] From 1945 to the end of 1953 the U.S. population will have risen by 20 millions or 12½%, the U.K. population only 1·3 millions, or 2½%.

of 'junking' machines and of replacing them with better machines, more rapidly than anywhere else; and therefore of making machinery in order to make more and more machinery, in order to demand less and less of human toil. That does not mean that 'junking' is always right or fruitful. It does, however, mean that—other things being equal—newer machines coupled with newer methods of organizing human work will 'pay off' in lower unit costs.

The need to develop America's natural resources, the unprecedented growth of her wide internal markets, her freedom from damage by warfare for three generations, her vast expansion of population, and her technical progress, all combined to put a heavy premium upon saving and investment, upon the profitability of industry and communications, and upon mechanical and technical productive apparatus. In that way, America developed the priceless asset of a set of industries and services, all connected with machinery and tool-making, technical research, chemistry, metallurgy and the maintenance of plants and equipment. The snowball of capital gathered more and more new capital as it rolled on. The number of professional workers in research laboratories today is already almost five times larger than it was twenty years ago, and expenditure on research has risen even faster. Indeed it is probable that the investment opportunities created by technological research will in most years exceed the supply of investment-seeking funds provided by corporate and personal savings and pension funds.[1]

Thus the American system has succeeded in keeping its rate of capital-creation more rapid than Russia or any other nation has ever been able to do. The logical result has been the opposite to that so far achieved in Russia. In America the machines are treated inhumanly, and human beings humanely. The human beings in America are paid the highest real wages on earth, in order to let the machines do most of the real toil and make more machines. It is, moreover, highly profitable to all concerned.

This is far from theoretical. How otherwise can the history

[1] Figures and assessment from article by Prof. Sumner H. Schlichter of Harvard University in *Daily Telegraph*, April 29, 1952.

and current experience of the American and Russian economic systems be explained—in terms which hold water? Accordingly, what is implied for the rest of us in Western Europe, particularly in Britain, who are neither Russian nor American, neither completely competitive and free-enterprise nor completely totalitarian? To answer that in broad outline is the aim of this book.

The population in the productive age-group in Britain—perhaps alone among Western countries—has virtually ceased to grow.[1] Moreover, Britain will be an ageing country in any case until 1970. Those of the citizens who are in productive age-groups will constantly have to support more pensioners; and if they reverse recent trends and have more babies, they will have to support them, too, for at least another eighteen years or so. In Britain, the electorate between twenty-one and forty-four is no longer bigger than that aged forty-five and over. That fact has already led British governments of opposing political outlook to urge an extension of the retirement age and a postponement of the age at which full retirement pensions should become payable by the State. At the other end of human life, among the young, West Europeans seem to want the longer terms of costlier yet freer education that Americans have—which, again, means more 'passengers' on the backs of the productive portion of the population. That productive portion seems also to want, as in America, shorter working-hours and higher pay. All this means much more capital equipment.

Despite American and other aid from abroad, and despite the highest taxation in the Western world, it seems probable that the productive capital apparatus of British industry (both State and privately owned) had just about reached its pre-war proportions *per head of working population* by the end of 1952.[2] One cannot be dogmatic on so elusive an economic concept. But one can be quite dogmatic in comparing the *rates* of creation and installation of net new productive capital equipment in America and in Britain as between 1938 and 1952—that is, the rate of *increase* in the total of available productive capital equipment in the two countries as a whole, whether it

[1] Only 400,000 are expected to be added to the 23 millions of 'gainfully occupied' in the next ten years.   [2] See Appendix B.

24

was publicly or privately owned. The rate of increase has been steady, swift and vastly cumulative in America. In Britain it has been wildly erratic (a negative quantity for years during the war, when capital was consumed and not even maintained); and even if the calculation be subject to wide margins of error, it remains safe to say that if there has been any net increase in capital equipment *per worker employed* at all since 1938, it is insignificant beside the magnitude and rate of increase in capital apparatus per worker employed in America.

Two examples should suffice. In 1951, housing, schools and electricity supply together took more new capital than the whole of British manufacturing industry[1]; yet the economic contribution of manufacturing industry, both to exports and to the total of home trade, is incomparably greater than that of housing, education and electricity supply together. In America, housing, schools and electricity supply took but a fraction (about one-third) of manufacturing industry's total of new capital. Again, private investment (alone) in America since 1949–50 has been running at the rate of some $50,000 millions a year (nearly twice Britain's total national *output* in a year), and total American investment at about $63,000 millions a year. That means that American productive *capacity* is increasing by about the equivalent of some $10,000 millions to $15,000 millions a year: i.e. by at least one-third to one-half Britain's total output in a year. Yet America has only three times Britain's population. That would indicate for Britain an annual outlay on capital of about £4,000 millions to £5,500 millions—which is two and a half to three times the actual outlay on *all* capital in Britain (of which 25% is on housing alone).

Not all of these vast American additions to capital are in manufacturing industry: many are in basic utilities and services, in agriculture and mining, and in stocks and work in progress. But the comparative magnitudes are astounding, and the consequent *rate* of increase in American productivity per worker per year leaves British productivity far in the rear, and West European productivity as a whole even farther behind.

[1] Inaugural address to Institute of Transport by the President, Mr. C. T. Brunner, on October 14, 1952.

The disparity is of such a magnitude that scarcely any imaginable future cut-back in American investment in new equipment could bring the American and European rates of new investment parallel.[1]

Now if, as most people in West European nations seem to desire, the young are to have longer education (entering work later), the old are to retire earlier, pay for all working people is to rise nearer to the American levels, and hours of work are to be fewer, there will only be one ingredient of all production which can do the trick and produce the wherewithal to defray the cost. That ingredient is capital: productive equipment of all kinds—machinery, fuel and power, transport and every non-human adjunct to human labour. If that is not earned, worked for, 'saved for,' and fashioned, and installed, and organized to do the job, the job will not be done, because it cannot be done any other way.

To that extent, the Russians are logical. They cannot lighten the curse of Adam without capital; and to get capital *fast enough for their purposes*, the Russian people cannot be allowed to choose where, or how, or how long, or for what they work; how much they shall spend or save; or what their standard of everyday consumption shall be. To get real, appreciable, material progress, capital is the first priority. That is a common ground—the only common ground—between Moscow, Belgrade, Chicago, London, Delhi and Pekin. How best to get the capital, and who is to own it once it is 'saved' and in production—these are knotty and debatable points. But they do not affect the real issue. The real issue is clear and simple: no material progress, no easing of burdens, no increase in either publicly or privately distributed welfare, without better utilization of the capital you have—or, preferably, both that and the installation of new capital equipment as well.

The alternative to this is what the under-developed peoples and their governments have to do: namely, work their peoples harder, for lower standards of living. Countries swimming in natural resources cannot develop them—not even with populations that breed like flies—without hard work and forced

---

[1] This point receives more detailed attention in Chapter III.

'saving' on the part of their own people (or borrowing the results of work and saving from more developed peoples). Even the more developed peoples—Americans, Britons, Netherlanders, Swiss, Scandinavians, Frenchmen, Germans, Canadians —must still forgo some current consumption (or capital investment) at home if they are to send capital abroad to develop other peoples' resources.[1]

Today tools do most of the work, not men. The skill and energies of men are to a steadily increasing extent concentrated in making tools and seeing that they are powered to do their jobs. Masses of men and materials, by themselves, are not— and for all of human history have never been—enough.

Britain and Productivity

Britain's position in the world is peculiar. She has long been—and still is—more dependent on customers and suppliers all over the globe than any other great or middling power, and more than any other country except Denmark, Belgium and Switzerland. She was first in the so-called Industrial Revolution. She first discovered and applied virtually every one of the principles of mechanized manufacture which America now calls mass-production. She once had a monopoly of the manufacture and export of machines. Her people long—from 1890 to 1939—lived on a higher material standard than their current work and output warranted, because they imported much food and industrial raw material as the yearly interest and dividends on savings which their forefathers had invested abroad. They had to sell most of these investments—the very best of them— in 1914–18 and in 1939–45. After 1945, therefore, they came back with a jolt to a 'pay as you go' or 'pay as you can earn' basis, in an unsentimental world. It is worth recalling a little economic history today.

Charles Babbage, Lucasian Professor of Mathematics in the University of Cambridge, wrote and published in 1832 a

[1] British governments of both parties have been embarrassed in pointing this out to the electorate since the war ended. It is the short answer to all those —neo-imperialists and neo-totalitarians alike—who cry out for swift development of the Commonwealth's or sterling area's undeniably large natural resources.

treatise *On the Economy of Machinery and Manufactures*. In it can be found many of the principles of modern 'scientific management.' He set them out in such a way that they can be summarized thus:

Machine-manufactures economize in human effort and time. They increase human power. They convert raw materials into end-products in quantities which human hands could never compass. Now human efforts, even though they require trifling force, become intensely fatiguing—even torturing—after constant repetition. So machines should accomplish all such operations. But machines must have 'long runs' to be economical. All consumers' wants should therefore become standardized and simplified. Manufacture by machines can then be on such a scale that units of the end-product become very cheap. The machines themselves should become standardized, for the same reason. Those countries with the biggest reserve of machinery will then have the highest standards of living, the least human toil, the greatest material rewards, and the greatest material power.

But at the opening of this century the Mosely Industrial Commission of trade unionists, which visited the chief industrial areas of the United States, reported that in many cases American employers had more mechanization, or could run their work in more shifts per day or week, or used more fuel and power, or could show greater productivity per worker and per machine, than their opposite numbers in Britain could.[1] The only substantial criticism of American manufactures made by them, and by Dr. Shadwell in his *Industrial Efficiency*, which compared American industrial capacities with those of Germany and Britain, was that they were of poor finish compared with those of Britain and Germany.[2] (Even that criticism could not be made of American manufactures today.) American industrial and commercial progress during the last fifty years is striking. It must raise searching questions about the future of fifty-one million souls in the British Isles. And no practicable rate of emigration from these islands can solve the problem.

[1] These reports were published in 1903 by the Co-operative Printing Society Ltd., Manchester.

[2] *Industrial Efficiency*, Arthur Shadwell, Longmans, 2 vols., 1906.

It is still apparently necessary to remind ourselves that the First War dislocated the British economy to an extent that no other country experienced, and that the strain of ten years of world war in the last thirty-eight years should not be ignored in seeking an explanation of present difficulties. . . . Larger capital resources were needed. At the same time the pressure of taxation on profits, increased by war and post-war needs, slowed down the accumulation of capital in business hands. Resources have been further depleted, in the long period of rising prices which has followed the suspension of the gold standard, by inadequate allowances for depreciation of plant and replacement of stocks. . . . So much for the effects of war; for our present purpose they would not be so important if they did not re-inforce the influence of a fundamental change in industry operating in the present century independently of war— the enormously increased importance of fixed capital equipment. What American comparisons do bring out is the decisive influence on manufacturing costs of capital equipment. Industry is no longer carried on mainly by small or moderate-sized firms, relying on the skill of workpeople, and using an amount of capital per head which can be collected in a few months. If conditions can be established for the use of mechanical equipment—the 'mass-production' of popular discussion—and finance for the equipment can be secured, almost miraculous reductions in costs are possible. At varying rates, all industries in all countries are moving in the direction of more and more capital equipment per worker.[1]

Yet the two world wars were in fact only the major causes of delay in the accumulation of British capital equipment; of the running-down of capital, when America (and Canada and other countries) were enabled to build it up; and of the incurring of vast new external indebtedness (and of the loss of old and well-earning assets) which is now a new net drain upon Britain's output and resources. But before 1914 an unfavourable trend in Britain's economy had set in, about which economists in various countries were already writing. It was a relatively declining trend of capital-creation per worker employed, and of relative volume and terms of trade. It is not America alone which has caught up with, and surpassed, Britain in industrial matters. That was the evidence of many British experts—and

[1] 'The Campaign against Monopoly and Restrictive Practices,' by Sir Henry Clay, *Lloyds Bank Review*, April 1952, p. 17.

officials—between the two wars. The process has been long at work. It seems to have been a process the responsibility for which must be shared by successive governments of all political parties, and by successive generations; a process for which the nation as a whole must bear responsibility.

It is quite wrong for anyone to nourish the idea that 'productivity' is some secret which can put Britain back almost overnight at the head of the field in the industrial stakes. History never really repeats itself. Times, peoples, circumstances and relationships are always changing. As we hope to show later, deep differences of philosophy, social outlook, politics and national custom enter into this picture. So do human valuations—things by which men set more than material or economic store. For example, leisure and lack of fuss and fuming and flurry is worth *some* (though how much?) sacrifice in material standards of living to the overwhelming majority of Englishmen.

Yet the British *want* higher material standards of living; they want the State to be able to undertake more of this or that on their behalf, from defence to State welfare; and they want less work, an easier life, more leisure and pleasure. To this extent they are as human and 'materialistic' as any Swede, Swiss, or American. Do they, however, see the implications of their wants? And if they see them, will they act on them accordingly?

Without the two world wars, Britain would have had 'world enough and time' to make gradual social and economic adjustments to her changing position in a changing world. But the Second World War caused a graver convulsion in the British economy than the British people at first suspected. The gravity of that abrupt change was screened from them by loans and lend-lease from others during the war, by living on capital (the vanishing of which did not become apparent till much later), and by the swift and vast incurring of British debts to other countries. After the war, when the Allied subsidies ceased, huge new borrowings, the Marshall Plan, and (more recently) increased borrowings from the sterling area countries, masked the essential nakedness of the land.

Not until 1952—the original end-year of the European

Recovery Programme, financed by the U.S.A.—did it begin to become plain to the overwhelming majority of the British people that post-war Britain would have to earn her material standards of life competitively, in a world in which the terms of trade had set against her, and in which both her military and economic vulnerability had immeasurably increased. It is not a question whether persons and institutions tried to warn the British public. Their warnings were largely ineffectual because most of the British people continued from 1945 to 1951–52 to live better, and they were not prepared to listen till productivity fell—and standards with it—after 1951–52 and the end of E.R.P. Drastically limited in her soil and the power to feed her teeming urban masses, intent on retaining something like her familiar democracy and anxious to avoid losing the social gains of the last fifty years (demanding, in fact, even better services and amenities for her people), Britain must look to one solution: higher productivity.

Higher productivity *can* be achieved in Britain, and in many ways. It is the most promising way to higher standards of living and lower economic burdens. But *American* standards of productivity cannot be achieved over-night. And something else should be said. It touches the less tangible elements mentioned above—human valuations, ideals, sentiments. Higher productivity can be achieved in any industrial country without having to imitate, slavishly, every ingredient in 'the American way of life.' American production methods are largely the familiar production methods of other countries, carried to the highest degree of application, with most mechanization. They do not necessitate the adoption of American social habits, any more than they demand the American legal or political system for their working out.

To have more simplification, specialization and standardization—or to have more intense use of machinery—you do not need to turn out American-style end-products. A simplified, standardized, specialized product can still look and be British, or French, or German. The proof of this is in the distinction, quality and high productivity of Swiss and Scandinavian manufacturing. And it must always be borne in mind that Britain can show some branches of manufacturing in which

31

quality and productivity are higher, and selling prices and costs lower, than any which American makers can furnish—such utterly unlike manufactures as ships, biscuits and bicycles spring to mind.

The arguments, the comparisons, turn upon the *average* performance. It is the overwhelming evidence of the A.A.C.P. Teams that the *average* performance in American productivity is far higher than the average in Britain. (Indeed, it must be so; otherwise the global figures of output and man-power would make nonsense.) How the British average can best be raised— by a widely dispersed improvement in each industry, or by concentrating on improvements among the medium and small-size firms—ought not to be discussed here; but it is right to mark its position on our stage before we raise the curtain.

If fifty-one million souls are to survive in a country which can be tucked into Texas; if they are to maintain even their present standards of living, let alone advance them; if they are to preserve a democratic way of life, a system of State welfare costly in administrative man-power, and a network of family relationships stretching all over the globe (which forms much of Britain's economic and defensive strength)—then they must at least do one of the following things, and they may find themselves having to do all three at once:

(*a*) use all their productive equipment (old and new) more intensively, make it work faster and more fruitfully;

(*b*) save more as a nation, and plough the savings into net new *productive* (and not only social or consumers') capital equipment for both State and private enterprise —road and rail equipment, ships, machines, tools, plant;

(*c*) make human beings work more effectively in the same hours, or work longer hours.[1]

---

[1] Work—even hard work—is not an evil. That we might all learn in unpleasant ways if there were none of it! Given the interest and the identification of the worker's creative sense in the work, it approximates to that of an artist; and artists are notoriously more wedded to their work than to anyone or anything else, and get their keenest pleasure from it despite the fact that they try more of the other pleasures than most men do. For everyone to work harder for longer hours would, of course, be a reversal of human progress; but it might

But productive capital equipment is available in Britain. It can be increased fairly quickly without real hardship. And it can be much more intensively used than it is used at present. It is only sensible to get the best out of existing plant before adding to it: to make existing equipment yield all of which it is capable, without straining any human being.

Apart from these alternatives, Britain faces only one possibility: to abandon her post-war attempts to maintain her position as a significant Power in a dark and dangerous world. This we do not seriously consider. Such a policy amounts to doing nothing. If Britain does nothing to raise her economic efficiency while present economic trends in the world continue, her people will lose even their present standards of living—and vastly worsen their and their children's position in the world— in a few years, and at most in a generation. Once that happens, revolutionary changes in many other British institutions would have to happen. For example, democracy, freedom to bargain and move and choose work, the rule of law as the West knows it, and so on, would have to go by the board. Remorseless and rapid reductions in nations' standards of life have always quickly led to dictatorships. The rigidities of feudalism and serfdom sprang from the collapsing Roman empire, and lasted a millennium. After all, only dictatorships can enforce utter economic equality at lower standards of life upon all citizens— as in cities (or countries) besieged, in all ages.

Whether one approaches the British economic problem by comparisons with Russia and America and other countries, whether one does so by examining Britain's own internal needs, or whether one does so from the angle of Britain's position in the post-war world, one is driven to the conclusion that the only long-run solution of problems which have already recurred, with alarming frequency and ominously increasing intensity, is continuously to raise the productivity of British industry,

---

well bring vast progress. The fact that in many instances more work could easily be done by Britons now, without working extra hours, may be an indication not of progress, but of regress. In the short run, more work per man may be the only solution of the country's present difficulties. It seems silly not to face and canvass these ultimate issues impartially since they are not strictly issues of economic values but of human valuations.

farming and other basic services.[1] There is no solution waiting off-stage in the wings. British management and work, British quality and inventiveness, must do the job. The most efficient, least burdensome, way of doing it is to organize human management and labour in such ways that machinery can do much more work.

[1] This book is not concerned with agriculture and cannot consider its problems. But the need to raise the productivity of British agriculture—already raised substantially, though at great cost—is a matter of common knowledge.

2
Better Management, Higher Productivity

All qualified observers agree that American industrial management is on the average more effective than British management.
It is different; in many ways it might even offend British ideas
or susceptibilities; but it is demonstrably more effective. It gets
better results.[1] The generality of American management is
nearer the best than is the generality of British management
near its best. It is therefore worthwhile asking: Why, and what,
is management?

Why Management at all? What is its function?

In communist and capitalist countries, in Oriental as in
Western lands, there are now two identical trends: first,
increasingly to industrialize and mechanize; and secondly, to
form fewer and bigger productive units whether they are owned
by the State or by private persons. These trends inevitably
mean more responsibility for, and demand more skill from, the
'administration' and 'executive' of the productive units.

Everyone knows that enormous economies have been made
possible by mass-production. Fewer people know that mass-
production can also be massively wasteful—can make losses on
a gigantic scale—unless the administration and the executive
(the management) keep constant watch on the relative rates of
consumption of raw materials, labour, fuels, machine-service,
transport and so on.

[1] Cf. Conclusion No. 1 of *Management Accounting*: 'The most significant
factor in America leading to high production at low cost is efficient management'; and the imposing Appendix of twenty-two extracts from separate reports,
in the same sense, on p. 21 of *Education for Management*.

The more that processes which were formerly done by human labour are mechanized, the more it becomes necessary to keep the machines going—that is, if monumental losses are not to be made, and the goods are not to turn out dearer by the 'better' methods than by the old. Cheaper goods of the same quality, more goods entering into a worker's standard of living, a bigger yield of the same quality of goods for the same outlay of human labour and other ingredients of production—these results, desired by all peoples, can only occur as an outcome of close attention to productive processes. It is an attention as close as the individual craftsman gave to his work in the Middle Ages. That is management. The more skilled it is, the better the results for everybody.

The most effective management will naturally arise in the most favourable atmosphere. There are many ways of inducing good management. It is a pity that the managers of the vast Soviet industrial trusts—say, the textile or light engineering trusts—cannot exchange places for a year or two with managers in Britain and America. The atmosphere favouring good management in Russia is a very different atmosphere from that favouring it in Britain or America. The rewards for good management in Russia (relative to the rewards for skilled or unskilled labour) seem to be higher than they are (relative to the rewards for such labour) in Britain or America. But the penalties for bad management in Russia are very different.

Modern industrial management is both an art and a science; it partakes of a science in its concern with machinery and technique and of an art in its concern with human beings. Above all, the scope and responsibility of management are bound to increase with more mechanization. So the best kind of management will demand a particular kind of human being: he will be one who likes power and responsibility (which can be dangerous); but also one who is both artist and scientist enough not to do wrong and silly things with the human beings and the machines and processes under his control; and one who can work well as a member of a team. The kind of industrial management which is now developing—in Russia as in America, and everywhere where large-scale production takes place—puts more and more of a premium on the *marshalling*

36

and proper *combining*, the *varying* and appropriate *adapting*, the *planning* and due *changing* of all ingredients of production: of models, processes, tools, human skills, raw materials, and fuel and power.

Many people think it is the 'soulless corporation,' the limited liability company, the amorphous body of shareholders represented by a board of directors, or the public board answerable to nobody in particular, which is responsible for the complex and minutely planned methods of modern industry. It is nothing of the kind. Those methods—and the problems of modern management, the demands made on managers—would still be what they are if every large-scale unit were still owned by one man, who still worked in the shop and called his workers by their first names. The plain fact is that such a man today would have to employ just as complex a management as a big public concern, in order to cope successfully with the many-sided technicalities of large-scale production. The many-sidedness itself is responsible: the complexities, the inter-lockedness mentioned earlier, the ever-increasing round-about-ness of production, the interdependence of one process or material with another. All that is increasing, and must increase, as new and more intricate relationships—of things, processes and groups of men—are required (and invented) to turn out what the world needs.[1]

In short, modern industrial management becomes more and more detached from ownership of the enterprise, the larger the undertaking; and particularly so when the enterprise is publicly owned. It is an art and science on its own, in its own right. It has increasingly developed as the techniques of industry have developed. It has become a technical profession—as much of a productive service as skilled labour, which (in a sense) it is. Russia rightly lays the highest stress on it, and gives it the highest rewards. It increasingly resembles the administration of

[1] To mention one instance which has nothing to do with raising productivity (indeed it reduces it): most modern governments require both public and private enterprises to 'carry' a staff of clerical workers to act as tax-gatherers, keepers of records and statistics for government agencies, and file-clerks serving government departments responsible for health, unemployment relief and social services. The public may gain from all this. But it is at a cost in terms of physical output sacrificed, though the cost is not shown in any one account.

a country, of an army in battle, of a ship at sea. At its best it is a two-way process, reaching down from the top to the extremities, but reaching back from the extremities to the top. Only so can the ramifying complexities of modern industrial production be comprehended and 'managed.'

As these complexities arise both in the scientific and the human fields—in processes and technique as well as in industrial relations and organization—management itself has outstripped the capacities of any one man. No individual could possibly discharge the responsibility for running all the departments of even a medium-sized modern industrial concern. The increasing complexity, specialization and technicality of modern industrial processes have been reflected in parallel developments in management. Management itself, therefore, has had to become more complex, specialized and technical. As soon as that happens to any human function, more learning and skill are required to discharge the function successfully.

The most embarrassing aspect of all this is that techniques have progressed much faster than the organizations and institutions of human beings. Human minds may have kept pace. Their institutions have not. So a good management, trying to keep abreast of rapidly advancing techniques, must continuously learn new things, train new people (and re-train many of the old), alter familiar ways of doing things, upset traditional methods, and in general be prepared promptly to reorganize, adopt and adapt. The kind of men required to staff such a management are not ordinary. They may *begin* as ordinary, but they have to be trained to become extra-ordinary. Like good officers, they need training and much experience. Some must be familiar with the technical problems of the *non-human* ingredients in production—materials, machines, fuels, processes—and others with the far more intricate, and less scientifically soluble, problems of the *human* beings involved. They must respect each other's speciality and good faith, as technicians. And they must all be economically co-ordinated by good administration.[1] Otherwise a firm's, an industry's, a country's power and resources will fail, and its people's

[1] Administration today could be defined as the art of keeping specialists in order, in touch with each other, and in effective operation.

standards of life fall, as its techniques of production lag behind others.

Management in America

Many A.A.C.P. Teams beside the four concerned with training for management and technical education[1] found that industrial management in America was not only a business or a career, but was also recognized on all sides as the mainspring of the high American productivity, as a service crucial to national well-being, as a function deserving of social respect and esteem, and as the prime contributor to the nation's strength and progress. It was as much of a clearly marked profession as, say, that of a civil engineer, doctor or lawyer. And owing to the complexities of industrial production, it necessitated special training and experience, of many aptitudes and in many fields. It is useful to consider all this under separate heads.

Management is, by any European standard, extremely handsomely rewarded in America. It provides the quickest bridge to leadership in industry, and therefore to a comparatively quick fortune, at any rate for those who can 'make the grade' in a highly competitive society. Throughout this book, therefore, it is of the utmost importance to bear in mind that this superficially-seeming *internal* condition of American productivity—management—partakes very heavily of *external* factors, too. (These find their exposition in Chapters 8 and 9.) If the American people to a man, woman, and child did not so esteem industry, industrial techniques, industrial progress, machinery, inventiveness and initiative, newness, and the organization of all of these by management—if they did not respect them as the sources of their national defence, strength and well-being—there probably would not be the rewards for that management, or the keen competition among young men to enter it, or the ample and excellent facilities for their training.[2]

[1] *Education for Management; Training of Supervisors; Training of Operatives;* and *Universities and Industry.*
[2] But see p. 122 for a warning sign, which is appearing even in America, about the strain on management.

Every perceptive European visitor to America perceives that, in a society lacking Europe's aristocratic and medieval distinctions, the captain of industry is a hero-type for adult men and women. It is certainly so in American towns and cities; and it is nourished by not a few in American universities, colleges, high schools, and farms. (The young have never seeped away from the farms to the cities as rapidly and voluminously as during the last twenty years.) That is not to say that in America material rewards alone determine the high social status, 'social significance' and national esteem enjoyed by captains of industry, top-flight executives, and leading managers of industrial and commercial concerns. That would be tantamount to saying that in America *only* one's income determines one's social status or public esteem: a notable fallacy in view of *The Social Register*, 'society' south of Mason's and Dixon's line, and some other sources of social or public distinction.

The right order of reasoning seems to be that the industrial leader in America took over the role of the pioneer. A century ago the pioneer was the hero of most Americans—and of not a few European children. Today, the far horizons and the wide open spaces still lie ahead; but the pioneers are the leading technicians, the captains of industry (the very term 'captain' is reminiscent of pioneer days), and the ablest managers of the national resources. The goal has long been, and is still, a continuously rising material standard of welfare, more leisure in which to enjoy it, and a fuller and freer life. Americans may seem to Europeans to have reached and passed that goal. But Americans do not think so. And it ill becomes any European today to sneer at the American concept of management's duties, social status, and reward, when it 'pays off' so handsomely to every soul in a nation, and in addition helps half the world.

Another aspect of American management, noted by many Teams and other observers, is that the function, scope, and authority of management are more widely recognized and assented to *inside* the firm, factory or concern. Team after Team noted the cordial relations between operatives and management, and between different administrative departments

40

and management executives. 'The controller's department are on the whole regarded as friendly guides rather than as blood-hounds or watch-dogs.'[1] You would expect much of this to follow from the nation-wide acceptance of, and esteem for, the role of management. But it is immensely important in practice, because it enormously facilitates all processes of management, it saves time and energy, and it results in something like a first-class 'chain of command' in a ship, or an army, or first-class co-ordination and morale in a professional games team. This result is reached by many different ways: management in America means special training and knowledge; it is a universally recognized and esteemed skill; it means hard and competitive work; the manager has 'won his place'; he knows by experience what he is talking about and how the job should be done, because he has (more frequently than in this country) worked on, or come up from, the shop-floor; and so on. Many of these aspects will be examined later. Meanwhile it should be noted that the manifest competence of American management, its much greater extent of recruitment from the ranks, and its promotion by merit have clearly impressed themselves on organized labour—which, in turn, has more recently been adopting the scientific methods and studies used by management for training its own experts. It is impossible to reject the conclusion that there is better team-work in America during normal working—as many Teams observed. This phrase 'better team-work' does not mean 'better industrial relations as a whole.' It means merely better work as a management-labour team *while work is going on*. Indeed, as we shall see later, industrial relations as a whole since 1945 have been better in Britain than in America, where days of work lost through strikes and stoppages due to 'labour troubles' have been much greater (in proportion) than in Britain. The point is that *work as a team* is more effective in America. Almost all foreign observers in America have noted this in the past three generations.

The management of American industry generally seems to play a greater role in local community life than European

[1] No. 27 of Conclusions and Recommendations of *Management Accounting*, p. 15.

managements are expected to play. It recognizes and discharges obligations to the communities among which it works and which its workers help to form. Examples of this can be found on all sides: in the close working connection between managements (or *ad hoc* associations of them) and the local universities, college and high schools in the matter of curricula, training schemes, apprenticeship, amenities, visits to the plants, etc. (In Britain some of this is also found, but in the minority of first-class managements. The link between firms and technical colleges in regard to apprenticeship training is also good in Britain, and is fast improving. The setting up of canteens, crèches for children of married women workers and provision of transport to and from work—particularly since 1945—is also a 'service to the community.') In the leisure pursuits of workers the American management is not much concerned— neither there nor in Britain would such concern be welcome— but in the American local community there seem to be more abundant and general evidences of the charitableness, munificence, community spirit and farsightedness of industrial or commercial managements. This is naturally more evident in the smaller townships, where the plant or plants bulk large relative to the rest of the community. But the European visitor is surprised by the extent to which the life of the factory is neatly mortized into the life of the local community in America. It was not ever thus. It is now. And it is a factor which sociologists and psychologists are just beginning to weigh in their analysis of European workers' dislike of their work and workplace.

This factor, by the way, should always be borne in mind by Europeans who emphasize the lack of public welfare in America. There is less Federal welfare in certain ways—though there is not very much less public welfare in most American States today, once State welfare is added. But there is a far greater degree of what can be called individually insured and 'private-enterprise welfare and social security' in America, notably pensions and life and other insurance. Much of it is manifested in the local community's amenities.

The longer term of public education in America (at least, among the two-thirds of Americans who live in industrial regions) does not debar the relatively poor man's son, still less the majority of better-off working-men's sons, from entering and learning management or securing promotion. Extended education *helps* the less well-off to enter management. Public education begins later and ends later in America; but Europeans must remember that it is on the whole a *social* training, a social patterning of many different kinds of young Americans so that they can co-operate, a co-educational way of giving young people poise for the problems of adulthood, and only lastly an inculcation of basic knowledge and an education of basic skills or aptitudes. This process is nation-wide and general. It is on the whole consciously and deliberately rudimentary and 'inculcatory' up to the age of eighteen. It is only thereafter—in the main—that the techniques of thinking at university or college level, and also the techniques of management, can be learned. They are often acquired while the learner is engaged in some other work—either to 'pay his way through college' or to acquire qualifications while working in a factory. The upshot is that by the time a young man has a first degree or a technical qualification, he has also learned a good deal about the world of adults and its relationships, about industry itself, work in industrial conditions, and anything else from clerical work and salesmanship to the realities of politics. This kind of 'career open to the talents,' with its comparative ease of training while working for a living, is successful in securing talent for American management which might otherwise escape it. Even more, it is an aspect of American democracy often overlooked in Europe, where on the whole (with a notable minority of exceptions) more store is set by the content of an education, and less by its social or vocational effect.

The Skill of Management in America

Practically every Productivity Team which has visited the U.S. is agreed that productivity per man-year is higher than in Britain. They attribute this mainly to two factors. First, there is a climate of opinion which regards maximum effort by *every* individual as the primary guarantee not only of material standards but of the way of life of a free society. Second, there is a quality in management, inspired by this climate of opinion, and stimulated by the American system of higher education in general and, in particular, by that part of it which is devoted to administrative studies. American business employs graduates because it believes that higher education helps business. Strict adherence to promotion by merit avoids the danger that graduates will become a privileged class. . . . American experience has shown that productivity and education for management are closely related.[1]

(1) The A.A.C.P. Team which reported on Education for Management were impressed—perhaps most of all—by 'the steps taken by American business to educate, train and develop its future business leaders.' They noted in their findings the close connection between business and universities, colleges, technical schools, etc., and also the 'close co-operation between the trade unions and the universities which run courses for their officers.'[2]

This is only a projection into business life of the American concept of what education ought to be. It is all implied in the American notion that—if men are really to be freed (and not enslaved) by machines, to gain (and not lose) by technical progress—education must not stop dead at a certain age. It must go on to fit human beings to find the best-paying, most-rewarding positions in their society to which their capacities and talents entitle them. In terms of innate ability and capacity men are not born equal. Not even Americans believe that. But Americans do believe that men (and, be it noted, women) deserve to be educated as though their innate ability and capacity *were* equal, up to the point at which an adult decides not to pursue any more training for any occupation. The average intellectual standards of American public education at all ages—as the British and Europeans understand intellectual standards—are lower. But the purpose that education is intended to serve is different in America.[3] It certainly serves economic purposes better than British education does, and only in Scandinavia and Switzerland do the educational systems deliberately so serve the world of production and 'the everyday business of life.'

[1] *Education for Management*, Finding No. 1, p. 19.
[2] *Ibid.*, Finding No. 8, pp. 19–20.   [3] See p. 43.

At considerable expense to American industry, firm by firm, the higher and the technical education available in the industrial portions of America has been devised and developed to supply technicians who take up their responsible positions on various stages in the structure of management. A vast amount of the necessary funds for buildings, equipment, etc., came from industry—not from public treasuries. (The American economic and fiscal system permitted—and still permits—this, whereas in Britain today industry could not find the funds without starving some other allocation or securing remission of taxation.) Over the past twenty years, therefore, the number of professional workers in research laboratories alone multiplied by five, and the industrial outlays on research by even more.[1] The numbers of students attending business colleges over the same period, for full courses, has multiplied by three. Those studying technological subjects—the sciences, their subdivisions, and their applications in the useful arts—have multiplied by four. And these fantastic-seeming multipliers have all appeared in the last two decades alone.

(2) In America, different roles are assigned to members of the management; different terms are used for different functions. The purely administrative branches seem to serve more continuously the executive branches of management; e.g. the budgetary controllers, accountants, and planning staff seem to work more closely with the men responsible for each department, to secure more conscious co-operative effort, than is the case in Britain. The A.A.C.P. Team reporting on Management Accounting made some remarkable observations; but they tally with those of many another Team:

American industry . . . was convinced, with considerable justification, that productivity must be increased if the cost of the product was to fall . . . unit costs must be reduced each day and every day . . . The friendliness and understanding between the controller's department and the production department is [sic] remarkable. The controller's department is looked upon as an essential service to production. . . . From top management to foremen and charge-hands there is little fear of figures and there is a marked ability to

[1] Professor Sumner Schlichter, article cited on p. 23.

absorb information from tabular or graphical form . . . each man is expected to do his job and to meet his budget, or else have a very good explanation.[1]

This Team found that responsibility was much more devolved or decentralized in America; that accountants and managers worked more closely together; that the administrative and clerical staff were more flexible, ready to perform many more tasks; that management control was exercised throughout by costings and greater administrative controls, cross-checkings, etc.; and that the job and responsibility of each man was more clearly defined.

(3) One important feature of American industry is that foremen and supervisors are more generally recognized and rewarded as executives of management: officers in the front line with the men. Accordingly, foremen and supervisors are viewed as Very Important Persons. They are assimilated to management, paid as such, and their training is therefore viewed as an integral part of management training.

The American foreman . . . is regarded as part of the management by his superiors and is seen as such by his operatives . . . We formed the opinion that the range and thoroughness of supervisor training in the U.S. surpass corresponding activity in Britain.[2]

More emphasis is placed on training of foremen and others in the works, less on technical and other training outside—'Apart from some important research and survey work, relatively little supervisor training, as such, is available through universities and colleges of technology.'[3] There is, however, a tendency— not more than that—for more supervisors now to come from such institutions. That is a reflection of the far wider availability of university, college and technical higher education in America.

(4) Another important American characteristic is the greater general willingness of industry to share its experiences and 'know-how.' This also applies to training for management. Firms circularize each other with information and results;

1 *Management Accounting*, pp. 6–11, extracts.
2 *Training of Supervisors*, Summary Nos. 4 and 13.
3 *Ibid.*, Summary No. 25.

representatives meet at conferences and other places to pool their experience. So new developments or ideas quickly find their way round. And there is greater readiness of American management to change things. There is a greater ability to switch men and duties, both in administration and in the line of executive responsibility. New experiments and experience accompany a readiness to change anything, even abruptly and expensively, even during production if absolutely necessary.

(5) Everyone knows the importance accorded in America to salesmanship and selling. It has passed into language: 'sold on the idea.' It performs a most important function in a country where simplification, standardization and specialization result in cheap mass-production—but where the production must be sold to the last unit of the last model, before the next pre-planned models come off the production line. This is as true of toothpaste as it is of tractors. Accordingly the sales department is more closely dovetailed in with the planning and executive departments in America than in Europe: especially with such (generally hired) services as market research.

(6) The best management cannot do its best if the smooth flow of operations and materials is interrupted. So the best—and even the average—American pre-planning of production, down to the last foreseeable detail, involves the lay-out of sales and advertising campaigns corresponding to that of an army's order of battle, the most careful standard-costing of this and that detail in the proposed production, the closest consultation and collaboration between administrators and executives—just as in military affairs—from the supplies ('logistics') department to the foremen, and from the cost-accountants and controllers to the engineers. For these reasons the definition of functions seems sharper (even if more functions be given to one depart-ment or one man than in Britain); but the integration of all of them in action seems closer.

(7) Put thus succinctly, the comparisons flatter American industry as a whole; but European observers this century—and many Teams in the last few years—were impressed by the high efficiency of detailed planning and performance in average-sized American concerns, and even more impressed by the pitch of performance reached in the best or biggest concerns. These

things struck most of the Teams, in various ways. It is impressive to note the recommendations of each in its own field. Naturally, the Teams were not studying—they had not the time or the duty to study—the whole nature of American industry. They were sent out to study those things which could, in their opinion, most easily, cheaply, and quickly help to improve British productivity. All agreed that American management in general and on the average was more effective. When their recommendations are analysed under the heading of 'management,' it will be found that they picked out the improvements which in their own technical experience and on their own expert judgment could be expected to yield the best results in Britain with the least trouble.

Thus, the accountants were most impressed[1] by the budgetary control and standard-costing of operations in American firms, and recommended wider adoption of these aids to management in Britain 'to enable it to decentralize responsibility'—a significant explanation. The Teams studying training for management, American universities and industry, and training of supervisors recommended that 'training' or 'education' should be viewed more as a continuous process, and as part of working life, by industry itself, in order that better management and higher productivity should ensue; and that industry should identify itself much more with these training processes, both inside and outside workplaces. The Teams studying technical operations and processes—from cotton spinning to packaging—made recommendations which indicate a general belief in the improvement of management by means of more careful pre-planning, greater use of mechanical aids (which involve more careful pre-planning, administration, and executive functions), and a realignment of traditional duties and functions.

In short, viewing American management as a whole, the Teams saw ways of bringing the less effective average of British performance up to the higher average of American performance—and, indeed, up to the standards set by the best British managements, which in many cases challenge comparison with the best managements in America.

[1] *Management Accounting, passim.*

Management is Measurement

The extent to which good management must rely on measurements is not widely appreciated. But the majority of A.A.C.P. Teams emphasized it, and so did the Team of British trade-union officials which visited the U.S. and published its report through the T.U.C.:

Unions should seek to co-operate in the application of 'scientific management' which, even if not an exact science, can make a valuable contribution to increasing productivity in industry.[1]

The report of the Management Accounting Team, already cited, and the ancillary report *Productivity Measurement in British Industry*—together with the impressive (and related) reports of the Joint Committee of the Institution of Production Engineers and the Institute of Cost and Works Accountants on the measurement of productivity—make it plain that there is also, in this respect, no particular secret of American management. In fact, American management 'makes little attempt to measure productivity (as such), preferring to rely on unit costs.'[2]

American productivity rises so remarkably because *all* measurements are parts of the planning, costing or reaching of targets and because *only* those measurements are made which have relevance to those operations. This is as true of work-study measurements as it is of the figures for machine-utilization, material consumption, fuel consumption, and other operations or processes necessarily measured for purposes of costing, and therefore of budgetary and other control or for the reaching of targets. In brief, the measurements needed—and only those which are needed in the production plans—are themselves part of the plans, of the controls, and therefore of management.

There is no reason, inherent in the American economy or in American ability, why their management should be more efficient than British management. . . . The principles and methods which

[1] Report, *Trade Unions and Productivity*, published by the T.U.C., 1950.
[2] *Management Accounting* report, p. 6. The Federal Bureau of Labor Statistics, however, deserves mention for its valuable and regular studies of productivity.

D

American management applies are well known in this country but are practised much more universally and vigorously in America. . . . Their method is to set themselves targets which are as high as appear from facts and forecasts to be capable of achievement. They are continually measuring their actual results against the target they have set themselves. . . . These principles and methods are applied right down the line. . . . The actual techniques used to obtain the accounting and costing information are not new, but the application of the technical principles and the speed and service which the controller gives to the management are outstanding and impressive.[1]

The chief impression made on visitors by American methods of measurement for managerial purposes was that they were quick, bare, bald and strictly practical. Speed was the essence of measurement: speed for quick and practical comparisons. 'Management's first concern is with tomorrow.'[2] Often, rather than wait for an accurate monthly figure, American executives will estimate for the fourth week, and thus obtain an *approximate* monthly figure early enough to get out calculations to check the succeeding month's operations. (The correct monthly figure is established later, and this provides a cross-check for a check!) Such a swift supply of working figures is vital to the continuous control and checking which mark American management right down the line, from the office to the shopfloor. And everyone—whether in management or not, for example the operative himself—seems to be far more measurement-conscious than in British industry. That means comparison-conscious, result-conscious, productivity-conscious. More officers and members of trade unions seem also to be measurement-conscious and co-operative in calculating and checking management's figures (for their unions' own interests) —otherwise the American system could not operate so efficiently and effectively. Not all American unions and their officers are so effective and co-operative; but more of them seem to be so than in Britain—or, indeed, Europe. And the better unions are fast compelling the less efficient and less effective to follow suit.

Measurement of all kinds of performances in American

[1] *Management Accounting*, as cited, Conclusions and Recommendations, pp. 14 and 15.   [2] *Coal* report, p. 8.

management is carried to a high degree for a simple reason. It is a necessary part of the progress-mentality; a part of the drive always to reduce costs and increase output and sales. All the measurements of the various productive operations relate, ultimately, to costs: costs of the various kinds of services—of machines, of labour, of raw materials and of fuel and power—rendered in the productive process. American management on the whole—at least the best of it, the portion which competitively compels the remainder to copy it—does not want measurements, work-study figures ('time and motion study'), etc., mainly for comparisons with *past* performances. It wants them mainly as indicators, base-figures, and starting-points for comparisons with the possible *future* performance of the machines, or of the men tending and supervising them, or of the users of materials and fuel and power (these users being both men and machines). The overwhelming predominance of standard performances, standard costings, and standard budgets in American management is perhaps its most striking single feature. But it could not work without comprehensible and comprehensive measurement right down the line.

There are two important aspects of work-study and other measurements. (These subjects are more fully examined in Chapters 6 and 7.) First, upon management falls the inescapable responsibility of the manner and method of introducing and executing such measurements of human and mechanical performances—work-study, etc. This responsibility involves management's attitudes to trade unions in general, and to the particular trade unions and their officers and members in the particular plant. It is reflected in American management's emphasis on 'labour relations' and personnel management. Secondly, the workers' attitude to all such measurements arises from their degree of knowledge (or ignorance) of the part played by such measurements in securing higher productivity, higher pay, higher profits, higher efficiency in the use of machines, materials and fuel, and reduced hours of work or less strain on the operatives.

In many British trade-union and management circles, American management is thought to be 'tougher' and more ruthless towards the unions and their members than in Britain.

Yet in recent years more and more American managements have displayed a disposition to take pains in conveying to trade-union officials and members the fullest information on all aspects of measurements; and that is not confined to work-study, or measurements involving the workpeople alone. It is generally true of production, productivity, budgetary, and other measurements. Recently, also, more and more American trade-union officials—though by no means all or even the majority—have been playing the complementary role of bringing productive measurement to a fine art. They are beginning to train their own experts. They are studying and learning the skills of 'industrial engineers,' cost accountants, and other experts in measurement; and they are beginning to co-operate with management's measurement procedures, once these are comprehended and approved. Great progress was made along these lines in wartime. The collaborative process has perhaps been helped along in that American climate of opinion which favours the continuous raising of production, productivity, wages, profits, and machine-utilization; and which therefore favours better and more effective management of all these things.

Before we turn from the broad field of management it is important to set work-study, and measurements of machine-performance and other operations, in their proper place. In essence, they are not merely methods of calculating wage-rates, getting more work from the workers, introducing piece-rates or output-incentives, or otherwise driving the human operatives at the pace of the inhuman and mechanical operatives in a plant. They may have been so used, as a result of other circumstances in the past. Those other circumstances—the social and political atmosphere in industrial nations, the industrial set-up, and the state of industrial relations—have passed, we may hope, for good.

In our better circumstances today the need for more detailed and accurate measurement of the processes and operations of industrial production is much greater. It is to obtain more from the same equipment, and so to make the 'more' pay greater rewards to all concerned, and thus to make quicker material progress. It is no valid objection to work-measurement to say that it is 'only a way to get more out of the workers.' As we

52

show, that is necessarily a *part* of it; but the machines do most to produce more; and the effect of it is to give the workers more of the extra output from the equipment. Work-study thus enables the human worker's work to be more effective. In so doing, industry can afford better equipment sooner; and, thus, either to reduce hours of work, or to lighten work in the same hours and enable it to produce and be paid more in goods. The standard of life rises.

The reason, inherent in the very nature of industrial and mechanical progress, is instructive. It is that without better methods, and degrees, of such measurement it is impossible to determine—in a nation or in a firm—how greater productivity can most cheaply and speedily be achieved; and therefore how much more quickly material progress can be made. Without such measurement it is impossible to plan the most effective, economical and therefore rapid way of raising people's standards of living: to cut costs, increase output and employment, raise wages and general purchasing-power, and lower the amount of human effort required in the process from each individual employed.

The point has been well summarized by Mr. N. Pleming. He refers specifically to the objectives of work-study, yet each of his items is just as valid for all kinds of measurement in the industrial process. He sets out the objectives thus:

(*a*) To conserve operator effort;

(*b*) to obtain information which will enable the proper use of the time factor to be made in manufacturing;

(*c*) to secure proper deployment of labour so that there is a balanced volume of work available to each individual;

(*d*) to achieve effective use of the skills of operators;

(*e*) to conserve material;

(*f*) to control quality;

(*g*) to set up standards of output for control, costing and incentives.[1]

[1] 'The Application of the Results of Work Study,' by N. Pleming, B.Sc.(Eng.), Assoc.M.Inst.C.E., Chairman and Managing Director of Associated Industrial Consultants Ltd., Address to Conference of National Hosiery Manufacturers' Federation, Harrogate, October 10, 1949. For other useful information see *Work Study*, Production Management Series No. 2, British Institute of Management, by R. M. Currie, 3s. 6d.

As technical progress advances and accelerates, mechanization—which is capitalization—must increase too. Mechanization means more 'roundaboutness'[1] of the production process. More components or more operations are done by machinery, at an additional stage in the whole productive process. The new machinery for the new stage in that process must then be made, installed and operated. A nation, or a firm, which means to keep up in the industrial process—which means to maintain and improve employment and conditions of work and standards of living—must continuously measure the performance of its machines, because they are the primary consumers of human labour, raw materials and fuel and power. In many cases, such measurements cannot be accurate. 'The proper use of the time factor' in industry [see (b) above] does not permit complete accuracy; time itself is so precious that a reasonably accurate approximation must suffice. Estimation, sampling and approximation will often serve well enough. But afterwards—after the urgency of decisions during production is over—the slower, more accurate measurements must also emerge and provide a 'governor' to keep all current estimates within reasonable limits.

British Handicaps

Although criticism of British industry for its methods was fairly widespread between the wars, the second war imposed peculiar limitations on British industry. These are often ignored abroad. It is not just a question of direct war damage, and the enormous running-down of capital equipment. Supplies—of fuel and power and of raw materials—have been far more uncertain and irregular in post-war Britain than in America; and because of America's far greater natural resources, foreign trading and foreign currency do not play so inhibiting a role

[1] This was the word used in German, last century and this, to describe *the growing number of stages* inserted in the productive process by increasingly capitalistic methods (i.e. increased use of equipment, plant, machinery, etc.). Those who wish to browse in the pastures of productive principles—rather than of practice—may consult Prof. R. G. Hawtrey's *Capital and Employment* (Longmans) or Prof. F. A. Hayek's *The Pure Theory of Capital* (Routledge and Kegan Paul) and *Prices and Production*, where the term 'roundaboutness' received anglicization.

in American industry. Again, British manufacturing industry—though employing, as compared with America, a slightly larger proportion of the total population—works roughly one-third (and in very many cases over one-half) on export orders. Not one-tenth of American manufacturing industry works for foreigners. Since all foreign requirements differ, from each other and from home demands, Britain's end-products, even of more or less standard kinds like poplins or bicycles, have to undergo special processes or operations at one point or another; so that pre-planning, standardization, and sharply defined integration of management in Britain are necessarily subject to greater limitations. It is particularly galling to British industrialists to note that, owing to her new post-war indebtedness and her needs to develop sterling resources, Britain had to increase her exports of machinery after the war by a greater amount than she herself could afford to increase her own investment in new machinery. Moreover, in order to earn dollars at any cost, Britain exported to dollar countries much of the equipment badly needed by British industries; many of these new machines were invented in England and would have greatly increased British productivity if they could have been installed here.

This peculiar British situation has one advantage. For example, the intense degree of American pre-planning, integration of management, simplification, standardization and specialization necessarily makes it most difficult to modify—or for any other reason interrupt—the production of a model or end-product once production is in full scale. (It is sometimes done, as mentioned on p. 47, but it is very costly.) Such interruption is relatively as costly on a motor-car assembly-line in America as in the production of packaged foods, cigarettes or toothpaste. In British industry, however, there is one advantage to match the many other disadvantages—its processes can be more easily and cheaply modified. In shipbuilding, rearmament, and other lines of manufacture, this has often been found of benefit, and it is only right to draw attention to it.

Apart from the widely different situations in the two countries over supplies of raw materials, foreign trading, etc., a caution is necessary against any precise and literal translation of American management and its experience into British terms. We have stressed that measurement of all kinds is carried to a fine point in American industry. Clearly such a degree of measurement throughout the industrial process demands a new atmosphere in British industry—on both sides of it. But there are great obstacles to this.

The urgency and intensity of the measurement in American management arise from the greater spur of competition, the greater cost-consciousness, the higher capitalization and the relative dearness of human labour of all kinds. All of these lead to 'high efficiency for survival'; and efficiency can neither be gauged nor achieved without such measurements. One thing is, however, clear: there can be no progress without the fullest possible utilization of machinery. Therefore—quite apart from the *re*-equipment of British industry and the installation of *new* machinery—the long-continuing attitudes of many British managements and many British workers towards mechanical aids, redeployment of labour, modifications of relationships and rewards of crafts and skills, traditional differentials, and all sorts of 'restrictive practices' in general, would need to be revised before a general and average rise in British productivity could follow.[1] Prime Ministers of opposing political parties, trade-union leaders and leading industrialists have drawn attention to this as a fundamental post-war British problem. We must remember that restrictive practices are widespread in American industries and in some internationally notorious instances constitute 'world's records.' But it is important to note that the general industrial atmospheres in America and Britain differ substantially. They derive so much from their vastly differing national pasts. And it is even more important for British purposes to remember that the post-war British economy is overstrained, its resources are more straitened than those of America, and its ability to waste any labour, materials, or machine-capacity (and not miss it) is nil.

The hang-over of traditional, long-standing British attitudes on both sides of industry—however justified they may have seemed to their possessors one or two generations ago—is today

[1] In a minority of outstanding cases startling rises in productivity in British factories have occurred. Some examples are given on pp. 210–15.

56

the greatest single cause of the average and lower-than-average level of performance by British management and organized labour alike. It is not universal. The best British managements and trade-union leaderships have renounced and abjured it. But it is an evil heritage, an encumbrance.

The American economy has never expanded as fast as in the past ten years; never as fast as in the twenty years before that; and so on. Its output has broadly doubled every generation for a century and is still doing so. It is a cumulatively expanding economy, with a still expanding population and expanding opportunities for all. The experience of the British economy has been disastrous in the past ten years, and was bad for a generation before that. Unemployment, restricted domestic purchasing-power and the 'depressed areas' of export trade between the wars have been followed by an even more disastrous war, rigid controls and restrictions, rationing of many kinds for over a decade in the home market, and the cramping of initiative, enterprise, competitiveness and skills either by penal taxation or by automatic and standardized rewards. The effect of all this upon both sides of British industry has not been conducive to the highest output of individual skill and ability, the highest degree of competitive efficiency, the most intensive utilization of the existing plant and machinery, and the most rapid lowering of costs. America had to face some— though not all—of these recent handicaps, but she could also expand her productive capacity, her productivity, and her people's standards of living simultaneously. In America, the *purchasing power of workers and of profits, net of tax,* rose steadily as parts of a steadily rising national income. Britain's national income available at home, proportionately to her population, did not rise at all for over a decade, and even today it has barely risen compared with 1938 (see Appendix A). The British economic system needs cranking-up.

The Economy of American Management

One final aspect of American management merits examination: its paradoxical emphasis on economizing alongside much prodigal use of American national resources. This was noted

57

by many A.A.C.P. Teams in different connections. On the one hand there is an intense degree of research into the possible uses of by-products in America, the development of firms and even industries to use the by-products of other firms and industries, and the greater average ability of American management to make more flexible use of man- and machine-power in avoiding, or severely reducing, wastages. On the other hand, however, British managements are much more efficient conservers of national resources than most American managements.[1]

Perhaps the most striking example of economy-mindedness in America is the attitude of both management and trade unions, on the whole, to the utilization of man-power. Many observers of the American industrial scene—including the Teams—have long noted the tendency to break down 'strong backs, no brains' jobs into mechanical operations, and to break down greater skills into smaller or partial skills. That tendency, which has been going on for over fifty years, naturally has been paralleled by the tendency to break down tasks and jobs into smaller or partial processes and operations. It is a normal, necessary tendency in any progressive industrial nation, and it can safely be stated that it has developed rapidly in Russia—though not to the same extent as in America or Britain.

The logical end of this breaking-down process has always been, and must increasingly be, to render human tasks more and more capable of being done by machinery; that means, to raise the real wages of human labour, to reduce weekly hours of work, to increase the output of goods purchasable by those wages, and to lower the strain of work. The Americans enjoy the overwhelming advantage of an atmosphere in which gadgets, machines, mechanical power and energy, and labour-saving of all kinds are—and indeed, for a century, have been—viewed as the chief friends of mankind (and, indeed, of woman-kind at home). This goes some way to explain the more widespread American ability to work machines in double—and even

---

[1] See the report *Saving Scarce Materials*, especially pp. 11-13 and 17, for British superiority in this respect.

triple—shifts in a day in many of their leading industries.[1] And that, in turn, exemplifies their intense economy of man-power and machine-power. The process puts them on their toes, and competition keeps them there.

Economy of labour means almost a prodigality of machinery, which involves the highest degree of investment, which requires the highest efficiency of management, and so on. The only work which is not eased in this process is that of management itself! Thus, progress demands better management, and penalizes it.

Design and quality also yield economies. For what precise purpose is some article intended? To last how long? To stand up to what treatment? Here, too, the social atmosphere plays a part. Americans do not like to be seen using old things. Europeans do not mind so much. And the British cherish an affection for old things. (The notion of 'vintage quality'—in anything from wine to motor-cars—is European.) Distinction of quality for personal idiosyncrasies—tailor-mades, custom-built and hand-finished goods—these characteristics are European and play an insignificant role in America. American production looks mainly to 'long-runs' of goods; to standard-ization, simplification and specialization. In the American ready-made clothing trades the aim has been to compromise between standardization and variations of style: to offer as wide variation of the latter as is compatible with the demands of management for the lowering of unit-costs and prices to a minimum. Unnecessary frills, foibles and finishes are ruled out of American production as far as possible, so that the article can be composed of components easily made and assembled and so that the main purpose of the article can thus be served as cheaply as possible. In many cases, over-long duration of the article itself becomes an unnecessary frill, foible or finish. Yet, at the same time, the great size of the American market confers the boon of *many* competing suppliers of *individually standard-ized (and simplified) articles*; so that the customer, in fact, has variety from which to choose—a variety in stereotyped goods!

---

[1] For example, in textile spinning and weaving, automotive plants, printing, light engineering and making of containers, two or more daily shifts are far more common than in Britain (or Europe).

All the foregoing is a sketch: a few quick sweeps of the brush to catch broad outlines. Now the outlines must be filled in, and familiar details delineated, so that the picture of management can emerge. To the first of these details we must now turn: to machines and mechanical power.

3

More Power to the Elbow

If all material progress is towards evading the curse of Adam—
'in the sweat of thy brow shalt thou eat thy bread'—the
Americans have certainly outpaced humanity. They get more
bread for less sweat. But the proper question to ask at this
point is not 'Why more bread?' but 'Why less sweat?' And the
answer to that question is that they have, and use, more
machines and more mechanical power per industrial worker:
8 h.p. is behind the elbow of each American industrial worker;
between 3 and 4 h.p. is the British figure; and $2\frac{1}{2}$ h.p. for the
average of Western European industrial workers. These figures
for the *non*-human aid per worker go on diminishing, country
by country, down to the one-man-power of the three-quarters
of all humanity who are not industrialized and whose standards
of living are therefore lowest.

Few of the A.A.C.P. Teams failed to remark that right down
the line of American production, from general office to shop-
floor, much more horse-power and many more mechanical aids
(consuming that h.p.) were available and intensively utilized.
This is probably the most universally recognized of all American
industry's advantages. The whole subject requires, however,
examination and analysis. The amount of h.p. behind British
elbows in manufacturing industry is *less* than that behind
those of the Swiss and Swedes—as it was before the war.
Yet British productivity is not significantly different from
theirs. It is not merely a question of h.p. per elbow—as we
shall see.

Britain *could*—at some sacrifice of other things like defence,
standards of consumption, or hours and conditions of work—
rapidly develop her sources of h.p. The crux of the h.p. problem
in Britain is shortage of natural fuel and power resources apart

from coal, and of up-to-date generating plant. Britain *could*—
by sacrificing the strongly competing claims of defence, and
home and export industry, upon limited sources of men,
materials, and equipment—rapidly develop these sources of h.p.
But that is only a fraction of Britain's problem of mechanical
aids and h.p. Without new machines in her factories to use all
the new power—and use it as continuously and intensively as
possible—much of it would run to waste. On the other hand,
with the same sacrifices, Britain could rapidly make and install
a considerable quantity of new machinery. But if that machinery
were then under-utilized, owing to shortages or interruptions
of the supply of fuel and power, or of raw materials, or of
labour; or if it were under-utilized because of the hang-over
of old, traditional attitudes on the parts of both management
and operatives mentioned above; or if the new machinery were
of a kind that demanded for its most efficient use the introduction of a multiple-shift system in the working day, and the
men to man-up the second or other shifts were not available—
then even the fullest equipment of modern machinery would
not suffice to raise productivity. Indeed, unit-costs might well
rise, prices might rise, the wages of the men kept in work
might rise; but so might unemployment, as the end-products
became too costly to be sold in competition in the markets
abroad. The result would then be worse for the firm and nation
than before. This question of mechanization—which, as we
said, is the basis of material progress—is in fact far more
complicated than most glib discussion assumes.

Making Machines Work

   . . . it is the extra speed at which machinery is run, the high
specialization of work whereby each man becomes an expert in
his particular branch, which in itself means efficiency and an increased output, the economy of hands in attending machines, and
the excellent organization of the factories whereby the smallest item
of time and labour are [*sic*] saved, that make all the difference
between large profits and none, and a high rate of wages for the
men as against the comparatively low standard known in this
country.

That statement was made fifty years ago, in 1902, by Mr. A. Mosely, who sent a Commission of British trade unionists to the United States to investigate industrial methods.[1] Writing 'in the capacity of an ordinary business man,' Mr. Mosely also said this:

The manufacturers there do not hesitate to put in the very latest machinery at whatever cost, and from time to time sacrifice large sums by scrapping the old whenever improvements are brought out. . . . Labour-saving machinery is widely used everywhere and is encouraged by the unions and welcomed by the men, because experience has shown them that in reality machinery is their best friend. It saves the workman enormous manual exertion, raises his wages, tends towards a higher standard of life, and, further, rather creates work than reduces the number of hands employed. If there is one lesson that in my opinion has been amply demonstrated to the delegates on this Commission, it is this fact as to machinery—not, of course, that I think they themselves have ever opposed it (as that day is happily fast passing away amongst intelligent men), but they must have been pleased to see such positive proof of what they have for long past been trying to impress on the rank and file in their respective unions.

Fifty years later the A.A.C.P. Teams endorsed these findings. In the intervening half-century the American output per worker on the average rose about 2% (compound interest) per annum; total output has been multiplied four to five times since 1900; in the past fifteen years productivity has been rising by 3% per annum; standards of living of Americans of all kinds have doubled in the last fifty years; hours of work have been greatly reduced; and despite a big and rapid increase in population, the numbers employed have broken all records.

Behind most of this lies rapidly expanding capital equipment and good management. Good management has consisted overwhelmingly in making the machines work. The vast forward strides in industrial relations in America, in education at all levels, and in technical processes have been the *means* whereby

[1] *Mosely Industrial Commission to the United States of America*, October–December 1902, preface to Mr. W. C. Steadman's report by Mr. A. Mosely, Co-operative Printing Society Ltd., Manchester, 1903. This same preface precedes all the reports.

good management has achieved that end. All the other means serve the same end in management's hands—plant lay-out, the automatic serving of the workpeople ('Don't put anything on the floor; it doesn't pay to pay anyone to pick it up again!'), mechanical calculators and other office machinery, the smooth flow of work, the ability to pay high wages, training of all kinds within the factory, and so on. All are means to one end: making the machines work. Machines are not worth while unless they are allowed to do more and more work.

As soon as we look away from the over-all canvas to individual industries—which is what the A.A.C.P. Teams had to do—we find complete unanimity, both among the Teams and between both sides of British industry represented on them, about the universal availability in American industry of more and better tools, the extensive use of mechanical aids of all kinds, and the constant development of new methods involving greater use of mechanical power. The repetition becomes almost wearisome; machines doing all the lifting, moving, handling, packaging. From small units like sweets or foods, to big units like coal-trucks or chemical and metallurgical containers, the moving and preparation of them for processing or further operations were more highly mechanized than in Britain—or, for that matter, anywhere else except Canada. It is not, perhaps, so much in the basic machines of the factory— what can conveniently be called the basic mechanical operators —that the superior equipment of American manufacturing industry emerges; though in such outstanding industries as those making automobiles, containers, and durable domestic equipment the amount of 'basic mechanical operators' on factory floors, both absolutely and per worker employed, is larger than it is in Britain. The contrast really becomes striking, however, when you include all auxiliary and ancillary equipment: mechanical aids and tools for human labour, all helping to feed-in the ingredients at every stage of the productive process. Nothing is too lowly for machinery in America. The simpler and more everyday the process or operation, the more the need to mechanize it. And the more the urge, therefore, to break all operations down into simpler and more everyday elements.

Moreover, one of the important points about the greater quantity of machinery in American industry is that *it is planned to be used intensively*. The intensive use of machinery and mechanical power in America is the means to the end of high-volume, low-cost production. Another means to the same end is the planned *flow* of materials, skills, and processes. It all results in smooth and economical production. The flow of everything needed by machines—man-power and materials, mechanical energy and regular maintenance—must be carefully planned if those machines are to be intensively used. That is what struck many A.A.C.P. Teams—especially those from British industries in which many technical processes were important.

Machines and Men

The more machines are used, the better. That is true in both senses of the phrase; but it is doubly true once the machinery has been installed. The A.A.C.P. report on *Productivity Measurement in British Industry* and the other British reports on its measurement[1] emphasize this. To accountants it scarcely needs emphasis.

If a machine *can* be used forty-four hours a week on a one-shift system, eighty-eight hours a week on a two-shift system, and (allowing for time spent on maintenance, cleaning, etc.) 120 hours a week on a three-shift system, it can be written-off more quickly the more shifts are worked. It can then be more rapidly replaced by a more modern machine. But the man-power, fuel and power, materials, etc., must be available to work those shifts. And the relationships between the costs of the man-power on the various shifts, the costs to be charged for using the machine more intensively, and the costs of maintaining the machine under each shift-system, will indicate what is the most economical way of planning and performing the particular process. Accordingly—once plans, models, processes, and

[1] *Interim Report on Measurement of Productivity*, December 1949, and *Measurement of Productivity—Applications and Limitations*, 1951, both by the Joint Committee of the Institute of Cost and Works Accountants and of the Institution of Production Engineers.

E

operations are all laid down—four basic requirements for the intensive utilization of machinery remain:

(a) A secure volume of through-put for a specific time to come;
(b) a secure supply of energy for machinery;
(c) a secure supply of trained man-power (including supervision and management), and
(d) a secure, smooth supply of raw materials, components, etc.

Obviously any interruption to these four supplies would make the machinery idle for a portion of the time it could have been working. The cost per unit of output would then, inevitably, be higher than it need have been.

Another feature of American industrial life is the widespread acceptance—on both sides of industry—of the idea that the machines must be continuously invented, bought, and installed to help the men, and that the men must therefore organize and be organized to enable the machines to give of their untiring best. Naturally, a mechanical-minded, gadget-minded, labour-saving-minded nation gains in this respect, compared with one which places heavier emphasis upon the social or occupational distinctions of craftsmanship, skills, and 'custom-built quality.'

Today, as half a century ago, one of the outstanding features of American industry, compared with British industry, is that its equipment is generally far more intensively used, more rapidly written-off, more quickly replaced, and more rapidly expanded. Many of the A.A.C.P. Teams draw attention to this. 'American industry is now replacing its machinery at least twice as fast as is British industry; it is therefore lengthening its already long lead in competitive efficiency with every year that passes. This advantage may be partly offset by a faster increase in labour costs in America than Britain. . . . But in the modern world the advantage in exploitation of new inventions and new techniques will be with those who have the access to new capital equipment, not to cheaper labour.'[1] It

[1] *The Economist*, November 22, 1952, p. 583. Indeed, apart from politics entirely, the ability of any country's industry to raise wages—whether the

is a feature as marked in American spinning and weaving as in automobile plants, machine-tool factories and printing works, footwear factories and oil or chemical plants. Indeed, as far as can be ascertained, American equipment is more intensively used *even when only one shift a day uses it*. In other words, the percentage of 'available machine-hours' worked in one shift seems on the average to be higher in America and the pace of work in those hours is higher. Thus the total through-put of each machine is greater per hour, per shift, and per annum. This is what one might expect from the general dearness and long-run scarcity of labour—especially skilled labour—in America. But it is much more certain that American equipment *over the year* and *over its working life* is more intensively used. That working life is, on the whole, shorter, and the output from it is far higher per annum, than elsewhere. The explanation is twofold: first, despite the long-run dearness of labour in America, shift-working seems to be far more possible and common there, as some Teams pointed out;[1] and secondly, on any shift the equipment is more intensively used. An important part of the explanation for both these features is that higher wages and higher night-shift rates can be, and are, afforded in America. Clearly, the rate of pay for the universally unpopular late shifts is crucial. There are plenty of instances in Britain where it is reckoned natural to do shift-work as part of a continuous process—in steel, paper, rayon, glass, chemicals, and other industries—and little difficulty arises. But in industries in which no naturally continuous process is involved, there is almost a traditional or constitutional British—indeed, European —dislike of a multiple-shift system, even when shifts work to rota. It is probable that the big increase in productivity rendered possible by shift-work would enable European industries to pay wages high enough to overcome social and other resistances— provided enough of the extra pay remains with the worker and is not taken by taxes.

Even so, that does not explain why the use of machinery

industry is State-owned or privately owned—is in direct proportion to its ability to expand and renew its capital equipment. The more capital equipment, the higher the standard of living and the quicker it can rise.

[1] E.g. Litho printing, cotton spinning and weaving, etc.

should be in so many instances less intensive, and more wasteful, in a single-shift system in Britain. Shorter 'runs' are only part of the explanation. Management must look for other explanations in a list of causes: longer times taken to set-up or change machine-settings, longer time taken for ordinary work, delays or interruptions of the vital flows mentioned earlier, longer time taken for maintenance and cleaning, inadequate skills in tending or maintaining the equipment, and so on.

Britain has suffered a shortage of man-power since the war. Between the wars—tragically, because of vast unemployment—this handicap was not laid upon her. There has been a disinclination to work more machines per man, and so spread what man-power *is* available over two or more shifts. Partly this is the result of the over-all post-war inflation, which has prevented men from leaving less-important occupations and going to those, more important, which could have worked two shifts or more in a day. Partly it is due to the difficulty of managements and unions in reaching agreement on the re-adjustments of pay and duties required by shift systems. The earnings of unskilled and semi-skilled workers in Britain have risen so fast during the inflation that skill and differentials in wages to recompense greater skills have been substantially obliterated.

It is hard to see what were the real difficulties in the way of unions and managements. Profits were so inflationary after the war that differentials comparable to those paid in American industry could have been paid in Britain, to secure workers for second or third shifts. Perhaps the nation-wide negotiation of wage-rates for the leading British trade unions—as opposed to the more usual negotiation by plants (firms) in America—inhibited British managements from tackling this big problem. But if so, it seems a shortcoming of the managements. Perhaps it was that everybody, in management and in the unions, was 'doing quite nicely' in inflationary times. And the rapid rise in the incidence of the British income-tax may have played a part.[1] Partly, too, Britain's peculiar housing problem is responsible. British industrial labour—mainly for traditional, local, psychological reasons—has always been less mobile than labour in

[1] See p. 170.

America; but that relative immobility has been increased since the war by the precious possession of some house-room somewhere, and the fear of losing it.

This increased post-war immobility of industrial labour in Britain masks many anomalies. For example, the 'turnover of labour' from firm to firm, within one and the same locality, has risen enormously compared with pre-war times; yet the variations of earnings have not been very big. Compared with American industry—in which labour has always been mobile, but not as highly volatile as this—British industry since war ended has had to cover a 'labour-turnover-cost' of substantial proportions. This is a great obstacle to the steady intensive use of machinery. Covering this cost is possible in many ways— of which the best, to use an Irishism, is not to incur it at all. But if the national, local or industrial situation well-nigh necessitates a high labour turnover, and puts a premium on it, any well-managed firm must accept it and seek to offset its cost-raising effects by quicker and better training of workpeople, rearrangement of their work and duties in agreement with their unions, and generally more effective management.

One peculiar cost-raising item in British industry since war ended is due to this high and highly localized labour turnover. It puts a premium upon 'hoarding of labour,' 'concealed unemployment,' material inducements of many kinds to retain labour (often in the form of amenities, outings, and non-cash benefits), and so on. Either way, therefore, the tendency is to raise costs, and the proportion of indirect labour employed. There is nothing wrong with more inducements and amenities for workpeople: quite the contrary. But it is wrong to ignore the sudden effect of all these extra costs in a country bedevilled in six of the eight post-war years by inflation, acute shortages, currency crises, devaluation, vastly increased indebtedness to other countries, unfavourable terms of trade, rising armaments, and a greater dependence upon foreign trade as foreign competition increased. These post-war circumstances are largely the causes and symptoms of a long-continuing over-all inflation. It has suddenly upset the traditional *relationships* between, and rewards of, skills, grades, and qualities of man-power; and worse, it has distorted the normal ways of rewarding more vital jobs by higher pay. These circumstances can be expected to diminish as the inflationary pressure—both domestically generated and exerted from outside Britain—declines. But for as long as they, and the pressure, last, they make the tasks of management—and incidentally of the leadership of organized labour itself—more complex and difficult.

Serious as these tasks have been in America during the inflationary cycle there, they have been far more serious in Britain, where the other shortages and interruptions to the smooth flow of production caused by inflation have also, as we just saw, been more numerous. Continuous and intensive utilization of machinery in such a situation—let alone the efficient working-in of brand-new machinery—is not to be expected. Poor and backward as much of British industry was before the war, the wonder may well be that the management of British manufacturing industry since the war has done as well as it has.

Must the Machines run the Men?

This seems the right place in which to discuss the long-standing anxiety—not only on the part of the direct workers of machinery but also of philosophers, sociologists, psychologists, artists, and others—about the effects on the individual and society of faster and farther mechanization of life. It is idle to deny that under such rapid and extensive mechanization as has proceeded only in the last decade or two, and bids fair to proceed (at least in America) in the next, both the psychological reactions of individuals and groups are more tested than in former generations. The relationships between individuals and their groupings in society—even on the international scale— are also powerfully affected. For instance, the impact of the West upon Africa and Asia is likely to be far greater because of the potentialities of modern machines of all kinds, than was the impact of a more human (though not necessarily more humane) and less technical Western culture a century or two ago. Again, in the West itself, city and countryside now undergo faster, more far-reaching changes in ways of life and their mutual relationships as a result of greater mechanization and faster communications of all kinds. The uniformity of technical advances, spreading from fewer and bigger urban centres, obliterates much of the older traditional patterns of life, thought, and feeling. The anxiety just mentioned is often expressed in such simplified questions as 'Of course, mass-production and mechanization turn out enormous material benefits for people; but what price do people have to pay for them in the effect on their souls? Is it enough to be now a well-fed slave of the machine instead of, as most men were, ill-fed slaves of other men centuries ago?'

It is only right to emphasize that the use of more mechanical aids to production does not, of necessity, compel managements, nations or societies—however they be organized—to make the machines run their human beings. A simple example, already given in another connection, should suffice to prove this. Intensive use of machinery can often best be secured by a multiple-shift system; that means re-deploying the workers over the shifts, and often getting *more* workers; in turn, that results in lowering unit-costs so much that greater labour-costs (higher earnings) can be afforded from the greater productivity of both men and machines. But often, too, it results partly in giving the workers better earnings, partly in giving them more leisure (shorter hours in each shift), and partly in reducing selling-prices of the end-products, so that the workers' higher earnings and greater leisure become even more worthwhile by opening-up a wider range of amenities or consumers' goods and pleasures—a rise in standards of life.

What people *do* with their extra leisure and extra earnings, as the system of mass-production becomes (as it has become in America) widespread, is not the *result* of the system. The leisure and the extra pay, the higher material standard of life, are the result. To what ends that result is used by workers, the whole nation, or the whole civilization, is not the fault of the *means* whereby it is all obtained. It is—whether it is a fault or a merit—the result of that people's other-than-economic values: their values which only come into full play away from their work and workplaces, in their leisure: their values learned by tradition, education, and communication one with another through the multifarious channels of public communication.

71

Thus, a European looks at American culture—the patterns of American life—and, from gum to drinking habits, from housing and clothing to games and entertainments, is prone to conclude that an intensely industrial, urban, mechanized life naturally leads to these patterns. Yet one has only to read American and other documents about patterns of American life between, say, 1800 and the Civil War, to recognize many American characteristics and patterns of individual or social behaviour of today, although the America of a century or a century and a half ago was overwhelmingly rural, unmechanized, and ignorant of mass-production. Again, tastes—in the cinema, over the air, on the TV screen, in the Press, in eating and drinking, in dress and decoration—reflect national differences, although mechanization, h.p. per worker, urbanization, industrial occupations, and relations between cities and countryside may be almost exactly the same in any two countries. Compare and contrast, for example, Denmark and Sweden; or Australia and New Zealand; or the United States and Canada (where industrialization has been even more rapid than in the States); or Holland and Germany; or France and Belgium; or the United States and Britain.

Clearly, the more human life is mechanized or affected by mechanical techniques, the more is it likely to partake of a general over-all pattern due to those aids and techniques. That is implicit in the use of such phrases as 'Western industrialism,' 'Western civilization,' etc., and not merely Scandinavian, Swiss, or British industrialism and civilization. Yet Russia has shown that the aids, techniques, and methods of Western urban industrialism can be borrowed, copied, even more forcibly intensified, without necessarily importing into the patterns of Russian life the patterns of Western life. The same *means* of raising productivity and material standards of life cannot, and will not, be used everywhere to serve the same human *ends*. Those ends are values reached by other than economic avenues. The problem what people will do, or ought to do, with the greater leisure and higher material standards of life obtained through the higher productivity of mechanization, mass-production, etc., is one beyond the bounds of economic organization. Economic organization can only make the leisure and material improvements possible, with which men can—if they like—do more good or more ill. To this extent it is no more logical to blame the methods of reaching high productivity for the *kind* of life men decide to lead, than it is to blame physicists for discovering nuclear fission because it was used to make a bomb.

Nevertheless, more in Europe than in America—and more in Asia and Africa than in Europe—there is a distrust for machines. In America and Europe it is part of the social time-lag which expressed itself, for example, early last century in the wrecking of the first agricultural machinery by Luddites. This hangover persists both in American and British organized labour, though it is much less widespread than it used to be. In both countries, too, many managements still view machines as useful offsets to organized labour: another hangover from the days of the first machines.

Thus on both sides of industry instead of a sense of partnership in getting the utmost work out of machines to raise earnings and standards of leisure and life, the social time-lag maintains in both managements and unions considerable distrust of each other; and this distrust expresses itself perhaps most clearly over the role, intensity of use, and the effects of machines. They *are* Capital. The workers *are* Labour. And, with a touching but fallacious simplicity, many on both sides of industry, in both countries, still assume they must inevitably be opposed in their basic interests: just as the machines are thought to be 'opposed' to the men, and vice versa. Yet in Communist Russia and her industrialized (and industrializing) satellites—as in the socialized industries of neither-fully-private-enterprise-nor-fully-socialist Britain—the same human, administrative and economic problem of using the machines to their utmost productive advantage, while preventing men from being 'run' by them, has to be solved, by widely differing methods.[1]

[1] Many A.A.C.P. Teams reported that, despite the far greater mechanization in America, the human work itself seemed as hard as in Britain, but was shorter; and that the British workers seemed to work as hard as the Americans. In other cases, greater mechanization had made work easier and shorter. The important point is that mechanization makes work—whether it remains hard or not—far more productive of goods. On these points, and the social time-lag, an interesting symposium of views from 'both sides' is contained in the pamphlet *Unity in Industry* reprinted by the *Sunday Times*, containing articles in that paper in August and September of 1951 by leaders of British management and trade unions.

The speed and growth of mechanization have manifestly not resulted in setting a pace that kills in America; quite the contrary, they have increased the average of health, welfare, leisure, and longevity, more rapidly than in any other country. They have, however, thrown on the screen the shadows of vast social and cultural problems. Technological advances during the past ten years—like the application of electronics to industrial processes—show that easier daily work, still more leisure, still higher standards of consumption, and earlier retirement or longer old age in retirement are, *potentially*, just round the corner for Americans—and, indeed, for any people who are prepared to organize to secure these benefits. They depend on higher degrees of machine utilization, on investment in new equipment, on new ways of organizing work. If the machines, the slaves of the Western world, are really to do what they can for men, the reshaping of men's thinking and attitudes, of their own organization and behaviour, must be far-going.

Viewed in this way, the Industrial Revolution and the Machine Age are only just about to begin. That implies a revolution in many other ways: in working, thinking, and living. Once he had made a machine to bear his curse, Adam could no longer live as Adam did. Why does he still try to?

Horse-power and Man-power

The American figures of electricity used per worker throughout this century are striking. For manufacturing industry they are shown in Table I. It will be noted how the 'installed h.p.' *per unit of output* has increased from 1899 to 1939; and it is probable that—in view of the expansion of 'installed h.p.' during and after the war, and of the much slower rise in numbers engaged in manufacturing—the h.p. per worker in manufacturing industry has increased by about 14% since 1939. So the h.p. used *per unit of output* since 1939 must also have risen.

Electricity consumed per industrial worker (Table II) even during the past decade or so has risen by almost 75%. Electricity used *per unit of output* over the same period—particularly since war ended—has gone up by nearly 30%.

TABLE I

Horse-power per product in American Manufacturing Industry

Year	H.P.—rated capacity of		Total H.P.	Output Index of Manufactures	Installed h.p. per unit produced	Index (1939 = 100)
	Prime movers	Motors run by purchased energy				
	(1,000s)	(1,000s)	(1,000s)			
1899	9,633	178	9,811	100	98·11	72·5
1904	12,605	428	13,033	124	105·10	77·7
1909	16,393	1,669	18,062	158	114·32	84·5
1914	17,858	3,707	21,565	186	115·94	85·7
1919	19,432	8,965	28,397	222	127·91	94·6
1925	19,243	15,116	34,359	298	115·30	85·2
1927	18,901	18,224	37,125	217	117·11	86·6
1929	19,328	21,794	41,122	364	112·97	83·5
1939	21,239	29,213	50,452	373	135·26	100·0

Horse-power per Worker in American Manufacturing Industry

1939—6·4 h.p. per worker—(U.S. Census of Manufactures).
1951—7·4 h.p. per worker—(Estimated by projecting a series 1849–1947 appearing in *Electric Light and Power* magazine, January 1949—'Utility Financing Problems Can Be Solved,' by C. E. Kohlhepp).

75

There are special reasons for this. Despite the easier availability of almost every known form of heat and power in America, new processes and new products seem to rely more and more on electricity than on other forms of energy. Modern developments—like electro-chemical and electro-metallurgical processes

TABLE II

Electric Power per Production Worker in American Manufacturing Industry

Year	Average No. of production workers (Thousands)	Electric power used (mill. kWh)	kWh's per worker	Electric power used per unit of F.R.B. Index of mfg. production (mill. kWh) (3)
1939	8,192	70,518	8,608	650
1940	8,811	82,662	9,382	660
1941	10,877	103,109	9,480	610
1942	12,854	120,844	9,401	570
1943	15,014	143,964	9,589	560
1944	14,607	144,319	9,880	570
1945	12,864	129,183	10,042	600
1946	12,105	120,280	9,936	680
1947	12,794	141,919	11,093	730
1950	12,264 (1)	176,400 (2)	14,384	840

Principal Sources: National Industrial Conference Board; Monthly Labor Review of U.S. Dept. of Labor.
(1) U.S. Department of Commerce *Business Statistics.*
(2) Estimated by a group of industrial economists.
(3) Calculated by a group of industrial economists from second column and F.R.B. Index data as published in Federal Reserve Board *Bulletin.*

Note: figures for 1948–1949 are in process of revision.

—have increased the 'electricity-content' of many new products. This, together with the older trend to substitute electric motors for steam and other forms of power and transmission, have combined to raise the amounts of electricity used per worker.

It is also worth noting that—since hours of work per worker have steadily been reduced in America, and both h.p. and output per worker have steadily increased with the expansion of capital equipment—*electricity used per worker* in manu-

TABLE III

Gross Investment by Non-Agricultural Producers in Plant and Equipment in U.S.A. 1929–51
(in $000,000,000)

Year	Total	Equipment	Construction
1929	9·8	5·6	4·2
1930	7·6	4·3	3·4
1931	4·6	2·8	1·8
1932	2·5	1·6	1·0
1933	2·3	1·6	0·7
1934	3·1	2·2	0·9
1935	3·8	2·9	1·0
1936	5·2	3·9	1·3
1937	6·6	4·7	1·9
1938	4·7	3·4	1·4
1939	5·7	4·0	1·7
1940	7·4	5·3	2·1
1941	9·3	6·6	2·7
1942	5·8	4·1	1·7
1943	4·6	3·5	1·1
1944	6·3	4·7	1·6
1945	8·7	6·3	2·4
1946	15·5	10·7	4·8
1947	20·3	14·6	5·7
1948	23·4	16·7	6·7
1949	21·7	15·3	6·4
1950	25·4	18·4	7·0
1951	29·6	20·8	8·8

Source: Department of Commerce; from July 1952 Economic Report to the President, by Council of Economic Advisers.

facturing has not increased as rapidly as *electricity used per man-hour*.

One more indicator of the advancing importance of electricity in American industry is the ratio between 'prime movers'

77

(individual installations producing power) and 'motors run by purchased energy' in the first two columns of Table I. Since 1899, and at an accelerating rate, American h.p. per worker has come to depend more on electricity (and some other sources of energy) bought from outside the plant. The upshot has been that electricity used has roughly doubled every ten years, while the physical volume of output of the American economy has increased in the same periods by about one-third. This has very important implications for the future of American—and all other—industry.

In Britain, these same trends—or most of them—have also been followed; but far in the rear. For example, the rate of installing new generators to raise the total available output of electricity has been far slower; 'prime movers' have also been retained more, many of them older. The rate of installation of both h.p. and equipment per worker has been much slower— the new equipment rate affecting the rate at which resources of h.p. were developed.

All this is, of course, a vast canvas. It covers surprising differences. For example, mere horse-power, by itself, is no more necessarily an indicator of efficiency than mere brawn in a man. The efficiency of the use of the h.p. by the machinery, or of the brawn by the brain, is the important feature. More modern machines may well do more work with less h.p. Again, productivity may in certain cases move independently of the movement in h.p. per worker. In American industry before the war productivity had not increased, apparently, as fast as h.p. per worker in such branches as automobiles, cement, rayon, hosiery, tobacco, and breweries; productivity seemed to have increased more or less in direct proportion to h.p. per worker in certain iron and steel processes, woollen textiles, paper, and foot-wear; and it seemed to have increased faster than h.p. per worker in the making of biscuits and bread, and cotton textiles.[1] What is clearly required for higher productivity all round is that degree of specialized management which we have already analysed: management which treats fuel and power, raw materials, machines, and the various human skills as separate

[1] Rostas, L., *op. cit.*, pp. 54–8; see also his entire Chapter V on Factors affecting Productivity Differences.

(but not necessarily mixable) ingredients with productivities of their own. It is a question of high efficiency in the use of h.p. That factor alone could explain some of the poorer showing of British textile industries compared with those in America, which use h.p. less wastefully. A lot depends on the *quality* of management and of the workpeople's operation of the industry's equipment, fuel and power, and raw materials. 'Many an old loom made an unbeatable fabric'; but who tended the loom, and how? In short, brand new machinery and unlimited mechanical power may be essential parts of the answer, but are not the whole answer, to Britain's problem: the raising of the average level of her industrial productivity.

Plant and Machinery in America

Americans have recently tended to concentrate less on their buildings and plant, and more on machinery and equipment.[1] According to a special study by the U.S. Economic Co-operation Administration, *gross* fixed investment of all kinds in the U.K. increased by only £100 millions *at 1949 prices* between 1938 and 1949. For British manufacturing industry, this must mean a net decline in that period, in view of the big increase in gross investment in housing, coal-mining, electricity, etc.[2] In the same period American *manufacturing alone* increased its gross fixed investment by the equivalent of some £2,000 millions to £2,500 millions each year.

In Britain, especially since the war began, buildings, plant, and machinery—especially in manufacturing—have been badly in need of modernization and replacement. In some older industries—textiles, pottery, hosiery, and general engineering in private enterprise, and the railways, docks, Post Office, B.B.C., and other agencies of State enterprise—Britain's need of new plant, machinery, and buildings is clamant. On the other hand, in certain of Britain's newer industries—light engineering, automobiles, radio sets, rayon, clothing, and domestic equipment—there are lay-outs and installations which compare with

[1] Plant is anything built into a building (e.g. boilers, ovens, vats); equipment is hand tools, benches, lockers. Buildings and machinery are as commonly understood. [2] See Appendix B.

79

the most modern anywhere. In America, the whole of industry seems to be grouped closer to the average, and that average to be more up to date.

From 1910 to 1932—the latter year being the worst of the Great Depression—it seems that in America the *volume* (not value) of new buildings and plant and of new machinery and equipment (public and private) ran neck and neck. But from 1933 onwards, and with an enormous acceleration in and after the war, the volume of new machinery and equipment streaked ahead of the amount of new buildings and plant. From being about half of each year's total between 1910 and 1932, the new machinery and equipment accounts for as much as three-quarters of the total 'in-put' into buildings and plant between 1940 and 1951 inclusive. And the total amounts of both buildings and machinery have been rising steeply and sharply since 1940.

In Britain, since war ended, investment in new plant and equipment has been more possible than that in industrial buildings (apart from the making good of war damage)—for many reasons, including different Governments' housing programmes, controls over new industrial building, and general concentration of limited capital resources upon these items and the newly nationalized basic service industries (coal-mines, electricity, etc.). In Britain there has been nothing like the proportionate American investment in both buildings and plant, the proportionate heavy concentration on equipment, and the proportionate concentration of all of it upon *manufacturing* industry.

A significant aspect of this development, again, is the *absolute size* of the overwhelming recent American investment in equipment—mainly machinery. Here again the same advantages accrue as were noted above. The average *annual* 'in-put' of equipment alone exceeded $10,000 millions of 1950 value (£3,570 millions) between 1940 and 1945 inclusive, and exceeded $23,500 millions of 1950 value (£8,390 millions) between 1946 and 1951 inclusive. In 1951 alone, $20,000 millions of new equipment was invested in *private* enterprise. This is roughly three times the *proportion* of investment in new equipment for British private enterprise.

Clearly, so big an annual inflow of new equipment requires a vastly bigger machine-tool, engineering, and maintenance industry than in other countries, and the services and servants that go therewith. It represents a repository of experts and a reserve fund of artificers who can be assigned to solve all kinds of technical problems in production. But by the same token, of course, it represents the Achilles' heel of so highly geared a capitalistic system. The first wave of recession must break upon this machine-making and machine-servicing industry, as upon an exposed sand-bar; and in a real depression it would be engulfed. On the other hand it could be held of many of the older industries of Britain—and of Western Europe—that their machines were so gently, slowly and gradually used-up, that they remained technically efficient after decades, though absolutely and comparatively out of date by reference to current American models. There—of its kind—is a safeguard in depression for them. High wages, high productivity, high standards of living—high vulnerability; lower levels of all these—lower vulnerability. It is worth bearing in mind that the problem of securing stable and steady economic progress grows greater as the amount of up-to-date productive apparatus per worker grows greater. Human life at the lowest levels is certainly more stable!

The more industrialized a country becomes, the greater the economies under the heading of buildings and plant. In industrialized countries there is already apparent one significant aspect of this: the trend away from two—and more—storey factories, and towards one-storey extensive and extensible factories or plants. Therefore the trend is away from city-centres to the 'green belt' or suburbs, where land is cheaper; where local taxes (rates) are lower; and where, accordingly, new factories become almost uniformly standardized. Electric power and road transport have carried this trend much farther in America than in Britain; but even in Britain it is strikingly noticeable today—though the employees' bicycle racks take the place of the American workers' car parks.

It will not escape the observation of the technologically-minded that the more a country mechanizes, the less important and less relatively costly are its industrial buildings likely to be,

81   F

TABLE IV

Actual Input of New Industrial Capital (Gross) in U.S.A.
(at 1950 Prices, in $000,000,000)

Year	Total	Equipment	Plant
1910	9·7	5·7	4·0
1911	8·7	4·8	3·9
1912	10·0	5·8	4·2
1913	11·0	6·4	4·6
1914	9·3	5·1	4·2
1915	8·7	4·9	3·8
1916	11·5	7·0	4·5
1917	12·2	8·0	4·2
1918	11·0	7·7	3·2
1919	12·2	6·9	5·3
1920	12·8	7·4	5·3
1921	9·2	4·7	4·5
1922	11·2	5·9	5·3
1923	14·3	8·3	6·0
1924	13·6	7·5	6·1
1925	14·8	8·1	6·7
1926	16·6	8·8	7·8
1927	15·9	8·2	7·8
1928	16·6	8·9	7·7
1929	19·3	10·6	8·6
1930	16·2	8·6	7·6
1931	10·4	5·6	4·8
1932	6·1	3·2	2·9
1933	5·5	3·4	2·1
1934	7·5	5·0	2·5
1935	9·0	6·4	2·7
1936	12·0	8·6	3·5
1937	14·2	9·8	4·4
1938	10·2	6·9	3·4
1939	11·8	8·3	3·6
1940	14·8	10·6	4·2
1941	17·9	12·9	5·0
1942	13·5	10·5	3·0
1943	10·1	8·1	2·0
1944	12·8	10·1	2·6
1945	15·3	11·6	3·7
1946	27·5	19·8	7·6
1947	19·6	22·8	6·9
1948	31·0	23·5	7·5
1949	28·2	21·2	7·0
1950	32·6	25·7	6·9
1951	34·3	27·4	6·9

Source: Machinery and Allied Products Institute.
Data obtained through McGraw-Hill Publishing Co.

82

and the more relatively costly their contents. The less comforting corollary for Britain is that the larger the quantity of older buildings nearer city-centres, and the greater her need to mechanize and install new equipment, the more of a handicap are the old buildings and old workplaces likely to prove. In Britain, new buildings and new contents are already—and in future will increasingly be—needed simultaneously.

Renewals and Replacements

There seems to be little difference on the whole between the rates allowed by the U.S. Internal Revenue and the U.K. Inland Revenue for the annual depreciation of machinery. The American authorities allow twenty-five years as the normal 'useful life' of a textile loom; the American textile companies write off their looms even more quickly than that. Yet Lancashire and Yorkshire have written many of their looms off completely, but still find costs of production too high, and competition from many countries with newer cotton textile industries too severe. The possession of machinery standing at 'nil' in the balance sheet does not guarantee efficiency and competitiveness. Sometimes it does the very opposite.

On the other hand the U.S. Internal Revenue reckon four years as the official 'useful life' of television apparatus for transmission, five years for 'sound' studio microphones, and ten years for 'sound' studio equipment. That would explain, by itself, the vast technical strides made by TV and VHF and other broadcasting in America, compared with the TV equipment of the B.B.C., much of which was condemned before the war as 'obsolescent,' and most of the B.B.C.'s 'sound' equipment, which is also pre-war. This is a useful example, since American (unlike British) TV is wholly post-war; and the official attitude of the U.S. Internal Revenue towards (private enterprise) TV in America is typical of its attitudes to the equally typical all-American readiness to spend on research, new equipment, experiments, etc., and to utilize machinery intensively. Consider the following official 'useful lives' of American equipment:

83

	Years		Years
Salesman's automobile	3	Cigarette machines	15
Commercial motor-cycles	4	Commercial aircraft	5
Book-keeping machines	8	Coal-cutting machines	10
Typewriters	5	Belt-conveyors	15
Automobile tools, dies,		Broaching-machines	15
patterns, etc.	3–4	Blast furnaces	25

There is another important American official practice which helps obsolescence, replacement, and modernization. 'Certificates of necessity' can be obtained from the U.S. Internal Revenue (Treasury) if for any technical or other valid reason more rapid rates of depreciation ought to be granted to a firm—e.g. for certain defence plants and equipment, or if some disaster or some unexpected or new technical development has invalidated the normal rates of depreciation.

But, by and large, these official rates of obsolescence and depreciation are not significantly different from those in use in Britain. The big departure in American industry seems generally to have been taken by industry itself. It was always able, 'over the long haul,' to make and retain profits large enough to write-off its equipment more rapidly than any other in the world. It is important to note the factors contributing to this outcome:

(1) The volume of turnover and flow of through-put were big and steady enough, and the man-power ready, to use equipment intensively;

(2) the machinery was in fact more intensively used per annum, and therefore tended to wear out more rapidly;

(3) there was consequently a bigger regular demand for new equipment, with a consequent impetus to equipment-makers to experiment, develop, etc.;

(4) the lowering of unit-costs and expansion of the market enabled new investments in new equipment to pay-off more rapidly;

(5) over the years, the entire process acquired a 'snowballing' effect, building up bigger machine-making and machine-servicing facilities, and increasing and accelerating maintenance, renewals, and replacements;

(6) as this system develops, there is less and less work 'in process' as a consequence of 'flow production';

(7) and consequently more and more investment in machinery;

(8) and a more and more rapid turnover from that investment.

A rough American survey in 1949 showed that the majority of manufacturers thought equipment should pay back its

TABLE V

Percentage of U.S. Companies of the Opinion that Equipment should pay back its Cost in the Following Number of Years or less

	2 years	3 years	5 years	10 years
Steel	—	—	80	100
Petroleum	—	—	50	100
Electrical Machinery	11	44	89	100
Chemicals	10	20	60	100
Automobiles	29	57	72	86
Machinery	13	38	85	100
Food	7	27	67	100
Transport, etc.	—	29	100	100
Textiles	7	36	57	100
Coal-mining	20	35	65	95

original cost (including installation, etc.) in five years.[1] This is a more substantial and significant difference from British manufacturers' opinions and practice than the difference between the British Inland Revenue's and the American Internal Revenue's notions of depreciation rates.

In general it can be said—and most of the A.A.C.P. Teams concerned in industrial processes found—that both American managements and trade-union leaders and their members

[1] McGraw-Hill *Survey of Business Needs for New Plants and Equipment.* January 1949.

almost automatically look forward to, and assume, better performances by machines and men as part of an inevitable progress. It is also part of the American climate of opinion, more noticeable than it is in Europe. Their attitude in this respect is all of a pattern and a piece: whether to buy and install a new machine or item of equipment is decided by reference not only to past performances, but also to the *further potential* of the existing equipment as compared with the potential of the new. A nation so productivity-conscious that it always expects and strives for a 2% to 3% compound-interest advance in its output per head will naturally create a climate of opinion in which the emphasis is not only on more intensive use of equipment, but also on quicker replacements and renewals. The cumulative and accelerating process already mentioned has now reached the stage at which, in many cases, such greatly improved items of American equipment are available so rapidly that all formulae indicate the profitability—i.e. higher productivity—of even more rapid scrapping and replacement. The American rule has almost become 'when in doubt, scrap!'

The three overriding American advantages in all this, as compared with Britain, are:

(1) the steady and sure supplies of materials and man-power for high machine-utilization and smooth flow in all processes;
(2) the size and availability of the machine-making and machine-servicing 'ancillary' industries; and
(3) the profitability of manufacturing, and the ability to retain more of the profits, wherewith the more rapidly to take advantage of (2) above.

It is possible for British management and trade unions, on their own, to improve things considerably under (1). But (2) has been an 'end-of-the-queue' availability to British industry since war ended, and is worse than ever in 1952–53 owing to the placing of heavier rearmament and export requirements ahead of industry itself. And (3) is to some extent denied as a commensurate British source of finance, compared with American industry's funds, by the heaviest system of taxation of business 'profits' in the Western world.

Private savings in Britain did not suffice before the war for industry's needs. They have vanished (on balance, after off-setting them by the amount of spending of capital) since the war.[1] Somehow, somewhere, industry itself will have to find very heavy sums in the future, if it can ever get its hands on enough new equipment. And finally, the over-all *needs* of such new capital equipment in Britain are far higher—both in productive State enterprises like highways and railways, and in private enterprises—than the global amounts invested in all kinds of 'capital' since the war, in official British statistics, indicate.[2] Much of this 'capital' has been in housing, public buildings, welfare equipment (schools, hospitals, etc.)—all of them, within limits, desirable and necessary 'capital' goods. Much, also, has been in the necessary basic services of coal, electricity, and gas supply. But the new equipment of manufacturing industry—almost wholly owned by private enterprise—has been far less than is necessary to fulfil the demands and desires of British Governments, and citizens of all political persuasions, after the requirements of defence, debt payments, and development abroad have been met. In default of enough new equipment 'make do and mend' has been the order of the day. Therewith, the need to use the old equipment more intensively has actually increased. Yet it has not in fact been as intensively used as was both necessary and possible; and by now, in some British firms and industries, equipment is getting beyond the abilities of maintenance to keep it both efficient and competitive with that of other countries.

Maintenance and Management

All this century, observers have been impressed by the quick and efficient maintenance, repair, and overhaul of American equipment. The production-planning, which so largely makes for good management, would be frustrated without speedy and competent service to machinery. The standards of machine-maintenance, and the speed of all repairs (planned or in emergency), astonished many of the A.A.C.P. Teams. Yet these

[1] See Appendix B.   [2] *Ibid.*

87

things are necessary implications of the high utilization of machinery.

The proportion of employees engaged in maintenance, out of all those in production, seems on the average to be higher than in Britain. The Americans do not appear to be more advanced than the British in what is called 'preventive maintenance':[1] the kind of overhauls, checks, tests, etc., which look to the prevention, rather than cure, of breakdowns. But the schedules for maintenance in America are very strictly kept, and—as part of the common climate of attitudes in American factories— breakdowns are almost always viewed as a reflection on the skills and efficiency of the maintenance department. Again, there seemed to be a more general *awareness* of the need for preventive maintenance. The underlying principle inspiring all this is the same as we have already noted: to 'make machines work.' If the costly machines are made more idle than is absolutely necessary as a minimum, then the relatively more costly man-power is idle somewhere. The productive *capacity* of the firm is idle. There is waste. Productivity, and therefore Americans' personal prosperity, is held back. Accordingly it pays hand-somely to keep highly skilled technicians and maintenance men, and to use them frequently to ensure the smooth running of all equipment. A more recent development has been to call in maintenance and other specialists from outside. This could only arise in a system in which so much regular maintenance and new equipment were required, on so large an annual scale, that it paid to set up 'outside' firms of maintenance specialists.

The significance of this development—which is parallel to that of 'buying-out' components and many specialized services in America—should not be overlooked. 'Personal services' have been rapidly dying out from our industrial society and from its censuses of occupations. That is a process which Americans— naturally—felt first; domestic servants were always prohibitively costly in the Northern industrial States. And now that indus-trialization is sweeping ahead all over the world, all the world *begins* to enter the real machine age. So personal services are on the wane. Services for machines and 'public services' are rapidly taking their place.

[1] See *Plant Maintenance* report, especially pp. 5, 7, and 10.

4

Making Machines Work

In all international comparisons it is important to bear one thing in mind. Size is itself an advantage in certain ways—though by no means in every way. In the case of an industrial nation, it is an advantage to be big rather than small. In purely economic matters—and *only* in those—it is better to be America than Belgium or Switzerland, even though these last two countries have achieved the highest average material standards of living in Europe since war ended, and something like the highest productivity per industrial worker. The reason is simple, and becomes more cogent as our era becomes more technologically complex. The big absolute size of a nation's industry makes possible a congeries of subservicing trades and industries. These furnish components, machine-tools, and other specialized (and standardized) products or services. Such ancillary technological trades also engage in research, simplification, standardization, and sub-specialization—until the primary industries' research and techniques, *plus* those of the ancillary trades and services, form an advantageously big fund of technical facilities and 'know-how,' ready for any experiment or emergency.

Accordingly, the 'buying-out' of components—and even of specialized services, like local transport, maintenance of machinery and plant (or parts thereof), and even of research and management-training—is quite usual in America, because the size and scope of industrial operations in that vast market make such independent specialized services profitable. It is dubious if such ancillary trades could ever pay in Switzerland, Denmark, Sweden or Belgium—though their manufacturing industries are both comparatively small *and* efficient. The size of Britain's world-wide 'market,' however, should theoretically

89

allow such services to pay in Britain or somewhere else; but our imperfect world of insulated economic systems, of controls and currency restrictions, does not offer anyone enough of a reliable *international* market in which to offer such facilities. He could never be confident that he could defray his costs and pocket his reward, in any currency. This is a striking example of the shortcomings of anyone's heavy dependence upon a foreign market today—even upon a world market.

No international ancillary industry therefore exists to serve the ordinary industries of West European countries, as the large American ancillary industry of technical services and tool and component-manufacture serves the big manufacturing industry there. The individual European economic systems are too small to warrant the setting-up of such ancillary trades and services as flourish in America; and even if they did so, currency and other obstacles would jeopardize those trades. The result is a compromise—namely, the largest amount of such sub-specializing and 'service' trades and industries (not to be confused with personal service of consumers) as each West European country can 'afford.' In such circumstances it is not surprising that in Western Europe the nearest approximation to the American ancillary trades, serving ordinary industries, is a multiplicity of special (and probably costly) departments owned and run by the larger enterprises themselves. Thus, there is to some extent both duplication and unnecessary maintenance of partly-idle facilities in European countries.

Another advantage of absolute size of units and operations in America is the degree of research which this facilitates.[1] With size of productive unit go wider facilities for research and training of all kinds; and this is, proportionately, as true in Britain as it is in America.[2] The difference is that the size of the big units and their scope in so many different American industries is much larger than those of the corresponding big units in the corresponding British industries. Therefore many research activities pay in America which cannot pay in smaller

[1] It is perhaps necessary to emphasize that size has little to do with competition; production units can become bigger and fewer, yet the competition between them can become fiercer.
[2] See article by Sir Henry Clay cited on p. 29.

units or on a narrower scale; and much of the American results and practices which issue from this research is shared, very quickly, throughout the industries concerned.

Size, Scale, and Organization

The quickest road to high productivity, as we have shown, does not lie merely through new equipment, though more and better equipment is a necessary condition. Rather does it lie through forethought, careful pre-planning of all the flows in production processes and the fullest possible use of equipment. The machines must be made to do more and more of the work. It is easy to say that. What is implied in it for an industrial nation, and for the day-to-day practice of its managements?

If one plunges into the official statistics, censuses of production, and other special studies of industry in America and Britain, one emerges, after an 'under the water' feeling, with a strong sense of surprise that the *structures* of both firms and industries in the two countries are so similar.

First, industry by industry, there is a bewildering variety of separate producers of all sizes. There is no such thing as an ideal size or kind of production unit which can be laid down for all firms and industries to copy. The typical size of firm varies from industry to industry. In some industries—in America as in Britain—one can broadly divide the firms into big, medium, and small; in those industries, as indeed in all industries, the majority of the separate firms is composed of small businesses; and the biggest businesses are the fewest. But in many industries the majority of the *persons* employed is to be found in the group of medium-sized firms. In other industries, it is to be found in the smaller group of big firms.[1] Moreover, the size of the

---

[1] Details of the distribution of production units, by size, will be found for the U.K. in the Censuses of Production, and in the article 'Statistics of the Censuses of Production and Distribution,' by H. Leak, C.B.E., in the *Journal* of the Royal Statistical Society, Series A (General), Vol. CXII, Part I, 1949, p. 67; for the U.S.A. in the reports of the Temporary National Economic Committee (T.N.E.C.), of the Federal Trade Commission, and of the Joint Congressional Committee on the Economic Report. For the U.S.A. also, Professor J. K. Galbraith's *American Capitalism* (London, Hamish Hamilton, 1952), Chapters 4 and 5, will be found both informative and provocative.

separate business, by itself, is no final criterion of that firm's economic power, for it may operate in association with other units, for all kinds of purposes. And the degree of competitiveness between the units in any industry, American or British, has little to do with the numbers of those units, or their grouping into firms of differing sizes: you often find the fiercest competition when the number of producers diminishes and their individual sizes become bigger.

If any generalization is permissible about American and British industry and its working, it is that there is more competitiveness in British industry than Americans think and less competitiveness in American industry than the British think.[1] Apart from that, the next permissible generalization about size, scale, and business organization in the two countries would be that the much greater production and productivity of American industry is achieved by more *concentration* of industry upon much bigger production units, industry by industry. British industry can show far fewer giants—even relative to the output of each industry and to numbers employed in each industry. This naturally results in a much greater degree and scale of research, specialization, and experimentation in American industry. Much more of all of them can be afforded, and defrayed, because of the much bigger scale of operations.[2]

Secondly, the *organization* of production is remarkably alike in the two countries: the differences (strikingly enough) are in the *scale of operation* and the *degrees of application* of this or that method, process, equipment, etc. They are not differences of economic principle but of practice. In short, as we saw earlier, the far higher productivity in America is not achieved as a result of some American secret, but as the outcome of better application of commonly known methods and aids.

Thirdly, as to organization of industry: marketing, distribution, selling, and their problems naturally differ between the two countries, as their proportions of city and rural population,

---

[1] For American practice see Galbraith, *loc. cit.*, and—in more popular vein— *The World the Dollar Built*, by Gunther Stein (London, Dobson, 1952), especially Chapter 2 on 'Corporate Power.'
[2] See Galbraith, *loc. cit.*, for details and development of the argument in favour of large-scale economies, and large-scale research and experiment.

their climates, diets, habits, and institutions differ. But it is quite wrong to suppose that Wall Street 'high finance' (or 'the bankers') control American industry and its methods, to a greater extent than 'high finance' controls British industry. On the contrary, 'the bankers' control proportionately less of American industry than they did fifty or a hundred years ago. Again, while the industrial giants of American industrial concentration wield enormous economic power, the *degree* of their domination of each industry—as of their competitiveness one with another—is generally exaggerated; and in any case they do not dominate American industry as a whole. Only in a very few industries—chemicals, automobiles, steel, and (oddly enough) 'the movies'—do a handful of big units really dominate the scene, and then they often operate in keener competition than is the case in Britain or Western Europe. One trend of American industry over the last twenty years (since the Great Depression) is different from British practice, and is important. It is the tendency to form more and more separate, partly controlled, and competing subsidiaries.[1]

This last American development *is* strikingly different from British experience and experiment; and, since it has led to far more 'buying-out,' use of components, and applications of the 'three S's,' in American industry, it merits brief examination. In essence, it is simply the logical conclusion of cost-and-productivity-consciousness. The breaking-down of jobs, skills, operations, and of big units into 'confederations' of smaller units, leads logically to the setting-up of subsidiaries.[2] As we said, there is no 'ideal' size for a firm, any more than there is for a country. But it has been found—by the Russians and Americans more than any, who can show the biggest production units—that 'firms' or units can be too big. The trend towards 'confederations', complexes of firms, with loose associations of subsidiaries and a greater degree of specialization and 'buying-out,' is the outcome of this lesson of experience. It should not be lost upon British industry, whether it is organized as a number of privately owned businesses or as a State monopoly.

[1] *Big Business*, by Peter F. Drucker (London, Heinemann, 1947), gives a popular exposition of these American developments and trends.
[2] See p. 98–99 for an example.

The higher ratio of technical research and experiment in America as compared with Britain—in both industry and educational institutions—shows that there is an advantage in being of a certain size in industry: a size large enough to be able to afford the degree of research, experiment, and application of new methods. To a considerable extent the peculiarly British system of industrial and other research associations—which have no equivalent in America—bridges the gap in British industrial practice. These research associations help the smallest member-firms in the industry, as well as the larger firms.

One offsetting advantage of the small firm needs to be mentioned: that is its lack of rigidity, its flexibility: its ability swiftly to change, to maintain close personal relationships between management and workers, to switch men and machines, to interrupt production, to cut losses quickly. In brief, its chief advantage lies in its non-commitment to heavy overheads, capital, and other costs.

These advantages and disadvantages of the various sizes of firms in the two countries are the same. The differences of productivity are not mainly due to differences of size—though they are to some extent due to the much greater absolute scale and size of American outputs, of financial resources, research, machine-making, ancillary services for industry, etc. Here, size by itself allows certain things to be *generally* done which are *exceptional* in Britain.

Manufacturing—for What and for Whom?

One sidelight on this comparison of machine-utilization between America and Britain is worth making, even as a digression. Few people know that the increase in the numbers of workpeople *in manufacturing industry* in Britain since 1939 has been very large. Between 1939 and 1952 Britain added 1,000,000 more workers to manufacturing—an increase of some 15 to 20%. She reduced the men in her distributive trades by as many as 400,000, only some of their places being taken by women; and the proportion of workers in manufacturing as compared with distribution therefore rose from $2 \cdot 5 - 1 \cdot 0$ in

1939, to 3·3–1·0 in 1952.[1] Britain's exports are overwhelmingly manufactures. This is how and why the *volume* (not value) of British exports was so swiftly raised to a level 80% higher in 1951–52 than in 1939. Yet it has not bought the British more imports for their own domestic consumption; it has bought them fewer. It has not provided them with more of their own manufactures; per head of population, it has provided them with fewer.

Part of this rapid and enormous expansion of Britain's exports of manufactures has had to pay the relatively higher world prices for Britain's vital imports of food and raw materials. The imports of food have been kept down by controls, in order to pay for the much higher volume of raw materials required compared with pre-war requirements. Another part of the expansion in exports of manufactures has been repayment of war-time sterling indebtedness, export of new capital equipment to develop under-developed lands and resources, etc. The remainder should normally offset the bill for imports; and as the *value* of that bill has risen so much more than Britain's bill to the world for her expanded exports of manufactures, the *volume* of her imports has remained, since war ended, below or at the pre-war figures. Thus, in sum, 175% of pre-war British exports now only buys 100% of pre-war imports—and fewer of those for Britons themselves.

This has a vital bearing on the utilization of British industrial equipment. As we saw earlier, controls, 'cuts,' shortages, and taxes have kept down the quantity and rate of re-equipment of British manufacturing industry, highways, railroads, etc. The output of that industry has expanded rather more than its man-power since 1939—much more than 15 or 20%, and nearer to 40%. The extra output has gone abroad. Two conclusions emerge: first, *any quick increase in domestic consumption of manufactures can only come from better utilization of existing equipment;* and secondly—owing to the comparative stability of the working population, its rapid ageing,[2] the pruning of the

1 *Hansard*, House of Lords, May 7, 1952, statement by Lord Swinton, Minister of Materials.
2 In 1911, 53 out of 1,000 people in Britain were 65 and over; in 1947, 105; and in 1977 the estimate is 160. Meanwhile young recruits into industry have

distributive trades and the increased burden of 'indirect labour' for administrative purposes—*better utilization of this equipment calls for better utilization of strictly limited industrial man-power.* American industry has never yet been driven back upon these two possibilities alone. It has always enjoyed greater possibilities of offsetting this or that temporary difficulty by increasing the amount and rate of re-equipment. The flow of recruits to industry, when required, is relatively bigger, faster, and more variable (the role of agriculture as a reserve of man-power being so much greater in America than in Britain); and that flow is also one of young recruits, with longer industrial 'lives' ahead of them. These are big advantages. They are often over-looked; but they do not diminish—rather, they increase—the urgency of the British need to utilize existing productive equipment more intensively.

The Three 'S's'

Mass-production, smooth 'long-runs,' assembly-line methods, pre-planning of production, high utilization of machinery, quick writing-off and replacement of equipment—all these conditions of low unit-costs demand in their turn three special factors. These are Simplification, Standardization, and Special-ization. They are the three charmed 'S's' of high productivity. They are equally applicable to materials, to machines, to motive power, and (through training, and breaking-down of tasks and skills) to men: indeed, to management as well as to work-people. As so many of the A.A.C.P. Teams refer enthusiastically to the effect of these 'three S's' in achieving the peaks of American productivity, it is worth first examining them in connection with the highest possible utilization of machines and equipment. It is predominantly in this connection that they play their beneficent part.

Simplification is the deliberate reduction of variety of manufac-ture, whether of component or end-product. Specialization denotes

declined, and will do so until 1960; longer education and military service claim them; and after 1966 the 'post-war bulge' of young people will disappear, and the absolute decline will again set in. See also p. 24.

the concentration of factory or production-unit on a very narrow range of products—the consequence of simplification pressed to the limit. Standardization, a term often used as an alternative to simplification, is here taken to mean organized agreement upon and definition of performance, quality, composition, dimensions, method of manufacture or testing of a product. For example, if a motor-car manufacturer were to decide to reduce his range of models from, say, ten to three, that would be simplification. The decision to make certain parts of the cars common and interchangeable would be standardization. The supplier of sparking-plugs would probably be making only that one product, and that would be specialization.[1]

Much confusion has been caused in British minds by the popular use of the words Standardization and Simplification to mean one and the same thing; yet they should be kept distinct. In industry, the words denote distinct methods or processes; and in American industry those distinct methods or processes can be traced through many decades of economic development.

In the past three or four years, the British automobile industry has remarkably narrowed the range of different models of motor-cars. That process of simplification has been carried faster and farther by the Austin–Nuffield merger. But at the same time, as compared with conditions before the war, the makers of components of motor-cars—the firms responsible for greater and wider specialization in components—have also *simplified* their ranges of products, and *standardized* their own sub- and sub-sub-components. Accordingly you now find in the British automobile industry greater Simplification (narrower ranges) of both end-products (complete cars) and of components; more Standardization of parts both for competing and the same makes of cars and components; and a greater degree of Specialization by various firms serving the entire industry with special parts, from pressed bodies to instruments, tyres, springs, and coverings. This interlocking of the three S's is carried to a greater extent—over wider tracts of industry—in America. Since war ended it has also been developed to a considerable

---

[1] This succinct distinction between the three 'S's' appeared in the first of two articles in *The Economist* on 'the three S's,' December 29, 1951, pp. 1593–4. The A.A.C.P. *Simplification in Industry* report should also be consulted, especially the definition on p. 2.

extent in other British industries than that making automobiles, e.g. furniture, radio sets, metal and glass containers. On the other hand certain British industries are outstanding for their lack of the three S's: e.g. building and contracting, building components, textiles, household equipment, electrical apparatus and switchgear, tools and implements.

Simplification needs a broad base of *Standardization* and *Specialization* on which to operate. Given that base, the Simplification of processes, components, equipment, etc., can achieve prodigies of production when carried to practicable and logical limits. For example, the famous American system known as 'the interchangeability of component parts' would be senseless without Standardization of, and Specialization on, those interchangeable parts.

It is worth noting that the American degree of simplified production is attained in an atmosphere of keener competitiveness than exists in Britain. It does not involve 'doing away with competition,' or 'stereotyping' consumers' demand. In fact, there is also a greater width of variety of American *simplified* goods—from ready-made clothing to equipment—in America. Generally speaking—and this is particularly true of consumers' goods—it is their components which are simplified, standardized, and specialized; the ultimate finish, or arrangement of the components, distinguishes the end-product and secures variety. On the other hand, in European countries where consumers' rationing in the past ten or more years might have been expected to reduce costs (by restricting quality and choice) costs have *not* fallen—far from it. The reason for this superficially paradoxical contrast was partly given in the *Simplification in Industry* report. It found that *Standardization* was on the whole no more advanced in American industry than in British. It was *Simplification* that had been carried so much farther in America. Accordingly, *Specialization* had also been carried much farther there.

Specialization of machine-making, machine-servicing and of many other component parts or services by separate firms or industries—and by separate departments of the same firm—is most obvious in American industry. For example, the specializing process has reached the stage at which it pays to

98

associate the specialist producer of a component (or service) with the main producer who uses his specialized products. An end-product-manufacturer will thus associate with his pre-planning staff one (or more) representatives of the specialist firms providing him with component parts or services. These latter representatives are thus induced to bring about, and take part in, inter-factory co-operation—indeed, co-ordination—even as early as the drawing-board stage. This is perhaps the most effective way of reaping the fruits of specialist services. And the great technical advance which America enjoys over other countries' industries is thereby lengthened, with all the added opportunities for research into, and application of, new methods and new equipment.

Clearly, all this was in the minds of the Simplification Team when they concluded that there was so much more scope for Simplification in British industry, and that the contribution which might thus be made to British productivity was probably bigger than that of any other single factor. Until Simplification has gone much farther in British industrial processes as a whole —until it is carried much farther by the generality of (and not the few outstanding) firms—it is idle to expect adequate Specialization. And without adequate Simplification, Speciali-zation and Standardization, the full fruits of these three S's, in the shape of higher productivity, cannot be achieved.

The three S's produce these fruits by a combination of their respective processes in this summarized fashion:

(1) Longer runs of production are facilitated, with fewer changings-over, greater mechanization, higher pro-ductivity, and lower unit-costs as a result;
(2) human skills can be broken down into part-skills, more easily learned;
(3) quality can be maintained more easily and consistently, with easier and less costly inspection;
(4) less capital need be tied-up in idle plant, equipment, tools, stock, work in progress, supplies, and floor space;
(5) costly special services in the firm's other departments can be reduced, e.g. drawing office time;
(6) clerical and administrative procedures can be simplified;

(7) the servicing and maintenance of plant and machinery can be simplified;
(8) sales and advertising departments can concentrate on the simplified, narrower ranges;
(9) the ensuing lower unit-costs and higher productivity facilitate more sales, readier availability and deliveries, quicker turnover, and therefore better services to customers and an improved competitive position.

It should perhaps be added that the customers, workers, and owners of the firm concerned may share in the benefits of higher productivity and lower unit-costs in proportions varying with their respective competitive positions. But at least with higher productivity there is more for them to share.

This does not imply that Britain's consumers—at home and abroad—must, first and foremost, accept a narrower range of what are popularly (and wrongly) called 'standardized products.' It means that a substantial fall in British unit-costs and selling prices *can* be secured by more general and better planning, organization, equipment, and methods. If that much-to-be-desired fall in costs and prices were so secured, the three S's could make the same good quality, at lower prices, command wider markets everywhere; in which case, as in America, consumers' choice would remain wide; and *compulsory* changes of custom or taste would not be needed. They would occur anyway, because of the far better value offered. The three S's did not follow in America from a prior conditioning or stereotyping of American consumers' tastes. Consumers' tastes were to only a small extent conditioned and stereotyped in the envied American high standard of consumption, as a result of the productivity of the three S's. Indeed, the three S's have constantly widened American consumers' choices, by raising the *total* of consumption, through lowering costs and prices. There are longer runs and wider ranges of simplified products in America, at comparatively lower prices, than anywhere else on earth.

After all, American consumers of motor-cars, tractors, ready-made clothing (very little other clothing is available!), household equipment, radio sets, footwear, etc. etc., have as wide a range of consumers' choice as anybody: yet these products—relative to incomes—are cheaper than anywhere else on earth. That is the same thing as saying that with so many hours of work an American can buy more of them than any other worker on earth. And he is not aware of having to buy what we loosely call 'standardized products.' What is true for Americans' consumer-conscious industry can, with proper methods, be made true for British industry, although it so largely serves the consumers of the whole trading world.

At a time when Britain's exports can scarcely hold their own in a more competitive world market—and when capital goods badly needed at home are helping to plug the deficit on Britain's international account—it is important to remember that both *higher quality and quantity* are the fruits of productivity. Volume of turnover can easily be given by machines, once they are properly supplied and utilized. The job of management—to make machines work—has not been well done until the 'three S's' have created better value out of better volume. That is real material progress.

Making the Market

The average of industrial productivity is much higher in America than in Britain; yet the *average* American manufacturer works for broadly the same number of customers as the *average* British manufacturer. He does not, in the main and proportionately, have to reconcile many foreigners' requirements with those of his own compatriots, as the British manufacturer must do. He does, however, study his home market—its nature, potentialities, and tolerances—with extreme care. It is not, for the American manufacturer, merely a question of market research, of questionnaires, of analysis of income-brackets, and of consumption habits. The A.A.C.P. Teams involved in the marketing of manufactures emphasized the scrupulous American attention to the *potentialities* of markets. Most of them also emphasized the part it plays in the pre-planning of production.

Market research, selling, and salesmanship, to which we turn later in this chapter, must not be confused with the *making* of the market—though in the pre-planning of production in

101

America the market-researchers' and sales-executives' opinions on what *can* be sold, when, where, and how, play an important part. Selling and salesmanship are mainly by-products of the keener American competitiveness. Essentially the *making* of the market involves the proper laying-out of production by planned processes and stages, in order to use machines and man-power more intensively, in order to lower unit-costs, in order thus to widen or create a market. The first and still supreme example of this market-making was the father of modern mass-production: Henry Ford.[1] All American manufacturers therefore employ these methods, and then seek to secure greater through-put by selling more than their competitors.

In this productive process, all the items of good management with which we have already become familiar play their parts: the training and use of the various skills; the appropriate designing—in which salesmanship and market research have much to say; the planned and intensive use of all the ingredients of production—machinery, fuel and power, man-power, raw materials—with the least waste; and the consequent employment of the 'three S's' to a maximum (Simplification, Standardization, and Specialization). Selling, marketing, advertising, and distributing are vital processes; but not of production as such.

Most Europeans would probably say that the assembly-line method—vaguely known as mass-production—was most typical of American industry; that it was the biggest single contribution of that industry to the modern world. They are probably right. But the significant aspect of this to an economist—and to all who wish to raise the material standards of living of mankind— is that assembly-line methods, the assembly of component parts (whether from inside the same firm or from outside), *cannot be justified without the 'three S's', and in turn permit them to function.* There would be no economy—there would only be gross waste —in standardizing, simplifying, and specializing sub-assemblies, components, etc., which were then only put into a bewildering variety of models, end-products, and processes.

The British excel at shipbuilding. The Americans cannot

[1] See *The Wild Wheel: the World of Henry Ford*, by Garet Garrett (London, Cresset Press, 1952).

102

approach them in this respect in efficiency and economy.[1] Yet shipbuilding in Britain is almost exclusively an 'assembly job.' Engines, plates, rivets, woodwork, members, fittings, furnishings, electrical gear, paint, everything is 'bought out' and assembled —not exactly on an 'assembly line' of the familiar kind, but nevertheless on something like it in principle. All the components and sub-assemblies which go to make a ship are in Britain the end-products of specialization. To a much greater extent than before the war they are now standardized and simplified (though still capable of far more standardization and simplification before they reach the American pitch of the 'three S's'). It is worth noting, moreover, that British shipbuilders do not generally own or control the firms making all these components. So successful and economical an outcome is the result of careful pre-planning. And such pre-planning can only be successful when and where specialization on components is possible.

An example of almost the opposite kind can be seen in British house-building. Bewildering varieties of (public and private) designs, of components, raw materials, etc., vie with irregular supplies of skilled or unskilled man-power, uncertain licensing and permits from Governmental and public bodies, and an inordinately wide range of standards, to prevent a proper and possible degree of pre-planning on the job, and scale of operations.[2]

In the automobile industries of the two countries there was a much bigger difference formerly than now. Yet even today— despite the ability of one or two British factories to show as efficient operation as, if not more than, the fewer and larger American plants—American automobile manufacture is still more of an 'assembly job.' The 'three S's' there play a much bigger part. This is still true despite the strikingly big recent British reductions in types of headlamps, carburettors, starter

[1] It was estimated both in America and Britain that the new (1952) American liner *United States* could have been built to specification in British yards for two-thirds of the dollar cost, and more quickly.

[2] See A.A.C.P. *Building* report, which contains a table showing the remarkable extent to which the U.S. National Bureau of Standards has been able to reduce types and sizes of building equipment and components. The *average* extent of such reduction is broadly 75% over recent years.

motors, distributors, windscreen wipers, dynamos, batteries, etc.: and despite the Austin–Nuffield merger, the British motor-car manufacturers still make many more models relative to the size of markets involved. The same comparison and comment can be made about domestic equipment, electrical apparatus, motors and engines, etc.

The working-out of the 'three S's' is indeed viewed in America as a vital process in the making of markets. As we have seen, it does not necessarily—though it can—result in narrowing the range of consumers' choice. In America, the multiplicity of competing manufacturers of consumers' goods provides a wide range of choice in most mass-produced products. But where the 'three S's' operate most effectively is not so much in the *consumers'* goods market as in those narrower markets for *producers'* goods: the markets for the necessary components, tools, sub-assemblies, and services. They are turned out at comparatively low prices. Their use in assembly jobs results in that remarkably high American utilization of machinery, materials, and man-power which in turn means high and rising productivity and expanding markets.

Standardization and Simplification must necessarily result in Specialization; and in such a degree of Specialization, the number of competing firms becomes fewer. Indeed, in many cases, it can only pay one firm to specialize in one particular component, service, or sub-assembly, in any one American marketing region, since there is only enough business to justify the capital employed for that one very specialized sub-process. Specialization on the *simplified* operations, processes, and equipment of British industry has not been carried to anything like the American extent. As we saw earlier, this is partly—but only partly—due to the advantages of scale in the bigger American home market.

There is also the question of specialization in *managerial* skills and functions: the specialisms which have given rise to industrial and managerial consultants in America and Britain. Despite the ubiquity of separate firms of 'industrial engineers' in America, the bigger firms naturally tend to keep their own specialists 'inside the house,' as indeed the largest and most modern British factories have their own production engineers, work-study specialists, etc. While separate consulting specialists have much to offer, there is the natural danger that the medium-sized and smaller firms—who make up the bulk of their clientele both here and in America—will tend to bring in the 'outside consultants' and think that, therewith, the need to improve the firm's own management as a whole has been met. Management itself today needs to be staffed with at least *some* specialists in the art, skills, and techniques of modern industrial management—even if, for no other reason, in that way the regular management will know which 'outside consultants' it can most profitably employ. Thus, since the large businesses in both America and Britain tend to be self-sufficient in all *managerial* specialists, and since new managerial specialisms are being rapidly developed, there is now plenty of room for such specialists. They are needed both 'inside' and 'outside.'

Since the size of the market itself decides the number of specialist firms, and since the 'three S's' and good management in general make or widen markets, the continuous American tendency is for markets to expand. Therewith the American degree of pre-planned production becomes more and more detailed and intense. The one makes the market; and the market intensifies the one! The process is in the long run reciprocal, cumulative, and accelerating.

Competition and Private Enterprise

Americans have been consistent in their attachment to economic freedom in everything—except over their tariff. Within their frontiers, they have written the competitiveness of private enterprise into their law. Their businesses can even, for certain purposes, enter cartels outside their frontiers; but not inside them. The Sherman and Clayton Acts long lay as dead letters on the statute book; but they have become more lively elements in the past generation. As many an American economist has pointed out, the fear of the odium attaching to an anti-trust case—the fear of the damage caused to a firm's 'public relations'—has sufficed to stop any *open and general* price-fixing and private restraints upon competitive trade in America. Such practices certainly do occur underground and exceptionally. The sameness of certain basic commodities' prices throughout the well-defined marketing regions of America is not the result of mere accident. But such price-fixing and restraints upon competition by businesses themselves are not general. The frequency of Anti-Trust prosecutions might give the impression that monopoly and restriction are rampant in American industry, but the impression would be very misleading; it is precisely because of the well-advertised risk of prosecution that there is so little of these things in American industry. They involve risks which really and regularly materialize, year by year, as the Anti-Trust Division of the Department of Justice brings firms into the Federal Courts. They therefore provide and maintain something of *a frame-work of competition* for commerce and industry throughout the country. Whether the concentration of American industry itself allows competition to be pure, unrestricted and effective is more open to doubt.[1] There is much to be said for the contention that British and American industry are more alike than British and American industrialists realize, or will admit, in this matter of competitiveness.

It seems paradoxical to Europeans, however, that Americans will thus make competitiveness constitutional, yet heavily subsidize the whole of their relatively big agricultural community, their shipping, and certain other important branches of economic activity. (Subsidies to shipping and synthetic rubber manufacture can be excused on strategic—but not on economic —grounds). Their bi-partisan (and almost wholly political) subsidizing of the *agricultural* community actually holds back American *industrial* productivity; it artificially maintains small agricultural units, and retains on the farms numbers of unnecessary workers whose output in industry would be far higher. It must be viewed as an aspect of the time-lag in the American people's otherwise rapid change of attitude to world affairs: they still find it constitutionally difficult to import heavily, especially to import foods. But at least in industry, competition and keen—what an earlier generation of British and European businessmen called 'cut-throat'—competition prevails. How can it prevail, persist, and promote higher and

[1] See Galbraith, *loc. cit.*, and pp. 91–92 above.

106

higher productivity, without causing the nightmare of European businessmen, beggar-my-neighbour bankruptcies? There have been, in fact, and per head of companies, no more bankruptcies in America than in Britain over the past generation. How is it that this constitutionally compulsory American competitiveness proves so profitable? Why are so few throats cut?

The answer lies in the performance. 'Nothing succeeds like success': *solvitur ambulando*, 'solve it by going ahead.' An economic system which expects to, and does, expand its productivity by 2% compound interest per annum for fifty years, and by 3% per annum for the last fifteen, can 'carry' a high degree of competitiveness. Such a high degree of competitiveness ensures that such an economic system will expand its productivity by 2% compound interest per annum. If that proposition sounds 'just clever,' consider the contrary: an economic system which is organized to conserve what has already been gained, to guarantee to all participants portions of an existing market, and to their employees traditional rates of pay and other conditions, may prevent cut-throat competition and bankruptcies. But it will not expand its productivity even by 1% compound interest per annum, and not even for ten years. It will merely tend to share out an income rising parallel with population, and almost static per head.

Nevertheless there are obvious differences between the *kinds* of industrial competition which American and British industry have to meet. We have already seen that British manufacturing industry—perhaps as much as 50% of it—has to meet a more vague, more nebulous, more dissipated, less immediately perceptible kind of competition in innumerable foreign markets, where prices are compared in many currencies and no general system of tastes, or climate of opinion, applies. Often the British manufacturer cannot get to know exactly what has rendered his goods unacceptable, or someone else's goods more attractive. A greater number of causes outside his own country's control—and therefore outside the uniform set of legal and other circumstances applying to all other British manufacturers of the same products—surrounds him.

The American manufacturer, on the other hand, can easily assess almost all circumstances affecting himself and all his fellow-competitors; for they all work far more for the American (the home) markets. True, there is for most American manufacturers and their manufactures no single, wide, unitary 'American home market'; they work for many regionalized markets inside America; but the great advantage for them is that all those markets are within one contiguous national area, subject to the same set of national circumstances, conducting their business with one currency, and with a unitary set of public and other communications. We have already noted in another context—that of 'long runs' of production, specialization, and the 'buying-out' of components and services— what a great advantage so big a contiguous national market affords.

There is, however, one aspect of competitiveness—also of machine-utilization and of the scale and organization of industry—which calls for comment in the post-war British situation. It is the degree to which shift-working is possible in Britain. In it may lie much of the explanation for the long lag in British productivity during the past twenty-five to thirty years. One or two A.A.C.P. Teams touched on it, tangentially: especially the Letterpress Printing Team in its references and recommendations about shift-working.[1]

In the British printing industry a single shift is general; in the American, two and three shifts per day, with fewer operatives per shift, and therefore greater machine-utilization. This practice, through decades, has resulted in a concentration in America—firm by firm—on better equipment, the scrapping of the old very rapidly, and the distribution of man-power (which is *relatively* just as skilled and highly paid as, and *absolutely* far more highly paid than, in Britain) over more up-to-date equipment throughout the country. Now printing—like most highly mechanized American industries, and like industries everywhere as machines do more work for men—requires high capital investment per employee. Accordingly, in comparison with the American system, *any single-shift system which maintains in an under-utilized state twice the equipment really necessary under a two-shift system*, will waste both man-power

[1] *Letterpress Printing* report, paras. 46, 193–196 inclusive, and Recommendation 8.

and machine-power. Earnings will then necessarily be lower than they could be, output will be less, and machines will have to be replaced more slowly.

This seems to be a widespread, deep-seated characteristic of British industry: the spreading of man-power over a *proportionately* larger amount of less-utilized machinery. If so, the comparative absence of keen competition in Britain—the emphasis on stability, security, and maintenance of familiar conditions—must have the effect of conserving both the under-utilized man-power and the under-utilized equipment. When, in addition, a larger proportion of that equipment happens to be old—as it is in many British industries—the uneconomic effect, the holding-down of productivity, is enhanced. Concentration of the available man-power and other factors on *less* machinery (and more of it new) in two or more shifts per day, *for fewer hours per shift in a week at higher wage-rates*, would be more efficient and more productive.

This, however, raises two ghosts: first, the spectre of old shareholders' capital which ought to be liquidated; and secondly the phantom of 'pacemaking by machines,' 'working yourself or a buddy out of a job,' 'working for the boss's profits,' and other familiar fears of intensive use of machinery by British workpeople. These are examined elsewhere.[1] It is enough to emphasize here that there is a serious and peculiar problem of British industry behind all this—not, of course, in all industry, since most of the modern industries or the minority of modern firms in older industries can be excepted. That problem must grow proportionately larger as the older part of British industrial equipment grows bigger, re-equipment is retarded, and other countries make more rapid industrial progress.

A Difference of Application—not of Principle

All this may help to explain the general American tendency— already mentioned—to rely more and more on the principle of 'assembly.' Successful application of this principle, in an atmosphere of keen competition, compels good management to smooth out the flow of production into more and more

[1] See p. 176.

pre-planned processes and stages. The three S's then come into operation. They make components cheaper. The good management then tends to make fewer components 'in the house,' to 'buy-out' more of them because they are cheaper; to 'buy-out' more and more specialized services (e.g. maintenance of machinery, market and other research, the services of 'industrial engineers' and other production experts, etc.); and therefore to concentrate on the fullest utilization of the ingredients of production, the avoidance of wastages, and the minimum of locked-up working capital in stores of materials, components, spare parts, and other items in the stores or supply departments. In this way a modern factory increasingly tends to become a place of final assembly.

The 'structural' risks in any line of manufacture thus tend to be spread over many separate companies, all servicing the final assembly-factory. The same spreading of risks occurs over industry as a whole. And—a noteworthy result—more of a premium is thus put upon medium-sized units of production, and less upon giant concerns. Accordingly, here also emerges a part of the explanation for the tendency of American manufacturing industry to break down production into more machine-work, into semi-skilled jobs, and into smaller and more competing production units (even though the latter remain under one concern's ultimate control). The exception, already mentioned, is the kind of process-industry which demands a large-scale production unit for high productivity— e.g. certain chemical processes, oil-refining, papermaking, and the more obvious case of atomic energy.

In all of this, the portents for British industry—granted all other necessary improvements—could be remarkably favourable; for in manufacturing Britain possesses a concentration of average medium-sized firms. She has—as she showed in war-time—the flexible and expandable resources of many small firms making components and sub-assemblies. She also has a nation-wide distribution of skilled and semi-skilled factory man-power. She lacks the organization of these resources into the appropriate channels of pre-planned production, industry by industry; the degree and scope of training for management and man-power alike; and the keen competitive sense of urgency in raising efficiency and productivity all round. But there is no inherent, national, or indeed any other, reason why, for example, British visitors to America should find 'bought-out' bushings delivered already drilled-out, while in Britain they have to be drilled-out in the factory after delivery; or why the outstanding degrees of efficiency, economy, and productivity in such disparate industries as British shipbuilding, biscuit-making, confectionery-manufacture, and the assembly of bicycles should not be attained throughout British industry.

As trade association after trade association, and trade union after trade union, now gauge the magnitude of the improvements and changes which must take place to raise British productivity—in the face of handicaps which Americans do not have to face—so the various requirements emerge. These requirements are: better training of operatives, supervisors, and other management executives; more and better-trained pre-planning staffs; more and better-trained production engineers, work-study experts, controllers, and factory, cost, and works accountants; more trained designers, engineers, technicians of all kinds; in short, more and more specialists.

In this way, the ideal and successful management reaches out on all sides—to the schools and universities, to the trade associations and trade unions, to Government and public services, to research institutions and social and psychological analysts—seeking greater simplification of work by way of more standardized and specialized operations. It is not a process which can be made successful by management alone—though 'management is the only group whose *actions* can be decisive in bringing about the desired increase in prosperity.'[1] If not the actions, at least the attitudes and assumptions of other groups in the nation—consumers, trade unions, political parties, governments and public services, universities and schools, professional bodies—will be equally decisive in the solution of Britain's No. 1 priority problem. For competitive efficiency and rising productivity can only come from better management if the general climate of opinion favours them.[2] The general climate of opinion does so in America.

[1] *Management Accounting* report, p. 6. Italics not in the original.
[2] See Chapter 8.

The American people—businessman and trade unionist alike—seem to be more productivity-conscious, even cost-conscious, than the British. The British businessman and trade unionist for a long time—perhaps for the past fifty years—have not been under such social and other pressures to become so. The climate of general opinion was against them; and they had a big say in forming it. Stability, assurance, the bird in the hand—these filled the horizon of industrial and commercial opinion—for owners, management, and trade unions. The team of British trade-union officials which visited America under the Economic Co-operation Administration's auspices, and not under the A.A.C.P., could well report that 'Efficient management set the pace of productivity in American industry—not because of altruistic belief in social progress but from necessity.'[1] But that necessity has been, and still is, the product of general opinion in America, in all groups and political parties. It produces the highest material standards of life in the world. The overwhelming majority of A.A.C.P. Teams sensed it, and said so. And the raising of productivity necessarily involves such a general attitude as favours the making and widening of markets through all the methods we have hitherto examined.

Demand is Moulded and Met

There seems to be an apologetic note in the oft-repeated British businessman's reference to 'the vast American home market.' As we showed earlier, it is not this 'vast home market' for which the average American manufacturer works. Moreover, that market could only be safe, secure, stable, and guaranteed for the American manufacturer if he were shielded in it from competition with his fellows—which he is not. On the contrary, it seems that American manufacturers compete with each other in the same market quite as intensely as, and probably more keenly than, British manufacturers. In many industries (e.g. confectionery, brewing, radio sets, men's wear, publishing) competition is keener, and the range of consumers' choice even wider, than in Britain. American advertising would not have bulked so proportionately large unless these things had been so.

[1] *Trade Unions and Productivity*, published by the T.U.C., London, 1950.

That is not to say that there are no advantages in the over-all size of a nation's home market. If conditions of transport are favourable, if the end-product lends itself to distribution in the same styles and qualities throughout a big country, and if climatic or racial or other local differences do not invalidate large-scale operations, those operations can result in large-scale economies. But offsetting all this are the costs of distribution, marketing, and merchandising. And throughout the Western world distribution, inland transport, merchandising, and advertising have long been looming larger as a proportion of total cost.

The decisive advantage, therefore, of a vast contiguous home market lies in the same ability which we encountered earlier to enlist the 'three S's' in production *and in distribution*; standardization, simplification, and specialization. It can guarantee to the best managements the best shares of the home market, and therefore the greater through-put for their models or products. This in turn renders mass-production cheaper, and helps it to tap lower income-brackets, and so to widen markets and raise standards of living.

The gamble of management in America is on being able to sell enough to secure enough through-put, for long enough, and for the given model or product. If it can bring off that gamble, unit-costs will fall with cumulative rapidity, the particular operational equipment (e.g. tools, jigs, dies, etc.) can pay-off quickly, and the best budgeting of the best accountants and controllers will prove to have been pessimistic. That is why, in unfortunate cases, it always pays an American management to scrap an entire model or product—over which some mis-calculation has been made—cut the loss, and get on with a new one which *will* pay-off.

It is clearly within this setting that advertising, market research, etc., play their important parts. Their primary roles need to be much better understood in Europe—where, none the less, they have made seven-league-strides forward in the past generation, and in particular since the war. We said earlier that industry everywhere must know, as fully as possible, the nature, potentialities, and tolerances of its markets. The only way in which an industry's products can be certain of being taken by consumers—whether final consumers or other producers—is by a dictatorship. Everywhere else, markets are subject to unforeseen variations, stresses, tolerances, and limits which can invalidate the best assumptions of producers for those markets. If those producers have sunk much capital, labour, and managerial skills in pre-planning some product, the throwing of the entire production out of gear by some voluntary variation of the market itself amounts to a disaster. In the trading world of today, even the acts of Governments, like those of God, are very often in the schoolboy's definition 'acts which no reasonable person is expected to perform'!

Sound statistical analysis of the levels of incomes, which form markets; the gauging of potential demand at differing prices; the projection into the near future of demand-curves—these items of market research are necessary *data* for the planning of production. They are of great use to the sales department and to distribution and merchandising in general. But in strict logic there is much to be said for viewing market research as part of pre-planning; part of the necessary prior staff-work of production, and not part of distribution. In the same way, the design department (though making use of the sales department's experience) is properly part of production and planning. Thus, to the extent that American manufacturers now tend to 'buy-out' the more specialized services of market research, and to plan with their aid, market research must be sharply distinguished from advertising, marketing and distribution.

Are American Consumers 'Conditioned'?

All this has an important bearing on a widespread European misconception: that American market research, advertising, merchandising, etc., in some mysterious manner compel consumers (or, indeed, customers who are other producers) to buy what manufacturers want them to buy. This is to take the stick by the wrong end.

The use of market research in the pre-planning of production is to *ascertain* what the potential customers are most likely to want, and therefore to buy. The use of advertising, marketing,

114

salesmanship, merchandising, etc., is to tell, persuade and convince the potential customers—once the products are made—that they are, in fact, what are best suited to their needs, and that in any case they are better than those of competitors. The one service is part of production; the other, of distribution. The use of advertising, marketing, salesmanship, and merchandising in Britain is precisely the same—though not carried to the same extent—as in America. But the use of market research is not nearly so developed, and is not so integrated with the pre-planning of production.

Visitors to America have always remarked the ubiquity and volume of advertising, the insistence on salesmanship, the prevalence of the old motto 'Don't knock, boost!'[1] This seems partly to have been due to the unprecedented populating and rapid economic development of an agricultural pioneer country, and its conversion into a predominantly urban, industrial one, within a generation (1865 to 1890). Partly, also, it is due to the subsequent further populating of the new cities with foreign immigrants who, with their children, naturally demanded very many more of the pre-existing American manufactured products as cheaply as they could be turned out (i.e. by a thus early emphasis on the 'three S's').

But the function and scale of American advertising and sales organizations are mainly due to the high degree of mechanization in all industries. Thus, just as the 'three S's' serve, and combine with, this degree of mechanization to make mass-production so efficient, so do American advertising and distributive organizations play their part in keeping an industry's productive capacity, chiefly its fixed capital, employed as near its full potential as possible. That, in turn, means keeping as many workers employed as possible. The efficiency, the productivity, the lowering of unit-costs and selling-prices, the high wages—all these desirable things are the results of the highest possible utilization of productive equipment. Therefore what seems to Europeans as unduly costly American sales promotion and advertising campaigns are often, in fact, justified hand-

---

[1] *Anglice*: 'Don't cry stinking fish, advertise!' Dr. Shadwell, *op. cit.*, on p. 29 of his most valuable (and oddly up-to-date) first chapter of Vol. I, wrongly cites this phrase as 'Don't grumble, boost!'

over-fist by their success in making sure of a steady and high through-put of materials and human work. In turn, that keeps all the mechanized equipment busy up to, or near, its full capacity. American methods of advertising and selling must be viewed against this technical, economic background.

There are also other American conditions, which help to place this emphasis upon advertising, marketing, merchandising, and distribution in general.

First, where competition is more open and keener, these aids to distribution must loom larger. Secondly—in a nation far more given to novelty, change, and variety—manufacturers have to change their models and products more often. In an atmosphere of greater competition, that too will necessitate more intense, and more extensive, advertising, merchandising, and distributive methods. Thirdly, these aids and methods of distributing goods will themselves become more competitive— and therefore produce another 'snowballing' effect than the one already mentioned. One manufacturer's established product will be fighting against another's new one. Both will then invoke distributive aids, the one to hold on to the market he has hitherto enjoyed, the other to break into it. Fourthly, 'make a better mousetrap, and the world will beat a path to your door.' 'There is always room for more business at the bottom.' If unit-costs can be further cut, selling prices can be lowered. The aids and devices of distribution already mentioned are then brought into play; and 'telling the world' will result in the opening of a lower reach of the demand-curve, the tapping of a lower income-bracket which can now afford the particular product.

No one who studies the psychology—nay, the sociology—of American advertising and merchandising can fail to be struck by its institutional role and effects. It is a vital department of American industry. It is brought in, at a certain stage, to play a vital part. Yet, serving this industrial and purely economic purpose, it plays (almost aside, as it were, to the audience) an enormous social role, a socially necessary function in the all-American scene.

116

Marketing and Productivity

One aspect of advertising—and of distribution in general— is worth emphasizing in connection with the measurement of productivity. Productivity of man-power, materials, machines, etc., is almost universally measured as a procedure in production. Distribution is almost universally kept out of the discussion. But it ought not to be kept out of it. For example, if transport and all distributive costs are included in costs of production as a whole (as of course they are by management) British industries and firms make a much better showing alongside their American counterparts. The reasons are not, however, very complimentary to the British, nor very derogatory to the Americans.

They are, indeed, almost wholly because of the objective, non-human, natural advantages and disadvantages of the two countries. The vast inland mass of America—apart from the Great Lakes for half the year—entails enormously high charges for land transport. Those charges in smaller Britain are relatively much lower and in any case subject to more competition from sea transport. Again, the geographical extent of what are called small marketing regions in America is so vast—compared with those of Britain, or in many cases with the whole of Britain— that the *proportionate* toll of advertising and distributive charges upon the selling price is much bigger than in Britain. It is, as mentioned above, more than offset by the fact that the total American market, due to constantly rising productivity, has gone on rising at 2% per annum at compound interest over the past two or three generations, and has risen at 3% in the past few years. That cushions a lot of losses—and offsets rising costs of distribution for everybody, winners or losers.

It must be said that Europeans on the whole have rather obstinately tended to view American advertising, merchandising, salesmanship, and even the distinct service of market research as unnecessary, or even as 'faintly immoral,' something like 'a racket.' The objection is still most frequently heard in Europe that 'It's all got to be paid for in the selling price!' No American would deny so obvious a fact. What he fails to understand is the widespread European inability to recognize the economic role of this element of pre-planned production and of

the orderly and rapid distribution of products. Europeans—
and in particular the more reserved British—have every right
to dislike what seems to them the American preference for
blatancy and bull-dozing in advertising, salesmanship, and
distribution in general. That is a matter of public and private
taste for one or another *method*. But they have no right to
ignore the economic role which these methods fulfil, and the
parts they play in raising material welfare.

Thus it is nearer the truth to say that simplification, standardization, and specialization have made American advertising
and distribution what they are, rather than to say that advertising
and distributive methods have made the 'three S's'—and all
that flows from them—possible. The same can be said of
competitiveness, of good management, of the general climate of
opinion in America. Advertising and merchandising methods
have followed on these things; they have not preceded them.
In their proper place they have powerfully helped management
to raise productivity. And it is worth adding that, in many an
American industry and firm, the way to the top has often been
taken by a man who started by knowing his market as a
salesman, an advertising man, or a specialist in distribution.

5

Ways and Means to Good Management

We have now examined the factors favouring high productivity which are wholly within the competence of management: the factors we called *internal* to management. It is a good point at which to pause and take stock of the argument, before we pass to factors *external* to management as such, factors within the competence of organized labour, and factors settled for management (and perhaps also for organized labour) by national and even international forces. We can start the interim stocktaking by looking at the ways and means to good management.

Management Means Measurement

It is impossible to conceive of good management without good measurement—of values, performances, efficiencies. And good measurements in turn assess the quality of management itself.

What makes physical output per head a good measurement of relative productivity is that it reflects the joint effect of a great number of influences on production. Relative physical output per head is influenced, for example, by differences in the skill and effort of the workers, but it is equally influenced by differences in managerial efficiency, different technical equipment, rate of operations, and various other factors.[1]

We have seen that British management, on the average, is not as cost-conscious, not as productivity-conscious, and not as aware of the need for measurement, budgeting, and other 'control devices' as American management. Yet the trend of

[1] Rostas, *op. cit.*, p. 2.

modern industry in all countries is towards more 'roundabout-ness of production,'[1] more mechanization, more intensive use of man-power and equipment, and more efficient use—i.e. more economical use—of materials, fuel and power, etc.

These premises point to a twofold conclusion: first, there should be more measurement, as such, in British industry, on the average; the average of measurement and costing in management must be substantially raised, if existing equipment and man-power are to be used more effectively. Secondly, such a raising of the average degree of measurement, costing, etc., in British management means much more technical training of that management and its personnel, from foremen to the board of directors.

There is already a sense of urgent need of these things in British industry. On the institutional side, the British Institute of Management and the Administrative Staff College—both post-war developments with industrial, trade-union and governmental support—are evidence. In the field of enterprise itself, the Training Within Industry scheme, the expansion of industrial consultants' work, work-study, etc., and the dearth of instructors in these new arts and sciences, testify to the rate at which individual firms are over-hauling their former methods and practices. The T.U.C. has initiated at Clapham courses in production and management techniques, and their industrial and trade-union implications.

The scale and scope of these developments in the sphere of private enterprise and trade unionism must be recognized. So must the protracted discussion—almost a dispute—over a related issue in the field of public education: the development of technical modern schools, technical colleges, technological 'universities' and university departments, and so on. Over all these new developments in Britain hangs the query: Are they keeping pace with the rate at which the problems of productivity arise? It is hard to answer that optimistically, in the light of three recurrent economic crises within five years, three successive sets of 'cuts' in the productive capital programmes of British industry, and the wiping-out of the effect of the devaluation of sterling in 1949 within two years by further inflation.

[1] See p. 54, footnote.

The *Education for Management* Team urged that a full examination 'of what is being done to teach administrative studies in universities and technical colleges should be undertaken as a matter of urgency.'[1] The 1949 Report of a Special Committee on Education for Commerce (called the Carr-Saunders Committee, after its Chairman Sir Alexander Carr-Saunders) recommended much more training of a more comprehensive kind for management.[2] The Report the same year of the Conference on Industry and the University, under the auspices of the Federation of British Industries, urged much the same expansion and extension of training for management.[3] The 2,500 and more firms which have adopted the Training Within Industry (T.W.I.) scheme—and therewith helped to put about 300,000 supervisors through one or more of the courses in Job Instruction, Job Relations, and Job Methods—could testify to the clamant need for extension and expansion of such managerial training. But it is not right to conclude that the facilities do not exist for such extension and expansion. To a large extent they do. The shortages are in instructors. The obstacles are largely matters of organization—for example, the appropriate arrangements for time off, shifts, etc. British industrial management needs to be brought more closely into relationship with the local universities, technical colleges and schools and other training institutions. And much of the expert instruction needs to come—as in fact it does up and down the industrial areas of America—from within management itself.

The demand for better managerial training in Britain does *not* mean reducing emphasis on 'the humanities,' the arts, and the graces of life. It is a fair criticism of American training for management—not of American education as a whole, but of the specific training for management—that it so largely disregards any ingredients of these 'cultural' elements. There are exceptions in America: the special courses in the arts and humanities at such technological institutions as the Massachusetts Institute of Technology, the similar foundation in California, etc. But, by and large, it is not unfair to say that the

---

[1] *Education for Management* report, 1951.
[2] His Majesty's Stationery Office, London, 1949.
[3] *Report of Conference on Industry and the University*, F.B.I., 1949.

high pitch of American perfection in the measuring and controlling of the processes of industrial production is achieved at the cost of extreme specialization. Indeed, public debate in industrial and academic circles in America has drawn attention to the dangers of too great an emphasis on technological training, to the exclusion of other forms of 'social adjustment.' And the pace of American management has, with more mechanization and more intensive machine-utilization and economy of resources, already become so hot—for the runners in that race —that in the past two or three years a demand has arisen, within American management, for a little humane easing of the tension.

It is one of the paradoxes of industrial progress that as machines ease the physical burden of the workpeople's work, the organization and administration rendered necessary by more mechanization increase the burden on the personnel of management. In terms of human relationships and industrial welfare, this is perhaps the central problem in industrialized countries today: the problem of finding, training, and suitably rewarding the best managers. Far from Mr. James Burnham's much-publicized 'managerial revolution' having created a new class of technocrats and bureaucrats, constantly swollen by new recruits, the necessary and desirable kind of 'managerial revolution' in Britain is being held up in Britain by a lack of recruits. American management itself is, for the first time, finding the recruiting of its ranks more difficult. The degree of skill now required—in all branches of managerial measurement and control—has become a major social problem in Britain, and may yet become such a problem in America.

Finally there is an aspect of what is properly the 'training' of management in Britain which often escapes management's notice. It is wholly psychological in cause and effect. It relates to the widely different attitude of British managers and owner-managers to their work and workplace from the American managers' and owner-managers' attitude. On the whole— certainly the majority of—American managers turn up at their workplaces, take time off for meals or breaks, and generally attend to 'the business of the nation, which is Business' with the same *application* as that shown by the American workpeople. This is almost as true, and was found to be so by many A.A.C.P. Teams and observers, of clerical staffs in America. The general atmosphere, the climate of intense application, of energy and drive on the job, impresses European observers in America. But it is of great psychological help to the workpeople to see management with its sleeves up, at its obviously exacting tasks, from the time the workpeople start to the time they finish—and beyond.

The Valves Team noted that '. . . the American executive often appeared at the plant at 8.0 or 8.30 in the morning',[1] and the Non-Ferrous Metals Team that '. . . company officials make a hobby of their job more than we do in this country.'[2] As the Metals Team commented, making a hobby of one's job is perhaps a dangerous degree of specialization, as mentioned above; but it certainly helps to raise productivity. Europeans who live in an American manufacturing city are always struck by the full 'commuters' trains' and motor-cars—the latter often being run in shifts through the week—which carry workpeople and managerial staff into and away from the factories at roughly the same hours. The 'democracy of the shop-floor' in American industry is carried to an 'equality before the eyes of the world' in a much broader sharing of the hours and conditions of work.

It is fair to conclude, under this heading, that British training for management should be more widespread and, in kind, more comprehensive. It should lay more stress upon practices, methods, and principles of measurement in the processes of production—more costings, more measurements of utilization of machinery and man-power and skills, more budgetary estimates and instruments of control, more methodical control over quality, wastages, rejects, performance-rates, and so on. The bulk of these measurements could, and should, be made more available—not only to the staffs and trade unions concerned in the particular firm, but also to competitors and to the press and public at large.

These are the real instruments of management. Without more of them, British industry cannot substantially raise its efficiency, for it cannot know where, when, and how to do it.

---

[1] *Valves* report, p. 7.   [2] *Non-Ferrous Metals* report, p. 7.

The Degree of Mechanization

American industry uses more mechanical power per worker. That is only another way of saying that the American worker uses more mechanical power. Simplification of processes and types, standardization, and the consequent specialization make this degree of mechanization—the breaking down of craft and other skills into semi-skills, and ultimately into machine-operations—possible and 'profitable' to everybody concerned. But the real governor or controller of the financial profitability of American mechanization is *the intensive use of the machinery.* The machinery would not pay-off, it would not be replaced so swiftly by more efficient models, the machine-makers and machine-servicers would not be able to afford to keep up the scale of their own ancillary industry, if capital equipment in America were not so intensively utilized. It is arguable that this is the biggest single advantage enjoyed by American industry over British. Even the *volume* of productive equipment per worker and the *rate of expansion* of capital equipment—the year-to-year, decade-to-decade increase in American productive machinery and horse-power per worker—are functions of, and depend on, the American degree of utilization of equipment per work-week and per year of the machine's life.

Management in American industry has long had to reckon with dear labour: labour which is costly *relative to* the costs of all other ingredients of production:

> Output per head shows how far at any given moment the different countries succeed in making use of their real resources: of their natural resources, their existing capital equipment and their labour resources, and how effectively labour—this scarcest of all real resources in highly-industrialized countries—is used in their national economies.[1]

The great advantage of more intensive use of machinery by the workpeople is that this builds up—perhaps cranks-up is the proper word—a better ancillary industry in the country, serving the already existing equipment of industry and the replacement of that equipment the more rapidly it is used up.

[1] Rostas, *op. cit.*, p. 7.

This is the snowball process responsible to a great extent for the unparalleled *rate* at which American productive equipment, and productivity, have expanded. The more quickly any country can crank-up this process and get it going, the more it can 'afford' to 'pay' to its workpeople a steadily rising *real* wage, i.e. the more goods and services it can 'pay' from the rising production to the workpeople.

It is pre-eminently the task of management to organize the country's industry—firm by firm—so that existing equipment is utilized to the fullest possible extent, the greatest economies of materials and fuel and power are made, and man-power is not wasted. That task is discharged in Britain today within severe limitations—many of which are unknown in America, some already mentioned, some yet to be examined. But there can be no doubt that over the whole of British industry it is not yet discharged as efficiently as the national crisis demands it should be discharged, or as the best British firms—of all sizes—discharge it.

Under this heading it is important to bear in mind one corollary of the high and rising American degree of mechanization. More machine-makers and machine-servers get drawn into the ancillary machine-making and machine-serving industry (and its adjuncts, like tool-making and maintenance in general), as man-power (reckoned in man-hours) falls *per unit of output* in the ordinary manufacturing industries. The more you mechanize your ordinary manufacturing industries, and the more intensively (e.g. by shifts) you utilize their equipment, the more you have to man-up the machine-making and machine-serving industry. That has been the result, the snowball element, in American industry. And it has been a big boon.

But before that boon can be won in Britain, substantial changes—in management, in the attitudes of organized labour, Governments, and the public at large—will have to occur. To some of these we turn later. But one, which powerfully affects management, merits attention here. It is the heavier taxation of 'profits' in Britain, combined with a degree of inflation which has also been responsible for 'accountancy profits' (i.e. writing-up the value of stock or work-in-progress, without any increase in business operations), and with a correspondingly rapid rise

TABLE VI

United Kingdom Savings 1946–1952

(£ million)

	1946	1947	1948	1949	1950	1951	Est. 1952
Public Authorities							
Surplus on Income Account	−923	−224	+464	+528	+672	+615	+350
Inventory Maintenance	(− 25)	(−100)	(− 60)	(− 50)	(−100)	(−150)	—
Net Savings, Public Authorities	−948	−324	+404	+478	+572	+465	+350
Private Companies							
Undistributed Profits	+354	+498	+596	+534	+682	+725	+750
Depreciation Adjustment	(−100)	(−100)	(−100)	(−170)	(−500)	(−800)	(−300)
Inventory Maintenance	(−100)	(−300)	(−200)				(+ 50)
Net Savings of Companies	+154	+ 98	+296	+364	+182	− 75	+500
Changes in Tax Reserves	−108	+166	+145	+ 4	+103	+537	+100
Changes in Dividend Reserves	+58	+35	− 15	+ 6	+60	+39	—
Capital Transfers	+552	+393	+219	+248	+160	+117	+ 80
Persons							
Gross Personal Savings	+259	+ 61	+ 75	+106	+177	+ 98	+ 40
Inventory Maintenance	(− 25)	(− 50)	(− 40)	(− 30)	(−100)	(−150)	—
Taxes on Capital	−143	−164	−215	−254	−190	−194	−170
Net Savings of Persons	+ 91	−153	−180	−178	−113	−246	−130
TOTAL NET SAVINGS	−201	+215	+869	+922	+964	+837	+900

126

in the replacement costs of productive equipment, materials, etc.[1] As long as such handicaps on mechanization and industrial progress in Britain are reinforced by positive 'cuts' in capital programmes, enforced by Governments, it is idle to expect productivity to rise *except by the more intensive utilization of existing equipment.* In short, if the more rapid rate of use and replacement of machinery is a necessity of the American situation, it is far more a necessity of the British situation.

Finally, British industry as a whole needs to give more managerial attention to the pre-planning of all production; the consequent extension of simplification, standardization, and specialization, and the greater 'planned assembly' of components; the greater use of market research and design in such pre-planning; the development of the 'smoother flow' principle in production; and the concentration upon the most efficient processes, equipment, and methods. Over and over again the A.A.C.P. Teams mention that American management excels in the *application* of methods, processes, equipment, and ways of organizing already familiar *in principle* in Britain.

Experiment, Research, Initiative, and 'Know-How'

There is not enough of these forward-looking progressive qualities in the average sample of British management. Such is the overwhelming testimony of the A.A.C.P. Teams and of casual observation in America. As to industrial research and experiment: it is worth emphasizing that so many of the technical inventions, processes, and even apparatus employed on a wide scale throughout American industries began in Britain or Western Europe, but were commercially developed—and above all applied—across the Atlantic. The handicaps upon British industry since the war—some of them greater now than

[1] See Appendix B, and the items 'Private Companies' in Table VI, for permission to reproduce which I am indebted to Professor F. W. Paish; see also his analysis *The U.K. as a Source of Capital* in District Bank *Review*, No. 105, March 1953.

The official Blue Book, *National Income and Expenditure 1946–51* (August 1952), is illuminating—particularly para. 10, p. 4, and Table 1, which shows 'Stock Appreciation' of £2,950 in 1946–51 inclusive, against total depreciation in that period of £3,832 millions. This £2,950 millions of inflationary 'paper-profit' yielded a heavy tax-revenue, about £1,500 millions over these six years.

in 1946–50—affect industrial research and experiment in particular: specific equipment is hard to obtain, it becomes increasingly complex and costly, much of the research and experiment is demonstrably not worth while financially as long as the resultant re-equipment cannot take place, and there is the over-all shortage of men with scientific and technical training which also bedevils management in general. Here, again, in theory or in principle much of British industry can show enough 'know-how'; but for many peculiar reasons it cannot *apply* that 'know-how' on a commercial scale. We shall have reason later to examine more of the *'external'* factors affecting industry. But it is only fair to say here that, though technical research and experiment lag in Britain, the explanations are neither few nor simple. The far larger proportion of American research to British research in both industry and educational or research institutions is largely the outcome of the many other American advantages (or advances) already mentioned.

But it is not the same with commercial initiative, enterprise, and salesmanship. These are independent of technical equipment. Indeed, to a large extent they can be independent of management—to the extent that a bad management can often be saved by a good sales department, at least for a time! It is hard to say definitely in what respects British commercial enterprise and initiative fall short of the degree required; but it is—and long has been—the common contention of British and foreign observers that they do fall short of it. Fifty years ago the story was told of the American and British salesmen who arrived simultaneously in an undeveloped market to sell shoes, only to find that the natives did not wear them; the Englishman cabled back 'Returning immediately natives unwear shoes'; the American cabled back 'Rush million pairs assorted shoes natives unwear them.' There is something of the national *'external'* factors in these subtle distinctions; but there is no gainsaying the British need, and the pressure from all sides to which it has given rise, for a higher degree of industrial and commercial enterprise. It ranges from designing to selling, from the merchandising of by-products to the manner and style of packaging, from advertising and market research to simplification of products and finish. Since war broke out in 1939

128

British industry has been snowed under with war-time and post-war inflationary demands, and salesmanship has been in danger of becoming a lost art.

Readiness to venture, to vary, to break with traditional practice, to innovate, to anticipate change in consumers' wants, or to create the change by correct anticipation of what the consumer can be induced to want—these are outstanding American characteristics. They were noted as such by one A.A.C.P. Team after another. But they are necessarily to a large extent bound up with the high productivity, the high utilization and efficiency, of industrial processes in general, anywhere. The particular end-products of those processes do not have to be the same. The models coming off the line in Britain and America, in Russia or in France, can be utterly unlike. But the methods and processes of line-production and of 'assembly' inexorably require a high pitch of initiative in distribution and selling.

The Implications of Good Management

At this point the requirements of good management can be listed as a kind of summary of the A.A.C.P. Teams' findings under this heading, and of the argument unfolded in this book hitherto. Thus good management demands—

(1) Training of its personnel, from shop-floor to office, in its special skills, both within and outside the firm;

(2) the appropriate organization to 'spot' managerial talent, train it, give it the right kind of experience, and promote it, with sole regard to its merit and efficiency;

(3) provision, awareness, and utilization of detailed measurements of all productive 'performances' and costings thereof;

(4) organization and administration of managerial skills to secure the most efficient, effective, and economical controls over productive processes;

(5) use of (1) to (4) inclusive to secure the highest possible degree of utilization of machinery (including maintenance), materials, fuel and power, man-power and any other ingredient in the productive processes;

I

(6) the pre-planning of all operations to ensure the smoothest and fastest flow through all the productive processes;

(7) the closest and best teamwork in and between all departments, and the measures to secure it;

(8) close and continuous pressure for greater standardization, simplification, and specialization of components or processes and of end-products;

(9) close and continuous pressure for research, experimentation, modifications, and improvements;

(10) an artist's awareness of the human tolerances within which all these conditions can be fulfilled.

Let it not be thought that this is the list of *all* conditions required by good management. It is a list of those required by good management *and within its own competence to provide*. But the best management, fulfilling all the requirements listed above, would fail if conditions *outside its competence* were not also fulfilled: for example, conditions required of Governments, or of organized labour, or of the attitudes and opinions of the public. To these factors we now turn.

6

Human Relations

Industry has revolutionized many of the most important human relationships—those between a man and his community, between 'master' and 'man,' between a man and his fellows engaged in what used to be craftsmanship, between men and women, between young and old (within and without the family), and between the falling numbers of people who work on the land and the increasing numbers of those who do not. The old Industrial Revolution, which made these changes, developed throughout the eighteenth and nineteenth centuries. The changes accelerated as our century opened. In the last generation industry itself has faced—but it has not yet undergone—the biggest technological revolution. Western—and many another —society will be remoulded by it. In that remoulding the human relations in industry will pay a leading part, and will themselves be powerfully affected.

Much misinterpretation has been given to the subject of human relationships within industry, as though new words and phrases for old things implied that no one had ever before recognized a problem in this field, or had tried to do anything to solve it. There is now a fashion of discussing 'personnel management,' 'industrial psychology,' 'industrial relations,' 'labour relations,' and 'industrial welfare,' in such jargon as to suggest that the discutants are unaware of the humanity of *all* the individuals concerned (including owners, managers, and office staffs). The abstract-sounding subjects just mentioned are concrete enough. The trouble is that such subjects form— indeed, they must now form—the raw material of necessary skills in industrial management, and of specialized or consultants' services. Thus, the problem tends to be removed to a rarified atmosphere, a high plane of responsibility-and-decision-taking. Then, all too frequently, management, which is *respon-*

131

sible for the decision, gets out of touch with the human beings who alone feel its effects. But once that kind of gap opens between management and other members, the harm to the relationships is done. Discontent, ignorance, frustration then crystallize, and a split in the firm's or industry's 'personality' develops to danger-point.

'The two sides of industry' is sometimes termed a bad phrase, because it implies a conflict of economic interests between them; sometimes a good phrase, because it recognizes that conflict of interest. In fact, modern industry is many-sided and covers many conflicts of economic interest. It has so many more well-defined groupings within it. All of them have one common interest in seeing that a firm or industry—even a State enterprise —'pays,' or is otherwise efficient, for on that depends everybody's living in that firm or industry. Yet there must continue to be 'two sides' who must (in a democracy) bargain with each other over their respective shares of their joint product. That is the economic conflict of interest which the 'two sides' reflect. It does not necessarily connote ill will. Collective bargaining between unions and management in Britain has, on the contrary, been marked by a high degree of goodwill, especially since the second World War broke out. It partakes of much more goodwill on the average than collective bargaining in America, just as there have been fewer strikes and days lost by stoppages of work in British industry than in American since the war. These things should be remembered. They are what might be expected in an older country, with less violence and extremism in its industrial relations, and with a much longer experience of collective bargaining. True, 'the sellers' market,' inflation, and the burdening of consumers with rising prices have combined in post-war Britain to make employers and trade unions take the easy way out—raising prices all round—instead of the harder way of harder bargaining for higher productivity and stable or lower prices to consumers, despite rising wages. But it remains true that industrial relations, as such, have seldom been better in Britain.

On the other hand it is as well, before we examine the roles of organized labour in British and American industrial productivity, to emphasize that *all* human relationships in industry can be improved or worsened. It is not just a question of human relations between 'two sides' alone, but of those between men engaged in managerial duties only, between management and labour, and those between members of the labour force itself. It is high time that the ordinary folk in modern industrialized nations began thinking about *all* human relationships which are affected by modern industrialism. The 'public relations' of a firm or industry with the public, with its own customers, with the agencies of government in the modern state, with universities and other institutions engaged in research on subjects vital to that industry or firm, and with other firms or specialists vital to its processes and progress, are all relationships which should be carefully nurtured if the firm or industry is to develop its best capacities. It is emphatically not enough, in our New Industrial Revolution, to cultivate merely the relations in one's own factory—vitally important though these are. The more modern industry forges technologically ahead—the more subdivided its skills and jobs, and the more specialized its ancillary service and requirements become—the more will its human relationships become complex and ramified. Then, if anything, even a minor thing, goes wrong with any of them, a kingdom may be lost for want of a horse-shoe nail.

In what follows, therefore, it is more helpful to conceive of these human relations and their role in productivity as human relations *affected by* industry; not merely (but certainly to some extent) of 'industrial relations,' 'labour relations' and the rest, in watertight compartments.

The Background of Industrial Relations

Britain was first, and for longest pre-eminent, in the old Industrial Revolution. The changes which this caused in the human patterns and relationships of the eighteenth-century world, before that Revolution, therefore occurred earlier in Britain and tended to become fixed earlier. There is an important paradox to note here if we are to unravel some of the causes holding back British industrial productivity, and creating the 'hang-over' in the attitudes of organized management and organized labour, which we mentioned earlier.

133

The British are a traditional, tradition-ridden, conservative people. They dislike change. They dislike it most when it happens to, or within, any familiar institution—social institutions, for example, and to a less extent conditions of work and play, relationships in the family, and so on. After great social changes, like those of the nineteenth-century Industrial Revolution, this British characteristic tended to 'fix' those changes. Later changes become more difficult than they would have been elsewhere (for instance, in America, or on the Continent) where industrialization came later, spread relatively faster, and was never a 'jelled' process. This, roughly, is what happened in Britain with the human relationships of industry, as compared with those in American industry. For long, they were far worse in American industry. There has been nothing in Britain for more than a century to compare with the pitched battles, the vigilantes, the strike-breaking and picket squads of the first twenty-five years of our own century in America. No such vast changes as occurred in the attitudes of organized labour and management in America in the second twenty-five years of our century occurred in Britain. They were not needed. They had occurred in Britain long before.

In 1902 American trade unionists—most of them in craft unions—formed a small percentage of workpeople in American industries, a percentage less than one-third of the British figure. Today the percentages of trade unionists in manufacturing industries in the two countries are roughly equal. In the past twenty years American trade unions have more than doubled their membership. They have multiplied their funds by ten. A few of the bigger, wealthier American unions, led by forceful and able men, have trained their own cost-accountants, industrial engineers (production engineers), work-study experts, and instructors. Such unions, though a minority of those in America, have—while waging hard-fought campaigns with management for their members' pay and conditions—co-operated with management to raise the intensity of use of machinery and man-power, the profitability of the firm or the industry (as the condition of further social gains, mechanization, and efficiency), and productivity. There has been a great increase in the power and responsibility of American unions since 1933.

From being weak and highly defensive-minded when the Great Depression began, the leading unions have become stronger and more positive, effective stimuli of technical improvement and economic progress. There are still widespread 'hangovers' of restrictive practices, 'feather-bedding,' 'making work' and 'sharing the work' in the majority of American unions. But the picture of trade unionism in America is unrecognizably different from that of twenty years ago.

Some idea of the growth of power, responsibility, and wealth of American unions in the past twenty years can be gauged from the report of the International Ladies Garment Workers' Union for the year 1951. This union, one of the most progressive in America, is an outstanding example of the changes in American unionism in that time. It has approximately 425,000 members, which puts it in the large-medium class of British unions. It publishes certified accounts, which is the exception in American unionism and is not required, as in Britain, by law. The membership is spread over 490 'locals,' or local unions. The payroll of its staff alone comes to nearly $6,000,000 annually, against about one-tenth of that for the biggest British union's staff. Its general office and affiliated local unions received and administered nearly $60,000,000 in its general and special welfare funds alone during 1951: say £25,000,000. The report showed that a record sum of $41,575,000 was collected from employers in 1951 in various funds which finance sickness, vacation, and retirement benefits. These facts not only throw into relief the greater material resources, power, and staffs of such leading American unions. They also show the effects of the much higher union dues in America, and the way private enterprise has been made to shoulder *directly* more of the social services which, in Britain, form 'the Welfare State.'

The change has been as great on the side of American management as on that of organized labour. Here, the other advantages of American management, already noted, have played a large part: relations with the local community, with universities and educational and technical institutions, and with research organizations or other firms of specialists, consultants, etc. Despite the awesome use of jargon, the actual *work* of American sociologists, psychologists, psychiatrists, anthropologists, and economists has been of great value in uncovering the roots of errors and evils which were formerly allowed to flourish in industrial society. There has been nothing in Britain—indeed, nothing in Western Europe—to compare with the work of the social anthropologist Lloyd Warner in his field studies of 'Yankee City' and its citizens' attitudes to their work, workplace, and workfellows; with Elton Mayo's teamwork, done by researchers from Harvard, at Western Electric (the Hawthorne Report); with the 'group dynamics' of training—an application of the team spirit—associated with the name of Kurt Lewin; with the Illinois University's 'experiment in industrial harmony' at the joint request of both the trade union and the management at the Buchsbaum plants in Chicago; or with the 'human relations research unit' set up by Sears, Roebuck & Co., the giant mail-order house, with the help of Chicago University's Committee on Human Relations.

It is easy to poke fun at this kind of thing in industry, just as it is to poke fun at the higher German criticism of everything from religion to literature or from art to philosophy. Jargon often clothes ponderousness and pompousness. Yet it can also mask great achievements; and there is reason to suppose that the Americans have been pushing along the right lines for two decades since the Great Depression. The significant thing is that the lines are logically those along which progress in the human relationships of industry—if it is to be achieved at all— must be made anywhere. They are lines implied by the intensive use of all the ingredients of production, the reorganization of big industrial units into complexes of smaller units, the breaking-down of skills and jobs into more simplified varieties, the increase of capital and mechanization, and the further application of the 'three S's'—simplification, standardization, and specialization.

These conditions of rising productivity and of material progress, by themselves, incur the risk of worsening the human relationships in industry, of having a de-humanizing effect on workpeople, of causing a loss of their pride and interest in work, a consequent deficiency in their self-respect and their sense of 'social significance,' and therefore a perilous intensification of frustration and pent-up dislikes. Such evils are apt

136

to multiply unless closer attention and greater skill in application are given to *all* human relationships involved in the firm. It is a remarkable tribute to the American belief in, and desire for, change, that both American industrial managements and trade unions have recently been undergoing research by 'outside' consultants, universities, and other researchers into the art and techniques of human relationships. This is the measure of American progress from the situation on both sides of industry (and between them) in America twenty-five years ago. The A.A.C.P. Teams, as such, were not charged with a duty to look into all this; yet from between the lines of many of their Reports peeps an obvious realization that these trends in American industry present a further challenge to British industry, and that in any case they play no little part in securing higher productivity:

Our industry is operating under full employment and under severe economic limitations. More than ever there is a need to explore energetically the individual and social satisfactions of work as a part of the quest for new incentives and the awakening of that 'productivity consciousness' which has impressed every British team visiting America. Co-operation in industry will not come in response to passionate rally-cries nor from national legislation alone. Eventually, the way to co-operation depends on the will of industry, on all sides and levels, to expose itself to self-analysis, and to be ready to alter its attitudes and habits of behaviour. In this sense, research in human relations might appear to be even more applicable here than in the United States.[1]

It is necessary to re-emphasize what we pointed out at the beginning of this book, and what we repeated as Requirement No. 10 of 'good management' at the close of the preceding chapter: industrial management becomes more and more of both a science and an art; a science of techniques, an art of skills. By no means the least element of that art is the maintenance and improvement both of the teamwork among human beings and of its foundation in morale.

[1] From the article by Mr. Peter Parker, 'Human Relations in Industry,' in *The Times Review of Industry*, February 1952, p. 17.

Productivity and Politics

The national atmosphere, the climate of opinion, is of immeasurable importance in favouring—or disfavouring— higher productivity. In the formation of a 'climate of opinion which thinks that productivity really matters'[1] the attitude of organized labour towards politics and political parties is of great importance. This is probably the biggest feature in the background of 'labour relations' in West European countries, but it is of insignificant dimensions in America and Canada. Why, and how, is this so?

The ordinary citizen of any European country has more sense of the continuity of history—that of his own country and of his continent—than an American, a Canadian, an Australian, or the citizen of any of the newer industrialized or industrializing countries overseas (with the exception of the older 'cultures' of Asia, like India, China, and Burma). The history of the newer industrialized or industrializing countries overseas which are mainly inhabited by people with white skins is so recent that it is scarcely history in a European sense, let alone in the sense of older Asia.

The average European today is unaware of the persistence into his own day of sociological, psychological, and cultural 'hangovers' from, say, the time when the Middle Ages created new classes, and fixed men in groupings of skills, 'orders,' and 'estates'; or when the first Industrial Revolution ushered in the triumphant *bourgeoisie* of the new towns and cities, with its privileged liberalism, its social reforms, and its sense of serious things to come. Yet those influences affect productivity through human relations and attitudes today: in a general awareness and esteem of class distinctions, like education, accent, manners, deportment, demeanour, social habits and customs, dress, and self-expression; or in class-consciousness, occupation-consciousness, the craftsmen's pride, the countrymen's attitude to townsmen; or in party politics which have become closely linked to occupation or economic 'status.' These social distinctions and economic alignments are scarcely traceable in America.

[1] Rt. Hon. Peter Thorneycroft, M.P., President of the Board of Trade, at the dinner of the Anglo-American Council on Productivity, May 8, 1952.

It is important to bear these non-economic, unbusinesslike things in mind in any serious comparison of American with British productivity. American society is new. It has never 'jelled' into historical classes, castes, 'estates,' and class-mentalities organized in political parties. It has not the task of emancipating itself from tradition, custom, and socially inherited attitudes—the most formative elements of the climate of opinion. In newly fused societies of immigrants, the emancipation took place in the first generation of immigrants (or at latest in the second when it went to its new schools). Nobody becomes an emigrant until he has already decided to emancipate himself from familiar attitudes. Emigration *is* emancipation.

The task of American society has been to assimilate, and to be assimilated: to adopt and adapt: to change and develop, but along standard lines and in standard American patterns. A glance at an American primary school's history book, and a glance at a similar book in Britain or France, tells a story. The new country accentuates what is required to be a good American; it emphasizes change, progress, opportunity, the future of the child and of the country. 'The past is a bucket of ashes' was said by an American. The 'old country' accentuates the age and traditions of the nation which the child is to inherit, the continuity of its history, the greatness of its past.

British and European class-consciousness, craft-consciousness, and 'estate'-consciousness have manifested themselves in political parties which tend to follow social divisions. This is not to say that Marxism is right; that the British Labour Party is entirely composed of Marxists; that the Conservative Party is entirely composed of landlords and industrialists; or that the urban proletariats of industrialized Britain, Belgium, France, Switzerland and so on are propertyless and continously becoming more 'miserificated' (the literal translation of Marx's *Ver-elendung*). On the contrary, all such statements are wrong. Their very opposites are right. But in comparing British with American organized labour, we must recognize that there are certain differences in their attitudes to management, 'the bosses,' 'profits,' and therefore to party politics. These differences largely reflect their peoples' historical background.

In Britain, as throughout Western Europe, the widespread

sense of 'class' in the Dark and Middle Ages, then in the Age of Reason, and lastly in the Age of Industrialism has bequeathed to organized labour today certain attitudes to manual work and other groupings in society—who also play economic parts, but who do not manually work—landlords, employers ('the bosses'), the clerical and office staffs ('white-collar workers'—in its origin, the manual workers' derogatory term for the non-manual workers), agricultural proprietors ('the farmer' in Britain, 'the peasant' on the Continent), and, above all, the 'middle class' (the *bourgeoisie* of Marxism, the professional and suburban class in Britain, the *Spiessbürger* of German-speaking countries). After all, it was in Europe that the term 'the workers' first meant manual workers; was first utilized for political party purposes; and first fostered the Marxist conception of class-conflict. It has had little place, it makes little sense today, in American society.

It is of small moment in this matter that in Britain—unlike most European countries—the trade unions affiliated to the T.U.C. and Labour Party embrace some office-workers and even some professional workers; that Marxism does not dominate the thinking of British organized labour, or even of the Labour Party; that there are trade unionists who vote Conservative; and that there are 'bosses,' managers, professional men, suburbanites, and farmers who vote Labour. The meaningful aspect of the matter here is that, compared with American organized labour, British organized labour is the backbone of one of the two main political parties in the State and that it is a class-conscious political organism. Its political attitude and its power have been built up in the past fifty to a hundred years by class-conscious leaders and followers, who showed intense loyalty and public spirit. As a natural consequence, the party-political loyalty of trade unionism was added to the older class-loyalties, and these attitudes invaded the workplaces and have thus formed the prevailing climate of opinion among workpeople in the British factory and office. There they have reigned for nearly two generations, during boom and slump, war and peace, until today the State reposes heavily upon organized labour for its political support and economic functioning, no matter what government is in power. The associations of owners or managers are relatively less influential than they were. Much the same is true throughout Western Europe.

None of these influences is as clear-cut or as developed in America. There, this or that union may be mainly Democrat or Republican, but union members' votes cannot be predicted— as the 1952 Presidential election showed. The 'bosses' may be mainly Republican: but in every Northern State and city it is unsafe to assume that any one 'boss' of any one firm is a Republican and quite wrong to do so in the South. The farmers veer from one party to another, election by election, State by State. So does a large fraction of the negroes. Economic occupations do not have as firm party-political implications as in Britain and Europe. Incomes count, and lead to social and other differences; but both main parties agree on 'the American way of life,' private enterprise, the social necessity and economic need of profits, the need for differential rewards of skills, output, and management; and so on. In Britain, it is probable on a modest estimate that half the trade unionists will nourish moral disapproval of private profit; believe in the greater moral value, and even in the greater economic efficiency, of public owner-ship; and deny merit to what they have been taught for generations to think of as 'the capitalist system.' Far more even than in Britain is this the common outlook of organized labour on the Continent of Europe, with the exception of labour in Scandinavia.

We have to recognize the greater rigidity of British and European institutions, the greater traditionalism, the greater immobility of workpeople, the lack of social fluidity, the greater hideboundness of party politics, the inheritance and acceptance of economic and political dogmas, the greater rarity of 'crossing of party lines' and cross-voting, and the great moral obloquy attaching to anybody 'disloyal to his class.' All these are characteristics of very old countries, very old societies. They may not necessarily be bad characteristics provided the loyalties are harnessed to co-operative endeavour—as Britain showed in war-time and has shown in purely industrial relations ever since. As long as they are manifested in attitudes, policies, and practices which divide, disrupt, and disintegrate, they cannot benefit

141

an increasingly industrial society, or a private enterprise, or a State undertaking.

There has, nevertheless, been a big advance in the rethinking of the fundamentals of production, productivity, and progress by both management and organized labour in Britain since the war. It was noteworthy between 1945 and 1948 and has more particularly been so since the A.A.C.P. Teams returned from America with their Reports and began to leaven the lump of older attitudes. But the process has far to go before it pays-off in material benefits. The greatest single obstacle in the way— on both sides of the way—is the big, long-built-up back-log of traditional fears and prejudices, dislike and distrust, between organized labour and management. The difficulty is enhanced —in Europe as in Britain—by the organization of political parties in the State along rigidly enforced, clear-cut lines of presumed economic interest. The good human qualities of loyalty, amity with one's fellows, crusading idealism, and self-sacrifice for a cause are thereby harnessed to division, dissension, and disintegration, instead of to co-operation, concerted endeavour, and common interest.

It is idle to expect any rapid change in all this. It is idle to expect men to become gods, or politicians to be superseded by philosopher-kings. Americans as a whole may be no readier to change social and political habits than the British; they do not apparently like State enterprise or the Welfare State as much as the British; but they do share a wider common ground of faith in what they call 'the American way'; they concur as a majority upon its economic requirements; they are in the main more experimental in economic methods; and in general, as a people, they are more buoyant, more self-assured, open, frank, and co-operative. These values, which operate in their industry and politics alike, create a climate of opinion favourable to productivity.

Both sides of industry in America seem to agree far more than Britons or Europeans on the requirements of their economic system, and then to secure them. In other words there seems to be more division in British and European industry and politics alike about what the British and European economic systems require to make them more efficient and productive.

Americans of both parties, and on both sides of industry, seem to distrust State action more than the British or Europeans do—though they seem more reconciled to it now, and distrust of the State still goes deep on both sides of industry in Britain. (The aims and ideals of the Co-operative movement in Britain are by no means always compatible with wholehearted Socialism or State-worship.) Again, it is often said that American unions help to raise productivity by being able to make special wage or other collective bargains locally, not nationally, plant by plant; that they distrust nation-wide collective bargaining, which is more common in Britain. Yet so many American unions are working towards it that in 1952 Senator Taft threatened to make it illegal; and in any case the more common 'local' or 'plant' wage and other bargains in America are generally approved by the headquarters of the organization concerned. Again, observers of organized labour in the two countries often over-look the great *regional* autonomy of the leading British unions, which are far from 'nationally centralized.' The regional British union organizations have power to make their own bargains in many cases, as 'locals' have in America. They also overlook the many local unions in the British textile trades. In Britain the common practice is to fix a nation-wide basic wage and leave the regional union organization and the firm, industry by industry, to fix bonuses.

From whatever standpoint one approaches the principles and practices of trade unionism in the two countries, one is struck more by their similarities than by their dissimilarities. The main explanation of the higher *general* level of industrial productivity in America does not lie in trade-union structure, principles or functions. It seems to have more to do with the deep conviction of both American management and labour that 'the American way' of high and rising wages, high and rising real material standards of living, and reasonably high and rising profits for private enterprise (including profits dis-tributed to private stockholders, who in America are more broadly spread among income-groups than in Britain), depends on their joint success in keeping productivity high and con-stantly rising. They also seem to be convinced that high and rising productivity depends on intense utilization of machines and men, which in turn depends on their own high co-operative efficiency. It was not, as we said, always thus among Americans. It is so now. And that is the measure of their ability to change.

Industrial Relations in Britain are as Good as in America—perhaps Better

The A.A.C.P. Teams generally recorded that 'labour relations' in America were good, but that those in Britain were just as good. Indeed, there is much evidence to show that they are even better. In many ways they are more humane relations, more human in that sense. America has always had a tougher, more violent society than Europe. This may seem surprising in view of what has gone before. It should not be so. Human relations in industry can improve or worsen independently of the political affiliations of human beings. At the highest level—that is, between management and the trade-union officials concerned —industrial relations work as smoothly in Britain as in America; perhaps more smoothly. Partly this is due to the traditionalism we have already mentioned: co-operation with, and recognition of, unions were general in Britain almost a century ago: much longer ago than they were in America. The drawbacks or short-comings in Britain, the brakes on productivity, are not due to the *quality* of 'industrial relations' between unions and manage-ments. Those relations are frequently of the best. The hindrances seem due to the more restricted *content* of those relations. It seems to take longer to get new methods tried. There is perhaps less of the crisp, clear-cut, and even ruthless efficiency in the preparation and presentation of a new proposal, which marks much of American industrial relations. However good the manner of industrial relations may be in Britain, the matter often fails to emerge: managements and unions often seem to 'stick' at a stage from which (it would seem from outside) big advances towards higher productivity ought to be made. And American managements and unions do not seem to 'stick' there. They may have worse industrial relations. But both sides in America seem to join forces—after a bad bout—and go ahead to put up new productivity records.

There would, however, be disadvantages in Britain if the

144

American system were taken over and applied, lock, stock, and barrel. For instance, Britain is small in area with intensely concentrated industrial districts. Measures to increase productivity, raise efficiency, increase earnings, or improve working conditions can easily be agreed on a national basis, and equally easily ensured throughout so small a country. It has hitherto been impossible—and perhaps inadvisable, if possible—to do so in as vast and varied a continent as America. There may also be one disadvantage of the small-scale, more compact, more centralized British industrial system. It is that within every firm or State enterprise, no matter where it is, there is more *uniformity* of attitudes on both sides. It is not so much a real remote control of the trade-union officials from a national centre, or remote control of management by the firm's membership in a trade association or other industrial organization. It is more subtle than that: an atmosphere of 'control by remote influence,' of 'keeping in national step' both by unions and managements, and firm by firm. The effect is to render British industry as a whole a little more bureaucratic, a little more rigid and inflexible on both sides.

One obvious effect of the greater American individualism, the greater freedom for the firm, the union's 'local,' the local community—indeed, for the units of a Federal State—is the informality of human relations between 'master and man,' management and workpeople, 'bosses' and union officials. This stems from the wider American recognition of the identity of interest between management and union, of the hard role and better rewards of management, and of the 'right' of the workman to earn all he is capable of earning without fearing that a grudging management will begin to scale-down his wage-rate as his earnings rise. It also stems from the workpeople's recognition that the executives of management have graduated to their positions by merit and experience (mainly shop-floor experience), and that their own promotion and advancement within the firm depend on their merit as workpeople.

Team after Team noted the interdependence in American industry of the 'sense of *camaraderie* and freedom of expression based on mutual respect,' the readiness to change working assignments and conditions, the willingness of unions to con-

145   K

form to new methods or apply new machinery (with hard bargaining for due reward!), and the all-pervading belief in the need to raise productivity.

Perhaps the only consideration we need add to this—at this stage—is that for not only the past two generations but for all American history this 'American way' has steadily paid-off in rising real wages, better material standards, and much more leisure for every individual and group in the community. For at least one generation the 'British way,' coupled with unfortunate and unhappy British experiences (most of which Americans have never been called upon to share), has paid-off more to workpeople by taking it in the main from other groupings in the community. The output and productivity *per head* and *per machine* has remained laggardly in Britain. The consequent redistribution of incomes—the phrase is so symptomatic of 'the British way' that we repeat it—the re-distribution of incomes has loomed larger in all discussion, in politics, and in industry in Britain for a generation, than the need to raise the national income more rapidly so that *all* can share in its rise.

As a pardonable exaggeration for the sake of brevity, one could say that the one system has been a dynamic society, the other has not; the one has self-assurance, co-operation, hope; the other has doubt, sectionalism, and—if not despair of the future—widespread dismay, and the desire to secure what can be secured from a more static industrial system while the going is good.

This widespread British attitude, climate of opinion, or situation is not justified by the facts or by the prospects. But it exists. It necessarily colours human relations in industry. It is perhaps the biggest single obstacle to British progress. It is almost wholly psychological and social. That it can change, and be changed, at least for short periods was remarkably demonstrated in the war, and again between 1948 and 1950. In the latter period, production and productivity rose rapidly, and despite the 'freezing' of wages and other incomes by the White Paper of February 1948. That is cogent testimony to British potentialities.

146

Trade Union Psychology

The broad purposes of trade unionism in both countries are (*a*) to secure better pay and conditions of work for members; (*b*) to strengthen unionism in collective bargaining for those purposes; and (*c*) to safeguard workpeople's status, skills, and interest. British trade unionism is more political, attached to one party in the State; American trade unionism is far less so, and unattached to any party. American trade unionism is still in the main less centralized and gives more local option to branches; British trade unionism is more centralized, giving less (though considerable) local authority for negotiations and bargains.

But one problem of British trade unionism today *is* singular. It is not quite unknown in American unionism; but it is now almost insignificant there. That is, the permeation and infiltration of trade unions by Communists. It is highly significant in European trade unionism. It affects to some extent the timing of improvements in industry, rate of technical progress, degrees of moral support for technical changes, and the efficiency with which changes—if and when agreed between union leaders and management—are carried out. These hazards are virtually absent from American union leaders' consciousness. In America the horizon of industrial bargaining is virtually clear of ideological clouds. In Britain, and throughout Western Europe, it is always misty, and it is hard to navigate towards straightforward industrial goals.

As we have seen, and as most of the Teams noted, American union leaders and their rank-and-file have no difficulty in seeing 'the business of America, which is Business' from the management's standpoint. The reason is simple: the ground on which they stand is the same. They merely stand on different sides of one and the same accepted industrial structure. As Americans believing in a materially better future, striving to realize that future, thinking of it in terms of greater material consumption and more leisure, both trade-union leaders and management approach their day-to-day problems in much the same spirit. They fight and bargain very toughly to safeguard their particular personal and collective interests. But 'the doctrine of the concurrent majority' applies here, just as it does in American attitudes towards the President's powers, America's defences, the value of the dollar, the introduction of new machinery, changing a home or a job, doing two or more different things during the same job, and a host of other subjects. Productivity-consciousness, output-consciousness, efficiency-consciousness—these have long been woven into the fabric of Americans' experience. So when it comes to the attitudes or practices of trade unions, it is idle to expect that experience not to manifest itself as it does everywhere else.

Productivity-consciousness is impossible of achievement if the workman feels that whenever he puts up his rate of output by his *own* effort the employer will scale down his time-rate or his piece-rate. It is just as impossible of achievement if the workman feels—for this is a question of feeling, emotion, sentiment, creed, almost of a secular faith, among European trade unionists—that if he works better he 'works himself out of a job,' or works 'a buddy' out of one; if he feels that a new machine or new method will do the same (the modern hang-over of Ludditism); or if he feels that all the fruits of extra productivity go to 'the bosses.'

These hang-overs colour European workpeople's conscious-ness, and condition even more their subconsciousness, far more than they colour or condition the consciousness of trade-union leaders. That is another handicap on union leadership in Europe, as compared with the leadership of American unions.[1] The causes lie deep and far back:

. . . the average American manufacturer runs his machinery at a much higher speed than is the usual practice in England—in other words, 'for all it is worth,' and the men ably second the employers' efforts in this direction. Do the workmen as a body do the same here? I think the answer must be in the negative. Why, then, is it that the systems are so different? In England it has been the rule for generations past that as soon as a man earns beyond a certain amount of wages, the price for his work is cut down. . . . If this be the case, can we blame the workman? . . . Machinery must be run at its highest speed whilst the workers must feel that they are reaping

[1] See p. 176 *et seq.*

148

the fruits of their labour, and that the fruits are secure not only for the present, but for the future.[1]

That was written in 1902. There has been marked progress in outlook, responsibility, and behaviour on the part of most British employers and managements since then; strikingly so since the war; and meanwhile Britain's trade unions have become very powerful. The most encouraging thing since the war is that the more go-ahead managements and the more go-ahead union leaders have hardly any difficulty in agreeing what should be done. Particularly has much progress been made between go-ahead trade unions and *groupings* of employers: for example, as long ago as 1919–20 the engineering employers gave pieceworkers (in all engineering unions recognizing piecework) considerable protection from rate-cutting, in national agreements.

The difficulty arises with the more recalcitrant trade unions and employers, whose feelings are still dominated by the hangovers. Truly, 'the greatest obstacles to increased productivity are psychological rather than technical.'[2] It is perhaps auspicious, a good omen, that in the A.A.C.P. Teams the psychological barriers were so quickly, naturally, and completely dropped. The unanimity of their reports has been remarkable. The hang-overs from the age-long distrust between the two sides in industry in Britain were scarcely even apparent.

The greatest difference between American and British trade unionism is that between their prevailing climates of opinion. American trade unionism is more recent; the leading unions are more specialized, more 'General Staff'd,' more exuberantly experimental. British trade unionism is older, cannier, more craft- or occupation-conscious, more status-safeguarding, more jealously separate and sovereign in each union's operations, less experimental. Much of these differences, as we saw, stems from national differences. But much does not.

The American workman has seen American unionism's attitudes pay-off handsomely in his own lifetime. He lives in an

[1] Mr. Mosely's Memorandum, Preface to the reports, Co-operative Printing Society Ltd., Manchester, 1903.
[2] *Productivity Measurement in British Industry* report.

expanding economy, in an atmosphere of 'Go get it!' and among a well-fed, energetic, enterprising people who are mobile, fluid, volatile.[1] The American worker lives more in the moment, looking not behind him. He has faced unemployment—as bad as any known in history—yet he is by nature sanguine. In his country there are always new opportunities; and 'the sky's the limit' for its productive system. It grows its own food. It depends less on other nations, economically, than any other industrial country in the world except Russia.

The British workman, on the other hand, is still aware of the past and its exploitation and mass-unemployment. He doubts whether leopards change spots;[2] whether Britain's future can be even as good as its past; and, above all, whether his present good fortune ('full employment') will last. Today the British workman—the rank-and-file of trade unionism—lives better than ever: much better than before the war. He works fewer hours and is paid (in real terms) relatively more per hour. He has better working conditions and amenities, longer paid holidays, easier work, subsidized housing, subsidized food, subsidized health and other social services. He consumes more leisure-time travel, more entertainments, reading-matter, radio, and tobacco. He pays to attend more games and shows, to bet, and to gamble more. And his and his family's welfare—education, health, social security—are greater, and less of a burden on his own income.

But grim figures lurk in the shadows; the fall in quality and quantity of meat, of coal, and of transport; the lowered qualities or small rations of cheese, fat, butter, and margarine; the reduced intake of sugar, sweets, bacon, and eggs; the fall in the quality of personal services, public and private; the running-down of highways, railways, and many other national or public installations. These things are the evidences of a country still precariously living—after a dozen years—by trade with other nations, in an ill-ordered world, and in a siege economy. It would be silly to ignore their effect in forming the attitude—the climate of opinion—of British organized labour as a whole.

---

[1] All observers have noted these characteristics of American society.

[2] See Shadwell, *op. cit.*, Vol. I, Ch. 1, for some remarkable observations on this over fifty years ago.

That attitude is still to a great extent that of men saving what can be saved from a wreck, instead of refloating and rerigging their ship.

Transatlantic Comparisons

The first Teams that visited America were struck by what appeared to them as the generally favourable attitude of American trade unions to improved techniques of production, the introduction of new methods and new machines, the problem of man-power displaced by them ('redundancy'), and so on. The very first report, for example, remarked that the Congress of Industrial Organizations 'offers no opposition to the inclusion or exclusion of specific duties from any man's performance, provided he is paid a rate of wages commensurate with his reponsibilities, skill, and effort.'[1]

It is important in any comparison or contrast between British and American unions and their respective roles in raising productivity to notice that phrase 'provided he is paid a rate of wages commensurate with his responsibilities, skill, and effort.' So many of the apparent differences of attitude and practice between the two countries' unions revolve about one central feature: namely, American managements and American unions can obviously agree on productive improvements, changes, rearrangements, etc., which prove so profitable that adequate wages, bonuses, compensation pay and other rewards can be paid, and full employment maintained. The two sides of American industry first make the profits, then haggle about them. The industrial relations may be worse in America than in Britain, or less 'human' and humane; collective bargaining may be more bitter; methods employed to 'influence' employers or workpeople may be more violent. But when all is said and done, the American industrial system goes ahead to set new high records for output, productivity, employment, and consumers' standards of life.

In 1950 the T.U.C. itself sent its own team of trade-union officials from many industries to study American unionism in action and to make recommendations to the British trade-union

---

[1] *Steelfounding* report.

movement.[1] (It was sponsored by the E.C.A., though not by the A.A.C.P.) The visitors had time only to study the practices of the biggest American unions, which are the leaders in the adoption of progressive methods, and therefore show American unionism at its greatest advantage. Nevertheless, that is also what the A.A.C.P. Teams did in American industry as a whole. They, too, saw much of American industry at its best. But the recommendations of the British trade-union officials merit as much attention as the A.A.C.P. reports.

In a paragraph of their preamble the British trade unionists said:

> This, then, is the real problem confronting Trade Unions: to find ways and means of increasing productivity—a problem concerned mainly with industrial policy and action as distinct from political pressure to achieve full employment and economic stability.

They do not decry—still less abjure—political pressure. But they fairly and squarely describe the raising of productivity as 'the real problem' before Britain's trade unionists. That is a momentous recognition of fact. This remarkable report goes on to say that most American unions

> regard comment on employers' profits as outside their provinces. ... However high, profits, at least in competitive industry, are not regarded as immoral or as a social evil; indeed they give proof of solvency and assured employment. Usually high profits are considered a sign of efficiency and relatively high output per man-hour, and the main concern of the Union is to obtain a fair share of them.

They go on to point out that on the whole American unions prefer to cope with the displacement of man-power (by new machines or methods) by compensation-pay; that they do not on the whole raise objections to work-study, job-evaluation, etc.; and that they (and their experts) concern themselves in the main with the fairness of the redeployment of labour or rearrangements of work, the resulting rewards, etc.

[1] *Trade Unions and Productivity*, London, T.U.C., 1950.

152

Among these British trade unionists' recommendations are to be found the following, which are summarized here:

(a) British trade unionists' interests can be harmed by the forcing of increases in pay unrelated to increases in output or productivity;

(b) a maximum of flexibility and mobility of labour is to be encouraged to meet demands on the British economy;

(c) training of the leading trade unions' officials in production engineering is to be encouraged and extended;

(d) the economic implications of an increase in the standard of living should be brought home to trade unionists more;

(e) they should not oppose technological advances, but should insist on full consultation before and during introduction of new techniques, methods, etc., and of adequate scales of pay for rearranged jobs.

There are of course detailed qualifications and modifications in the original T.U.C. report (to which reference should be made); but that is a fair summary of the outstanding recommendations. It chimes with the A.A.C.P. reports in two main particulars: first, in recognizing that productivity is the yardstick of material progress; and secondly, in recommending bigger, better, and faster overhauling of out-of-date or ill-adapted attitudes and methods.

In principle—and to a surprisingly large extent in practice—the process of collective bargaining for wage-rates and other working conditions follows much the same lines in British and American trade unionism.[1] The leading American trade unions —a minority both of unions and of total union membership— have led the way in co-operating with managements to make the most fruitful and profitable use of work-study, costings, and other measurements of productive efficiency, both of men and of machines. But over the entire field of American industry it is arguable whether there is greater readiness on the part of unions to co-operate in this way than there is among British unions in British industry. The wages, the rates of pay and

[1] See p. 143.

bonus, and other working conditions have still to be extracted from American managements, who are just as unwilling to concede the unions' demands as British managements; perhaps more so, if we take into account the greater toughness of collective bargaining and its methods in America. But the impression made on the 250 operatives and trade-union officials who went with the Teams to America was that there was, *on the average and in the sections of the many American industries visited by them*, a somewhat greater disposition on the part of the American unions to consider, favourably and to the greatest practicable extent, any and all propositions put to them by managements to raise productive efficiency.

On the other hand, both in Britain and across the water there are voices which say that what the A.A.C.P. Teams saw in American industry, and what we have described here, is non-existent: that relations between managements and unions are as bad as anywhere on earth; that obstructionism, obscurantism, 'feather-bedding,' waste of man-power, under-utilization of plant and machines, and non-co-operation are the hallmarks of American trade unionism.

It is hard to credit this. It may be the picture of one plant, one firm, perhaps even one industry. But, if so, it has been enlarged into a nation-wide generalization. It cannot be true of American manufacturing industry as a whole. The evidence against such a picture—from 1900 onwards—is crushing. The odds against sixty-six A.A.C.P. Teams (and their individual management and union members) having, during four years in all branches of American industry, encountered by sheer chance or uncritically absorbed precisely the same impressions, and all of them wrong, are incalculable.

Moreover the Teams noted that American trade unionists and their leaders seemed to be more co-operative in other ways than in work-study or measurement of performances. Take, for example, changes in union work-rules, changes in union restrictions on operations by other than certain operatives, the switching of jobs or duties temporarily, the temporary re-assignment of men or of duties, the changing of work-time or shift-time, the changing of teams or men from one task or shift to another. All of these changes help to raise productivity

154

if they can be quickly carried out. These variations, whether temporary or not, the American union leader or trade unionist seems to find more 'natural.' It cannot be put stronger than that. Perhaps that, too, is a reflection of the fluidity, mobility, adaptability, even volatility of American life, and of American management's greater ability to pay for what it wants. But the important facts to note are (*a*) that it has been so as long as American industry has flourished, and (*b*) that it pays-off in high productivity, high wages, and a high standard of life.

Voices are also heard on both sides of the water to the effect that the recent degree of co-operation between unions and management in America is temporary, 'marginal,' 'fair-weather sailing,' and will disintegrate in a depression. This, too, is hard to believe. For both management and trade unionists in America, adaptability and mobility are more natural. They are not mere watchwords or slogans. They are common experience, shared by all Americans. All urban Americans—and many farmers—are ever-ready to up-stakes, hitch their belongings together, and strike out for 'fresh woods and pastures new.' This aspect of the general fluidity of American society has a vast importance for industry. In America—in management or on the shop floor—men think little or nothing of changing their jobs, homes, firms, departments of the same firm, industries, and trade unions. True, the more widespread observance in America of most trade unions' 'seniority rule' puts a premium on the keeping of older workers; and this concentrates the greater mobility of American labour on those, say, under thirty, or on the unskilled. (To this extent, it can be argued that British trade unionism shows more humane 'human relations' in industry, since it does not make the seniority rule as sweeping as American trade unionism.) There seems little point in attempting to minimize the degree of general adaptability and mobility of labour and management in America, for it has always struck foreign observers.

As we pointed out earlier[1] this greater *degree* of mobility in America is to a large extent denied to post-war Britain—like a smooth and unlimited supply of fuel and power, of imported food, or of some imports of vital industrial raw materials. But

1 See Chapter 1.

within Britain's limitations there are still wide fields for endeavour, enterprise, and initiative; and in the ambit of the British trade unions' responsibilities a great deal is being done—though far more can, and should, yet be done—to raise productivity quickly, without strain upon any human being, and without making the euphemistic term 'redundancy' into widespread unemployment.

It is easy to overlook—indeed, to be ignorant of—the great advances made by British trade unionism since, say, 1939. Not many people in America, not many in Britain, know that the British trade-union movement is sending selected national officers into firms of industrial consultants for periods of training, in techniques for measuring efficiency, of up to four months; that some trade unions subscribe substantial sums to the research associations of British trades and industries; that the Trades Union Congress runs its own courses in London in work-study and other techniques of management and production engineering; and that, locality by locality, the British trade-union movement co-operates in the training work of technical colleges. Little of this can be found in American trade unionism. It is almost confined to the half-dozen big American unions alone. And to this must be added the achievements of British trade-union leadership in collaboration with managements, throughout the gravest social and economic testing-time of modern Britain, in securing a better state of industrial relations than any in the last two or three generations, and a freedom from national strikes and stoppages of work unsurpassed in Britain or any other industrial country at any other time in this century. There are some Americans who say British industrial relations *ought* to have been worse; that British employers and trade unions never 'got tough' over efficiency, and could afford to sink their differences and pass on to consumers all costs during a seller's market period. That period has passed. We shall see if this retrograde-seeming contention is right. But only those who know the British trade-union movement can appreciate how fast and how far the policies of its leaders have carried its campaign for higher productivity within the unions. The campaign has still far to go before the initial success inside the unions is translated to productive success in workplaces. That

156

is where relations with management come in. But without this essential initial success, all else would fail.

Progress is likely to be more easily made by steady pressure, all along the front, to carry recent advances farther ahead. Those advances have been at various points: the tackling of 'redundancy' due to new machines and new methods; persistence in seeking for compensation pay for the displaced labour; elaborating with far-sighted managements new and up-to-date systems of pay for rearranged jobs; increasing the utilization of machines both old and new; and the relaxation of familiar work-practices under new safeguards for the workpeople.

In listing these lines along which the advances of British trade unionism since the war have been made, it is only fair to emphasize three things. First, much of the recent emphasis in the more go-ahead American trade unions on work-study and job-evaluation was in order to find a way round a nominal national 'wage-freeze.' Secondly, more intense utilization of machines (in normal hours, by overtime, or on shifts) will always be expected to bring some extra reward to the workers of those machines. And thirdly, there is always an ultimate border-line between efficiency and good human relations in industry; and beyond that boundary trade-union leaders may well hesitate to urge their followers.

In any case, the necessary and desirable degree of advance along all these lines by British trade unionism cannot be achieved without changes in methods of evaluating and measuring work and of paying for it; in 'differentials,' grades and status of workpeople's skills; and in the quality and techniques of management. This, therefore, means that both sides of industry must improve the nature and content of the human relations in it. Who else can be expected to do that?

7

Incentives In and Out of Industry

There are long-recognized national differences between aptitudes for, and attitudes to, work. Sustained, persistent work—
kept up all day and at least five days a week, year in year out—
is mainly performed in the temperate or northern regions of the
world. Even when northerners settle in the tropics, they still
seem able to keep up their greater expenditure of nervous and
physical energy, whether at work or at play, than the natives are
able or willing to keep up.

Now America is almost a sub-tropical country. But Americans take in more calories than most dwellers in sub-tropical
climates. They take in more meat, protein, and sugar per head
than any other people. Over the week and year they enjoy more
leisure, on the average, than other of the world's workers. And
their mature adults seem to take less physical exercise and do
less *physical* work. The hardness of their work consists not in
brute force, not in brawn—though when it comes to brawn
Americans can startle many another nationality—but first in
careful application to a job which has been planned, secondly
in the use of many mechanical devices, and thirdly in the exercise of a carefully trained dexterity rather than of skill. That is
an old and deep-grained American characteristic:

. . . American workmen are more favourably disposed towards
machinery. Indeed, here lies the distinctive feature of American
industry, viz. the hankering after the latest machinery and best
methods of working, which pervade [*sic*] American industrialism.
Americans, both employer and employed, have realized more fully
than has been realized here that brains rather than brawn count in
most things; that mental rather than manual hustle is of primary
importance.[1]

[1] Report of Mr. (later Rt. Hon.) G. N. Barnes, Mosely Industrial Commission,
Co-operative Printing Society Ltd., Manchester, 1903, p. 24.

Every European who has written about America—and most who haven't—notice two ingredients of the American climate of opinion. These two ingredients powerfully help to produce the high standard of living: first, the nervous and physical energy of Americans; secondly, the harnessing of this energy—with more pleasure, or less displeasure, for human beings—to work.

One hundred and twenty years ago De Tocqueville asked 'Why are Americans so restless amid all their prosperity?' Half a century ago both Dr. Shadwell[1] and the Mosely Commission of British trade-union officials[2] noticed these things. During the last hundred years the national and racial composition of the American people has mightily changed; yet every European visitor has remarked on the 'hustle,' the *élan*, the pace and the persistence of American work; work by 'workers' and work by management.[3] During those hundred years the basic weekly hours of work in America have been reduced, and the American standard of living has been raised, faster and farther than anywhere else. But visitors to America have also remarked that *in the hours worked* the pace of American work is better, and is more sustained, than anywhere else. It is quicker, more fruitful work, in fewer hours. It is often easier work. It is not generally harder work. Many Teams found that British workers worked harder. They certainly work longer and they certainly do not work so fruitfully.

We must get this picture in proper perspective. The A.A.C.P. Teams' unanimous opinion was that American workers are not inherently superior in talents or faculties to British workers; nor can it be safely assumed that they are to French, Italian, German, Swiss or other European workers. After all, nine-tenths of American workers today are either first-generation Europeans, or descendants—from the second generation to the sixth, which is biologically a very recent business—of Europeans. Accordingly, if American workers render more productive work, if they waste less time getting on with the job or quitting it, if

---

[1] Shadwell, *op. cit.*, Vol. 1, Ch. 1.

[2] Mosely Commission reports, Co-operative Printing Society Ltd., 1903.

[3] 'The American manager is more enterprising . . . and he also works hard himself, being often himself the first in the workshop and the last out . . .' Report by Mr. (later Rt. Hon.) G. N. Barnes, Mosely Industrial Commission, 1903, Section (*b*) of answer to Question 21, p. 27.

they keep up a higher pace of work through the shorter hours of it—and on the average all these things seem to be established in American manufacturing industry—then the explanations must be sought not in American workpeople, but in the environment, the shorter hours rendered possible by more mechanization, the better industrial system that moulds their attitudes and their practices. That broad environment influences the behaviour of American industrial workers in many subtle ways, just as other national environments influence the workpeople of other nations.

Human work in American industry has been studied and integrated with all other industrial processes. It has thus been planned to perform more with less expenditure, to waste less, to get the most out of the least effort, and to make machines work more. The result, by and large, is that American workpeople do not seem to find their work such a strain that it prevents enjoyment of their greater leisure, or in any way detracts from their longer non-working life.

It used to be said[1] that American workpeople's lives were shortened by the intensity of their work: that their machines burned them up like candles; that the European worker lived longer. All the insurance figures now disprove this. The expectation of life for ordinary working men and women is longer in America than in Europe—though it may be doubted if that of a high-powered business executive is. It used to be said that American workpeople had to work until they were older than European workpeople. That, too, is untrue; the contrary is now the case. In Britain today the official policy is to induce workpeople to work after they are sixty-five or after retirement age is reached. It used to be said[2] that the American worker was more sober, more industrious, better educated than the British or European worker; that he saved more; that he was thriftier, keener to 'get on,' more energetic in general. Some of this may still be true—notably that he is more energetic (it would be difficult not to be on his average intake of protein and sugar) and that he saves much more. Higher taxes of all kinds, wider

---

[1] See Report by Mr. (later Rt. Hon.) G. N. Barnes, Mosely Industrial Commission, Co-operative Printing Society Ltd., Manchester, 1903, p. 31.

[2] Cf. Shadwell, *op. cit.*, and the Mosely Commission reports, 1903.

social and group insurance, and inflation have stopped all personal saving, on balance, in Britain today. In the last six years there has been, on balance, personal dis-saving, i.e. consumption of capital. On the other hand—despite inflation and the slower spread of group and other social insurance—Americans have persisted in saving, personally, up to 8% of their vast total of personal incomes in recent years.

But the American worker is certainly not 'better educated' in the sense of primary education. He is better trained, after schooling ceases;[1] and his schooling (on the whole, and in the majority of American States) ceases two years later than it does in Britain or Europe. He is not today more temperate than the British workman. The consumption per head of alcoholic beverages seems to have risen somewhat in America, and actually to have declined in Britain, during the past half-century.

The average British worker has perhaps physically less stamina than his American counterpart today; perhaps less stamina than he himself had before the war. This may be due to the twelve-year-long radical alteration in his diet (little meat and bacon, virtually no natural butter, very little cheese, a big increase in starches, bread, potatoes, etc., a reduction of sugar, and a drop in the quality of most items).

The dietetic statisticians—dealing in global calories—have not been able to take into account such disadvantageous developments as the fall in the quality of most British rationed foods as compared with before the war. (The fall in the food-quality of meat is notorious.) Nor has it been anyone's duty to study the effect of such abrupt changes in the feeding of working human organisms in a dull, generally sunless, northern climate. A guess—a guess, informed by knowledge of British and American workpeople before, during, and after the war—can be hazarded that an improvement in the British workpeople's diet would go far to overcoming the nervous and physical listlessness now observed by so many visitors from abroad. The displacement of the weather by food and feeding as the national topic of conversation is a significant feature of post-war British society.

These are probably—one hopes—temporary divergences

[1] *Training of Operatives* and *Training of Supervisors* reports.

between American and British nutrition. It seems fair to mention them, since they are so seldom taken into account. Even the A.A.C.P. reports only mentioned them here and there, with glancing references to the striking intake and general availability of American foods per head. But in a progressive industrial society which is increasingly mechanizing human work, climate and diet—within reasonable limits—should matter less and less. Brawn is not so much required. Brain is required more and more. And in the matter of brain, mental endowments, and potentiality for skilfulness, changes in climate and diet—even severe and abrupt changes—do not seem to have much effect. They certainly cannot have much effect as between America and Britain.

Such striking differences as the A.A.C.P. Teams and other visitors noted between the British and American workpeople's attitude to work and play, to effort of all kinds, and to learning or change, appear to be due to differences in the two *social* environments—differences in incentives and opportunity, status and responsibility at work, levels of taxation, the ability to increase earnings without strain on the earner, the power of earnings to command material enjoyments, the availability of those enjoyments, and so on. These are all man-made. They are independent of climates and natural conditions.

The American workman produces more in his hour, year, or life of work, not because of a higher American average of brain, brawn, skill, and potentiality, but because of much bigger (and easier) saving and capital investment, better arrangement of work, better application of the human being to the work as arranged, and better rewards for the work. That is the overwhelming and unanimous conclusion of the A.A.C.P. Teams. It is borne out by all the available evidence.

Breaking down Skill into Skilfulness

Throughout American industry the use of human work is better, 'more scientific,' more effective, more economical, and therefore more productive. It is a planned use of comparatively costly human skills and aptitudes. As we saw, these skills and aptitudes are carefully trained. But the principle underlying this

162

practice is old and familiar. It is implied by the use of any machinery. It was enunciated by Babbage one hundred and twenty years ago: repetitive, routine human action should be done by machinery, and goods should be designed so that they can be mechanically manufactured.

It is often said that more mechanization means less human skill, fewer craftsmen. In the early days of the Industrial Revolution, there were relatively few craftsmen and many unskilled workers. Today, in the heyday of machines, there are many more skilled occupations—designers, fitters, craftsmen, draughtsmen, process planners, production engineers, and so on. These are new skills; and the more we simplify, standardize, and specialize, the more specialisms and specialists we need, and the more the breaking-down of old jobs into simpler jobs widens the net of skill and dexterity. Even the so-called semi-skilled or unskilled worker in industry today has to be more skilful or dexterous than his forebears in the same grade of work were. The simplification of jobs may mean narrowing the *range* of a skilled man's skill into smaller operations, each demanding a *narrower range* of repetitive dexterity. But the skilfulness is still required, and so is the skill, throughout modern industry. One need only think of the first automobile and aircraft engines —indeed, the first cars and aeroplanes—early this century, and compare them with those of today, to see how many more complicated components, how many more products of machinery and human dexterity and skill, enter the finished product, how many more well-paid man-hours go to make these things today compared with a generation ago.

The problem of modern industry—its outstanding problem— is a human and humane matter. It is also a social matter: an affair of human relations. It is to bring back to workers, and to human relations in industry, the satisfaction and acclaim which craftsmen used to win by their work. And this problem certainly does become more intractable the more industry becomes mechanized, for the skills and skilfulness today are widely separated from each other. They are now performed by many different persons tending different machines, or tending one kind of machine which does many different things. And these ingredients of skilfulness will probably be performed miles away

163

from counterparts, which are assembled in one place to make the finished article. This is the hallmark of modern industry, in America and in Russia. None can escape it. It is bound to develop in ever-greater detail as industrial societies advance, and non-industrial societies become industrialized. It is therefore important to focus it in the perspective of our argument.

Most of the A.A.C.P. Teams, and most expert visitors from Europe who have examined American industry, detect a greater sense of community and common achievement in the average American factory. This sense seems to be shared by management and workpeople. It seems to be manifested as much in the worker's attitude to his work as in his feeling of participation in the firm's achievements and interests. It seems to be a greater sense of venturing together, of team-membership, of interdependence and mutual respect, than can be found in the average British or European factory. If this general European impression of American industry is true—and some American managements deny it—it has interesting implications.

First, why is it so in the country of Charlie Chaplin's *Modern Times*, of super-mechanization, of 'scientific-management,' work-study, and all such techniques? The answer would seem to be that it is partly *because* of these things; because the cumulative, accelerating simplification of human work into specialized mechanical operations has shortened hours of work, raised standards of life, and so obviously increased the common interests of management and organized labour. There may remain a lot to be done in restoring the human element to American industrial relations. Both sides of industry may distrust each other. Yet their overriding common material interest in maintaining and developing 'the American way of life' is obvious to each.

Secondly, Americans enjoy taking part in contests, competitive games, and exercises which test brawn and brain. Playing to win is viewed as a science worthy of meticulous study. It is not—and never has been—so viewed in Britain. The American audience applauds the winner more warmly; the British, the loser; and there may be some justification in the American wisecrack that the British make a virtue, an art, and a science of losing. There is even a recondite school of American

164

economists today which deduces all economic activity from a theory of competitive games, wagers, moves, and countermoves.

This American characteristic cannot be kept out of work, which looms so large in American life. When A.A.C.P. Team reports note that American managements, salesmen, and work-people seem competitively more 'on their toes,' it is highly probable that they are merely describing the reflection—within any one firm or factory—of this all-American enjoyment of competitive teamwork. Certainly no psychologist would deny that—from insects to human beings, from the bees to an orchestra—a special satisfaction can be obtained from com-munal endeavour, both in work and play. If American manage-ments—and union leaders—have realized this, and harnessed it to haul productivity higher, they are wise. If they have not, and if a sense of communal endeavour is incidental to the American atmosphere, it is none the less helpful and worth copying.

Here, also, America's youth and newness are a great advan-tage. The traditional, medieval, European craft-consciousness never obtained much of a hold there. When industrialism raced ahead—after the end of the Civil War in 1865—immigration raced ahead with it. The indigenous class of American crafts-men before the Civil War was small, and it was thereafter swamped by immigrant artisans and craftsmen of all kinds. Trade unionism—even of craftsmen—came late, by European standards. When American trade unionism grew rapidly after the First World War, the old craftsmen's skills were already being surpassed by the modern technological process of mass-production. Henry Ford can be said to have launched it in 1912. The process involved the breaking down of special skills into semi-skills which were more quickly and easily learned and into machine-minding, component-assembling, and narrower ranges of manual dexterity, in a planned lay-out of work. The rapid rise in productivity resulting from this process enabled managements to pay all human labour—skilled, semi-skilled, and unskilled—more handsomely than ever before or anywhere else.

American unions certainly preserved—and, as is right and proper, still preserve—the prerogatives and higher rewards of craftsmen's skills. But the important point is that the process itself progressively renders craftsmen's skills less *generally* necessary. Instead, it pushes the need of craftsmen's skills back, stage by stage, throughout the assembling-factory itself to the other factories where components are actually made, or the ever more numerous machines and mechanical tools are built.

As machines tend to do more, and to build more machines, the modern industrial process accordingly renders old, traditional practices—derived from the medieval learning of trades, crafts, and skills—obsolete. Therewith it tends to render more obsolete the old, traditional differentials of pay, the system of apprenticeship, and the old-fashioned 'wages lists' based on out-of-date grading of work by the workers (e.g. those of the British textile industries which were the first to be industrialized). The modern industrial process demands new methods of 'job evaluation,' of remuneration, and of differentiating scales of reward for differing performances. It outdates the medieval paraphernalia—paraphernalia both of mind and matter—which (in America less than in Europe, but everywhere in modern industrial society) still obstructs full productive use of the mechanical slaves which men have invented.

The reform, refashioning, and readaptation thus required, the unscrambling of the eggs, is bound to be harder in Britain than anywhere else. British industrial life, the attitudes on both sides of industry, and their traditional methods are older, more 'set.' But as the need to re-equip, modernize, and overhaul is more urgent in Britain than elsewhere, the two sides of industry face the problem together. Management and unions both need to revise principles, practices, and procedures of almost immemorial sanctity.

Incentives in Industry

In the American industrial system there are more man-made incentives to exercise skill, efficiency, dexterity, and skilfulness: that is, to do more effective work. This we have already observed. It is one of the loudest overtones in the chorus of the A.A.C.P. Teams. If deep-grained attitudes of European trade unionists are either not met with, or are being rapidly overcome in America, it must be because American workpeople find it to their advantage to participate effectively in their industrial system. What, then, are the ingredients of this greater advantage to them?

The overriding incentive to work is to live; and chiefly to keep alive and together a wife and family. It is the same—though the incentive varies widely—all over the world. We in the West may wonder at our own technological advances, or at the American standard of living; but it is a useful corrective to remember that Americans, Canadians, the British of white skins all over the globe, and all West Europeans form one-tenth of the world's people. They enjoy an average material standard of living double to five or ten times better than that of all other peoples. Even so, they spend a third of their waking adult lives at work; and their own (and *a fortiori* all other peoples') material wants are still nowhere near satisfaction. There is still much malnutrition, poverty, meanness, drabness, anxiety, unhappiness, and despair—which better material circumstances could help to eradicate—in America, as in Britain and Europe. In less fortunate countries it is more fatalistically accepted as the common lot of humanity.

Only the immature and the dogmatic believe that better material circumstances can solve *all* human evils and afflictions. But we think the contrasts just mentioned need to be borne in mind in the West, especially when it faces such heavy responsibilities for developing the health and welfare of the less developed peoples of the world. The unvarnished truth is that mankind is not, even in America, within faint sight of abolishing the need to work, and to work well; and that all the world's material resources, with all our machines and our work, would not today, if shared out, guarantee to humanity the material standards of living of a British shopkeeper or yeoman in the age of the first Queen Elizabeth.

For our immediate purpose, however, the salient contrast is between the material incentives offered for various grades of human work in American and British industry. Here, of course, it is impossible completely to divorce the system of industrial rewards in a nation from that nation's social and economic circumstances. They are inextricably bound up with each other. With this caution, we proceed to set out the findings of the

167

A.A.C.P. Teams and other experts. For this purpose we can set them out as initial statements, and then proceed to examine them.

(1) *The ladders of promotion in American industry are more numerous. They are longer. They are in more constant use 'both ways,' from bottom to top and from top to bottom. They can be used by all comers. And they have more rungs.*

This is perhaps only another version of the saying that every American executive's office has two doors: one through which he is promoted, the other through which he is kicked out. As we saw in Chapter 2, American management lays far more emphasis on the selection and training of managerial talent on the shop-floor, and on devolving managerial responsibility, down to the supervisor.

In the climate of American opinion, this merely puts into practice the cardinal doctrine that merit counts, that greater material rewards should go to greater output or skill, and that the best man should win. Virtually every A.A.C.P. Team remarked on the continuous American search for, and training of, talent; on the ease of promotion; and on the close correspondence between responsibilities and rewards. Some Teams—and many more observers—emphasized the advantages of the much longer period of formal education in America, and the much wider availability and use of university education. It provides a greater proportion of recruits for higher posts in industry, and for industry as a whole.

The American educational system and its facilities, arrangements within industry itself for training and promotion—these and other factors have influenced the attitudes of American workpeople and union leaders as well as those of managements to the calculation and grading of rewards. In the more rapidly varying industrial life of America—in an atmosphere of changing skills and specialisms, changing jobs, changing lay-outs of work and works—the opportunities, and the commensurately varying rewards, are greater. There is, in fact, more opportunity for the worker to rise in an American firm. The belief is therefore widespread that anyone *can* rise. And it is a small step from this to the general desire to 'get on,' which is so potent a stimulus in American life. When it is clearly so possible to 'get on,' it is not surprising that everybody—that in fact the entire nation—does 'get on.'[1]

(2) *Efficiency of work is more directly rewarded in America.*

This means a closer correspondence between rates of pay and duties, jobs, etc., both in management and manual work. We saw earlier that American management not only devolves responsibilities more, but defines duties more closely and sharply.[2] As a corollary to this, unions and management—more locally, more firm by firm, than in Britain or Europe—carefully elaborate and work out jobs and duties, scope of work, and contents of labour-contracts. The rewards are correspondingly more particularized.

There is something paradoxical in this, because—on the whole, and as far as can be ascertained—there is probably less piecework, less *direct* payment by results, in American than in British industry.[3] The American trend in recent years has been an advance from payment for piecework to a guaranteed high daily or hourly wage, in exchange for a guaranteed task (job, 'standard performance,' etc.) which is more and more frequently set by the capacity of machinery. This can be viewed as the logical development of piecework, as the machines increasingly assist the human work. It is more and more frequently based on the results of careful and precise work-study. Thus, American managements and trade unions on the whole have advanced towards higher productivity—and have put up higher and higher record performances of machines and men in combination—according as they have refashioned the traditional piecework into an up-to-date version of payment-by-results. It is thus far more a question of planning the work beforehand, in detail; agreeing rates of pay for well-defined work; and then securing the greatest possible degree of team-work and of smooth, uninterrupted operations. It is in this

[1] See *Training of Supervisors* report, p. 5.
[2] See Chapter 2, and *Education for Management* report. See also Conclusions and Recommendations of *Food Canning* report, p. 69.
[3] The International Labour Office's report, *Payment by Results*, 1951, was based on samples of industry in the two countries, U.S.A. and U.K. The findings were inconclusive.

169

sense of the phrase 'greater *efficiency* of work' that greater rewards are more directly related to it. In short, as is right and proper, the 'greater efficiency of work' is a product of both better management and better work by workpeople. Both of them should share in the fruits. And under such a system, the whole nation shares in them.

The leading British firms and trade unions, industry by industry, have already begun to work out—with the aid of consultants or their own work-study experts—up-to-date schedules on which earnings can be more directly related to both individual and group performances, over and above a guaranteed basic weekly minimum.[1] But—as in so much of British industry's troubles—the problem is created by the mass of average and sub-average firms and unions; not by the fewer firms and unions above the average.

(3) *Greater rewards for more effective work in America mean more real income than in Britain.*

This is due to the British system of income-tax and surtax, and the big upward jumps by which those taxes progress. Almost every A.A.C.P. Team mentioned this.

Even after the 1952 Budget, British income-tax begins at relatively lower levels of income than in America, rises more steeply with rising incomes, and (together with sur-tax) permits a *maximum* net income only a fraction of the maximum possible in America.[2] A workman with a wife and two children (the typical British family) pays income-tax on a smaller money income than his American counterpart. He also pays more direct (income-) tax and indirect tax (on goods and services) together. The *total of taxation* takes a much heavier toll of a typical British worker's income for all purposes (in State insurances, proportion of local taxes or 'rates,' indirect taxation of goods and services and direct taxation) than the total

[1] These are the 'standard times and performances,' 'work-loads,' etc., described in the reports on measurement of productivity already cited.

[2] This is true even if one converts tax-paid money-incomes into corresponding *real* income levels by taking into account the higher prices of most things in America. But the important fact is that *all* incomes in Britain are more heavily taxed, however low or high, than in America; so prices and exchange rates have nothing to do with this comparison.

taxation falling on the correspondingly typical income of an American worker.

The American worker can logically turn to the British worker and point out that a big proportion of all British tax-revenue goes to pay for a larger amount of State services to the British worker. In America a good deal, or all, of such services (medical services, the natural cost of foods, the natural rent of new house-room, etc.) is accordingly defrayed from the greater amount of pay which is left in the American worker's pay-packet. He pays, as we said earlier, more for private insurance, medical care, etc. The American logically says that the British worker cannot have it both ways: if he wants the higher degree of *State* welfare, he must give up some *private* welfare to help pay part of it.

When all corrections are made for this in the public and personal accounts of the British people, it remains true that the toll of all taxes in Britain is higher in all income-brackets than it is in America. And the disincentive effect of all British taxes together progresses very rapidly above a modest level of living—say £10 a week *net of income-tax*.[1] Thus, since the war, among the minority of the more penalized higher-income-earning persons, leisure in Britain tends to become worth more than extra work. This applies to British managers, professional men, and technical experts. But at the same time the heavy

[1] See *The Levelling of Incomes since 1938*, by Dudley Seers (Oxford, Basil Blackwell, 1951). This, and other studies, show that the overwhelming bulk of 'transfer-incomes' and State welfare, defrayed from the Budget, has been paid for by the upper, professional, and managerial incomes. See also Table 14, p. 26, of the official Blue Book, *National Income and Expenditure 1946–51*, August 1952. Of the moderate ranks of civil servants Mr. Seers says: 'We can say that a Principal in 1949 could only afford the living standard a higher Clerical Officer enjoyed pre-war. . . . The real value of the bonus on promotion had also declined. . . . Similar examples could be picked from other occupations' (p. 60). By 1952 the 'differentials' between real incomes had still further narrowed. The redistribution of the national income by taxation and inflation has thus penalized holders of more responsible executive positions; it has not, however, swollen the national income enough to make this penalization unnecessary. To that extent it cannot—yet—be said to have created a productive climate of opinion. In short, as we saw, the national output has, so far, been redistributed. It has not been greatly expanded per head of population; even less so in proportion to the increase in full-time employment in manufacturing.

taxation (chiefly indirect) of the mass of the workpeople results in widespread efforts to earn more by overtime, spare-time jobs, etc.—or to make tax-free gambling gains.

These wide-ranging problems involve social and political doctrines beyond the bounds of this book. But one thing can be pronounced, since many of the A.A.C.P. Teams also pronounced it. It is idle to expect people to do more work when they are paid less and less for more and more of it. Even today in America—where there is as much grumbling about the burden of taxation as in Britain—the managerial and professional groups can maintain a material standard of life, after paying all kinds of taxes, which is two or three times that of their counterparts in Britain. That kind of thing is bound to make *some* difference to the respective qualities of management, the recruitment for it, and its performance in the two countries. Since in other walks of life human nature has not yet proved capable of rising beyond earthly considerations, it seems over-exacting or over-optimistic to expect British industrialists to be unique.

(4) *Americans can buy more things with their pay; more consumers' goods and services are available.*

This is a truism. It was noted by almost all of the Teams. But—like the unfortunate British workman's or manager's higher taxation—much of it is due to the British people's new post-war indebtedness: to their need to tax themselves to stop themselves from consuming some of the things they make, in order that those things shall be sold abroad, so that (in turn) a siege standard of living at home can be maintained on a minimum of costly 'retained imports,' and debts paid.

That an American worker can forthwith buy more things if he earns more, is certainly important. But in our argument it would be necessary to show that *all* British workers knew this, compared their lot with that of Americans, and were swayed by it. This is dubious. The majority of British industrial workers are roughly 20% better off, materially, on balance—taking into account State welfare, 'transfer incomes,' longer paid holidays, and even in purchasing-power left to them after paying income-tax and welfare contributions—than they were

172

in 1939.[1] They are more likely to be conscious of that than of imaginary comparisons with foreigners.

What really constitutes a disincentive to British workers under this heading is the knowledge that such things as *are* available are indirectly so heavily taxed. Few Americans—possibly few British themselves—realize the automatic, subconsciously disincentive effect of a war-time system maintained by British Governments of both political parties since war ended. Under that system anyone could drink, smoke, legally gamble, go to paid entertainments, buy a television set, and do half a hundred things without let or hindrance—all of them taxed from 25% to 400% of their wholesale prices. Yet none could legally buy any more than a small portion of fresh meat a week a person, a few slices of bacon, a knob of butter, some margarine, a bit of cooking fat, and 10 oz. of sugar. However hard Britain's post-war lot, such economic fantasy is not really 'forced on Britain' by external circumstances. Anyone who thinks so need only consider the imports of dollar tobacco and films, which could equally be imports of fresh meat and other foods; or need only consider the relative costs of food and other imports; the availability of TV and radio sets, entertainments (the modern form of 'personal services'), and many other symbols of a highly advanced standard of life—all of them alongside siege-rations of elementary foodstuffs.

There is, however, a rejoinder to the wonder with which the British visitor regards the full (and dear) American food stores, the other full stores, and the extent to which American workers can still buy in them: 'Raise your productivity, and much of this can be added unto you, too!' Few British people realize the *proportionate* magnitude of their recurrent post-war economic crises. They were all 'ten per cent crises.' Ten per cent extra production, other things remaining the same, and there would have been no crises, but a better standard of life. Even

[1] See Seers, *op. cit.*; National Income Blue Book, 1952, cited, Table 14; *The Social Services*, by W. Hagenbuch, in London and Cambridge Economic Service *Bulletin*, November 1951; and *Changes in Size and Distribution of the National Real Product, 1938–1950*, by Prof. F. W. Paish, L. & C.Ec.S. *Bulletin* in *The Times Review of Industry*, March 1952, p. v, particularly Tables 6 and 7. The figure of a rough 20% increase in material standard of living for the bulk of industrial workers in Britain since 1939 does not take account of easier work.

if the extra 10% could not have been sold—abroad—it could have been invested. Ten per cent ought not to be a magnitude of national disaster.

(5) *There is more leisure-time in which to spend money in America.*

In fact, there is and there isn't; it depends on the industry or occupation. According to the official statistics, basic weekly hours in American industry are about 40, and in British industry are about 44. The figures are, in any case, approximations—and differ only by about 10%. Until recently the British worked more overtime. Today the Americans seem to be doing so, and the British less. On the whole, because of its organization, American industry can afford a basic working week 10% shorter than that of the British—and get all its other material benefits in addition.

Americans are, as we noted, more willing and accustomed to work in shifts—which gives them more apparent leisure in daytime for part of their working lives. There is, however, an aspect of this argument—the leisure-incentive argument— which does hold true. It is a real (though perhaps sub-conscious) incentive. The American climate of opinion has a large element of belief in the fullest utilization of machinery, in order to increase human leisure: not the enforced leisure of unemployment, but generalized leisure by way of reduced basic weekly hours of work. The A.A.C.P. Teams ran into this belief time and again, expressed in differing ways. The common and longstanding American view of the machine as the friend of man, and not his enemy, has helped to bring about the remarkable reductions in hours of work in American industry during the past generation. It can be expected to continue to do so, since mechanization is accelerating. To that extent it plays the part of an indirect incentive to the greater efficiency and productivity of American industry, by producing more leisure.

(6) *Since greater rewards arise in America from greater efficiency on the part of the firm, department, or team of workpeople, the greater awareness of team-approbation and the teamspirit are incentives to better pay and better work.*

There is something in this argument; but how much of it

174

works *as a direct incentive* on workpeople it would be hard to say. There is overwhelming evidence from the Teams and other experts of a greater degree of team-spirit, team-awareness, and team-approbation in American firms. Whether it is an incentive to better work and pay—i.e. a cause—or whether it follows as an effect from the better pay and better work, no one can really say. But what none can gainsay is that on the average those desirable characteristics exist to a greater degree than in British industry, and that they greatly help to raise productivity.

(7) *The incentives for foremen in America are much greater —in pay, responsibility, status, respect, and assimilation to management—and as American unions recognize this, it becomes an incentive of management and of foremen to greater efficiency, and an incentive of workpeople to become foremen.*

This is correct; but it is only a variant version of the argument about easier promotion under (1) above.[1] It is impossible to over-emphasize the importance of foremen in American industry. They are the acknowledged leaders of the work force on behalf of management, the dispensers and awarders of material incentives, and the practising psychologists on whom the morale of the factory reposes.[2] They cannot be members of the workpeople's unions, though they have a union of their own, for they are part of management in American industry.

In America great 'local' responsibility is devolved upon the foremen. Their rewards are commensurately great, and they are proportionately greater than those of American workpeople, whereas the rewards of British foremen and the rewards of British workpeople are closer together. American workpeople manifest the common American belief—already noted—that the best man wins, and that the ladder is open to all to climb, by respecting the foreman's role and reward. For all of this the American management's careful system of search, selection, and training of talent is largely responsible. Little doubt was left in the minds of Team members that the incentive to become foremen—the open ladder to that position and to all others above it—is one of the chief explanations of the much greater productivity of American industry.

[1] See p. 168.   [2] See *Training of Supervisors* report.

Unemployment, Redundancy, and Incentives

Unemployment—whatever its cause—exercises a powerful inhibiting, deterrent, and disincentive effect on the readiness of organized labour, everywhere, to adopt methods for raising the productivity of labour. Nowhere has this effect been more obvious, more lasting, and—it may be added—harder to remove, than in Britain. We cannot go into the reasons for it: the long and unparalleled degree of British dependence upon worldwide trading, and therefore on fluctuations in world trade, currency values, and other economic upsets; the 'threat' of those upsets, wars, and other long-run economic changes to old-established work-practices, ways of wage-calculation, differentials of skills, etc. etc.; and, more recently, the persistent British unemployment between the wars.

Economists all over the world recognize many differing causes of many kinds of short-run and long-run industrial unemployment. But in Britain (and Western Europe) there has always been a strong undercurrent in labour organizations—industrial and political—of distrust for machines, of fear of 'technological unemployment.' After all, Ludditism and machine-wrecking was European. It was virtually unknown in American industry. Where craftsmen are so important, as they are in Europe, traditions die hard. When slumps in world trade hit Germany or Britain, most organized workers in those countries traced their causes to the impact of labour-saving machinery at home or in other countries, to the Marxian 'miserification' resulting from competitive capitalistic mechanization, to 'imperialism,' and so on. Principle and practice, faith and works, doctrine and custom are all older—and more closely knit—among European than among American workpeople.

Much of this British and European attitude to new machines and new methods stems from historical causes, as does the general European alliance between trade unionism and political parties. Much, also, stems from the more 'set' or 'jelled' ideas, beliefs, and systems of ideas and beliefs (ideologies, dogmas, doctrines) common to Western Europeans of all social classes and income-groups. Such systems of belief and practice are rarer in America.

176

It is, however, necessary for us to face one aspect of unemployment which closely affects our argument: 'technological unemployment'; unemployment caused in a firm or industry by technological progress itself; or—euphemistically, as the fashion now is—'redundancy.' This is not long-run (or 'secular') unemployment, due to worldwide economic changes of an enduring kind. It is correctly termed 'transitional unemployment': the making redundant of some workpeople here and there by new machines and new methods of work. It has, of course, always gone on: motor-drivers replace horse-drivers, railwaymen bargees, and so on. No progress is possible without it. But in Europe this 'redundancy' due to new methods tends to be viewed more as an immediate threat to livelihoods, skills, statuses, and therefore to the interests of most trade unionists. In America, as many A.A.C.P. Teams found, such a view of it appears to be less common—though in America the trade unions rightly insist on, and vehemently bargain for, their share of the greater fruitfulness of new machines and new methods.

The A.A.C.P. Teams also found that new methods and new machines can *create* new jobs. The Freight Handling Team reported:

> In several instances it was found that the introduction of mechanical handling methods at depots had, by agreement with the union, resulted in some initial redundancy of labour. In most cases, however, within a short time the turnover of the depot increased so greatly that not only were these workers re-absorbed but additional labour was engaged.[1]

The Materials Handling Team collected evidence that U.S. 'employees displaced by the introduction of new methods were generally, due to expanding output, absorbed into employment as direct labour in manufacture.'[2]

As we pointed out, American managements seem to have progressed farther than those of Britain and Europe—in and after the war—in the development of compensation pay for such redundancy. It is still the exception rather than the rule in American industry; but the growing frequency of exceptions shows that old rules are being broken. Compensation generally

---

[1] *Freight Handling* report, p. 43.   [2] *Materials Handling* report, p. 39.

takes the form of the payment of agreed sums—based on degrees of skill, length of service with the firm, etc.—calculated to tide a displaced worker over until he or she gets another job. Alternatively, as the Teams saw, redundant workers are often absorbed into new jobs made necessary by a rise in turnover resulting from new machines and new methods. Indeed, that has also been the experience among the minority of British firms and unions which have tried this system.

There are, however, peculiar British problems in this context. The blocks and hindrances to physical mobility between jobs and localities in post-war Britain reduce a redundant worker's chances of a new job, if the redundancy occurs in a locality on a widespread scale (i.e. if it is generalized); or the locality is dependent on one industry or firm; or the new machines and methods make certain workers redundant whose peculiar skills (or lack of any skill) unfit them for such local work as *is* available.

Secondly, individuals and private enterprise in Britain already bear the highest taxation in the Western world, part of which—roughly one-third—is for State social security and welfare. No new net charge for compensation pay—comparable in magnitude to the charge on American enterprise—can therefore be laid upon British enterprises. The transitional unemployment necessary to technological progress was always in Britain supposed to be borne by the State unemployment funds.[1] The charge upon individuals and private enterprises for Britain's present public system of social security (and, it should be added, upon most of the public enterprises, too) were therefore calculated to 'carry' both transitional and abnormal unemployment. Further, the State 'national assistance' expenditure (outside the purview of unemployment insurance) was calculated to supplement pay, strictly so defined, in the event of necessity. These charges are already, as mentioned, proportionately heavier—and the benefits better and nearer to normal earnings—than those of any other industrial country.

Thus, better provision is made by the State in Britain for

[1] See, most recently, *Full Employment in a Free Society* by Lord Beveridge, London, 1944, particularly the statistical appendix by Mr. N. Kaldor and the calculations therein.

transitionally unemployed workers than in America. Yet American private enterprise and trade unions (with less social security guaranteed by public authorities) seem able to secure a greater readiness on the part of workpeople—to a greater extent and with more frequency—to change jobs, grades of skill, work-practices, and even occupations. This anomaly has to be resolved if productivity is to rise in Britain. Yet little study has hitherto been devoted to the revisions of practice and procedure involved for the State, for management, and for trade unions in Britain if a resolution of the anomaly, and a rise in productivity, are to occur.

Are British unions and managements—whether in public or private enterprises—to be left free to negotiate compensation for all redundancy? If so, will not random discriminations and anomalies occur, out of mesh with what the economy requires? Can managements raise the wages of the employed, and make compensation of the redundant big enough, without paying twice for transitional unemployment insurance? And what revisions in the practice of the State itself are implied—both on this score and on the score of the State's position as the largest employer of trade unionists? We mention these questions only to show that the problem involved in any effective tackling of redundancy in British industry is complex.

We have already emphasized the A.A.C.P. Teams' unanimous conclusion: the need for new measures and new methods in British industry. These demand more co-operation between both management and unions. Such new methods and measures— for example, the regrading of skills, job-evaluation, work-study, the revision of wages-lists and new methods of wage-payment accordingly—are all interrelated. None of them can really succeed without the successful operation of the others. If only one of them be attempted at a time, the ensuing degree of success (in raising the fruitfulness and the rewards of human work in Britain) will be smaller than if they had been taken as inter-related measures.

So it is, too, with measures and methods of wider scope: a degree of compensation pay which is reasonable and possible, firm by firm and industry by industry; the degree to which the State and its economic agencies help to smooth the transition

179

of technologically unemployed to other occupations; the degree to which the education of the great mass of the people in economic fundamentals proceeds;[1] and the degree to which the entire nation's energy and sense of urgency can be invoked to create a climate of opinion favouring the adoption of progressive methods by both sides of industry.

The British solution of the redundancy problem may lie partly in the adoption of some of the latest American measures by both sides of industry—collectively-bargained 'length of service' benefits, so that no worker need fear to lose seniority benefits by moving from job to job; guaranteed periods of labour; specific forms of bonus-incentives; or compensation pay. Some of these American measures increase mobility between jobs, others increase skill, and all of them increase efficiency. They would have to be modified to suit British conditions. In addition, a solution of the redundancy problem in Britain, as a stage in the more effective deployment of labour and utilization of machinery, would facilitate shift working. It would need to proceed along the lines of British practice and experience. It is certainly essential to the maintenance—let alone the advance— of Britain's standard of life that these improvements should be made quickly.

Yet we must admit that the conjuncture of economic affairs in the world is not as favourable to the attainment of these improvements in Britain as it was when the first A.A.C.P. Teams went to America. The judgment of the A.A.C.P. Teams, as of any economist, is that these improvements —and the ensuing rise in productivity—*can* be, if British people *will* that they be, achieved without the exploitation of individuals.

Many will applaud a passage in the maiden speech in the House of Lords of an old, revered, and admired trade unionist in the middle of the 1952 economic crisis:

We politicians—all of us, in all parties—have failed the workers in one important respect. We keep lecturing them about the need for increasing production and increasing exports. We have ladled out grave and gloomy warnings; we have wheedled them. What we

[1] See the T.U.C. Report's recommendations (c) and (d) on p. 153.

180

have not done is to explain in clear enough terms just what the consequences of a real economic breakdown mean. . . .[1]

Pessimists would say that, after three economic crises in five post-war years, the only effective explanation of a real economic breakdown would be the breakdown itself; the only effective lesson, the experience of it; the only effective set of improvements, that which is imposed on Britain by force of circumstances. All the members of the A.A.C.P. Teams were, on this showing, optimists. They believe that by taking thought cubits can be added to a nation's economic stature; that co-operative improvements can achieve successes greater than those achieved by 'force of circumstances'; and that 'ten per cent crises' need not be the symptoms of a national decline and fall.

But when all that is said, it remains true that the reforms, improvements, and changes needed—in principles and practices, in manners and methods, in activities and attitudes—are far-going. They represent a break with the accumulated rigidities and encumbrances of many decades. For this reason they are unlikely to be applied on the scale needed unless they are both devised and applied co-operatively by both sides of industry. That is the overwhelming and unanimous testimony of the A.A.C.P. Teams. That testimony itself, be it noted, was produced as the fruit of a co-operative venture. It is a good omen, a happy augury.

[1] Speech by Lord Kirkwood, *H.L. Debates*, May 7, 1952, p. 694.

8

The Climate of Productivity

There is one refrain throughout the A.A.C.P. Teams' reports. It is that Americans—trade unionists and management, consumers and producers, politicians and professional men, men and women, old and young—are more productivity-minded than Europeans. They seem on the whole to be more aware than their British or European counterparts of the need to raise efficiency, to raise the effectiveness of machines and men, to turn out more goods, and to turn them out at lower prices. This is not necessarily a conscious economic perception. But most foreign observers of American life have pointed it out in the last seventy-five years of rapid American industrialization.

West European countries are amazed when the United States decides—as it did in 1950—to expand its industrial output by 25% in the ensuing five years in order to bear the burdens of defence and of aid to foreigners. The President's Council of Economic Advisers assured him that such an expansion—on top of a doubling of industrial output in the preceding ten years—was well within the capacity of the American economic system. That means an increase in physical industrial output of 50% between 1950 and 1960, or of 100% between 1950 and 1970.

There is no reason why that rate should not continue, either for defence or for civilian development. American industrial output roughly doubled between 1939 and 1950. In the last hundred years the total American output has roughly doubled every twenty-five years, and by 1975 it is expected to be double its volume in 1950.

By the side of these figures, West German industrial output—thanks partly to a large accidental increase in the labour force from refugees—has surpassed its pre-war level by 33%. The increase of British industrial production has been of a similar order: about 35 to 40%. These comparisons are, however, crude. Qualities, ingredients, transport, numbers employed in industry, and many other factors have changed since 1939. In no country are we comparing like with like over the past fifteen years. Nevertheless there is one measure which no one can gainsay in international contrast and comparisons: the *rate of growth* of the total physical output of goods and services in each country compared with the *rate of growth* of its labour force.

If we take the crude figures of industrial output in each country, and correct them by the increase in the numbers of industrial workpeople employed since 1939, the resulting rough 'productivity' figures are less flattering to Britain. Britain had a larger proportion of industrial unemployed than the other countries in 1939 and has since completely absorbed them. Its total population has risen by more than 5%. The total employed in manufacturing industry in the U.K. accordingly increased between 1938 and 1952 by 23%. Its industrial output should, therefore, be expected to have risen to a higher level than those of countries whose employees in industry have not increased as much as those of Britain did between 1939 and 1951.

Members of the A.A.C.P. Teams were obviously impressed by this productivity-mindedness of Americans and the ways in which it 'paid-off,' without any large-scale and enduring industrial unemployment. It would not be straining sense to say that American society enthrones material well-being as its monarch, and allows it to rule in the name of national progress. The natural questions are 'How?' and 'Why?'

(1) *American society is new, young, 'unjelled' as yet, unridden by hang-overs of the European class-and-status system.*

This is an advantage in securing the most rapid and biggest expansion of material output in a relatively short time.

It is often said that American society is more 'democratic' than British or West European society. Some Team members said so. But by itself this is a dangerous use of words, a misconception. De Tocqueville was impressed by the all-pervading equality in the American atmosphere 120 years ago; and all visitors to America have been so since. Yet in some ways British, Swiss, Scandinavian, Dutch or French society is more 'democratic' than American: for instance, in degree and frequency of popular control over executive organs of government, in popular formation of national or trade union or other policies, and in degree of popular control over matters and enterprises 'affected with the public interest.' In many ways, however, American society *is* more 'democratic' than European: for instance, in education and co-education, in frequency of political elections, in political election of the judiciary (except to the Federal bench), and in a stricter and more universal application of the merit principle. But when all this is said, people must still decide whether pure and unmodified democracy—for example, the political election of judges—is 'a good thing.'

In the opinion of most observers, however, the American advantage does not lie in more or less of democracy. It lies in the absence of aristocratic principles and practices. Throughout Europe and (in another guise) Russia, a certain hangover of aristocratic principles and practices persists. The kind of education which parents are able or willing to give, or accent, or birth, or membership in privileged groupings, or demeanour due to social status and upbringing, plays a bigger part in deciding a European's social—and to a smaller extent his or her economic—status than in deciding that of an American.

In American society—on the average—the reverse tends to be true. There is a kind of hang-over of the 'log-cabin to White House' myth, and of the national conviction (becoming questioned today) that 'there's plenty of room at the top.' A man who has made himself rich by making a better mousetrap is laudable and acceptable in American society rather than the reverse. American society has certainly perfected euphemisms to disguise more indelicate or menial terms ('casings' for 'sausage-skins,' 'junior executives' for 'clerks,' and so on); but these are mere wordy differences. The hard fact is that comparatively fewer Americans are looked down on because of their occupations.

184

(2) *American society is far more fluid than European.*

This comparison follows from (1) above, the newness, youth and 'unjelledness' of American society. The fluidity of American society was remarked by De Tocqueville over 120 years ago;[1] by Shadwell, who was comparing 'industrial efficiency' half a century ago;[2] by such authorities as Arnold, Bryce, Muirhead, Brogan, from the 1870's until today; and by the A.A.C.P. Teams.

A significant result emerges from the combination of fluidity in American society with the comparative lack of 'aristocratic' and other values of a cultural *élite*. (This is not to deplore their absence in America, or to applaud their presence in European societies, including Russia.) The fluidity of American society, the mobility of persons and positions, and the greater pace of American life, are not directed towards the achievement of so many other-than-material rewards, or public recognitions of higher social or other status, as they are in all European societies (including Russia)—with the solitary exception of the Swiss. We have more to say of this below. For the moment we would emphasize that in France, Britain, Holland, Spain, Italy, and Germany—despite all ravages of war and revolution—there remain distinctions of social status, of popular recognition, of public power and influence, for which people of all income-levels will strive and for which they will even (on the average and within obvious reasonable limits) accept sacrifices of income or of material standards of living. It was so in the break-up of West European society under the Romans 1,500 years ago, and it is so still. It cannot be said to be 'a bad thing.' It exists as a social heritage, an inherited set of human values. But it is not so—to the same degree—in American society; nor indeed in any society of Europeans in the newer and younger countries beyond Europe's bounds.

The outcome is that the greater American social fluidity, mobility, and pace of life—the greater energy and initiative—are directed *in a greater degree* towards the production and acquisition of more and more *material* marks of achievement, of success, or of distinction. To a large extent this single factor is responsible for the long-standing American philosophy of

[1] *Democracy in America.*   [2] Shadwell, *op. cit.*, Vol. I, Ch. 1.

'two chickens in every pot'—and its modern equivalents, two cars in every garage and two TV sets in every home. Such an internal 'booster' to the big American home market—a 'booster,' be it noted, of non-economic origin but of powerful economic effect—has always operated there. It operated when America was mainly agrarian up to 1850; when it was industrializing, breaking new farmlands, and building up towns and cities by immigration, between the 1870's and 1914; and far more rapidly since 1920.

West European countries have rapidly adopted more Americanisms in language, behaviour, and methods since the Second World War. European children today copy modern Americanisms as once their forefathers, when children, played at cowboys and Indians. Nations copy Americans today as they did Britons last century. These are mannerisms, ways of doing things. But it is also only right to recognize that *for European society as a whole* it is impossible to become like American society as a whole. British society, European society, can become something rather different from what it was—as Russia has demonstrated. It can adopt and adapt American *methods*—but not for American ends and not in the direction of Americanism. 'The men of the New World are new men.' Europeans are not. Even Russian society is old, and seems to be manifesting more and more of its old characteristics. All European societies are old. They cannot reacquire the social arteries and sinews of youth. But they can adapt, adopt, and alter. The limits, and the ultimate direction, of their possible changes must nevertheless be recognized.

(3) *The American population is expanding more rapidly than any West European population, and far more rapidly than American demographers themselves expected.*

Part of the expansion is perhaps 'a draft of babies on the future.' Young people can afford to marry earlier in America. They do, and they have their families earlier. The average age at marriage, and at which mothers have their first and other babies, has fallen rapidly during the last fifteen years. The earlier advent of babies, due to these causes, may—but does not necessarily—mean that the expanding American population will slow down later on; perhaps just as rapidly as the un-expected expansion has occurred. Meanwhile the American population has risen by 15% (or 20 million souls) since the war ended. This produces more consumers—and (later) producers—in a vast market.

In Britain the post-war baby-boom is past and the pre-war trend towards an older, stable population has reasserted itself; the population is only 5% above its pre-war level, and is virtually already stable. In Western Europe—apart from an unexpected rise in the French birth-rate and the permanent big excess of births over deaths in Italy—the same trends towards stability of population are observable.

(4) *American society has certain quite different incentives from European.*

First, it is more 'vulgarized'—in the strict Latin sense of crowd-conscious, mass-conscious. That is what is usually meant when people say it is more democratic. American pleasures, relaxations, play, are all things of the crowd, things shared *en masse* and more so than in Europe. Golf—as in Scotland alone in Europe—is a relaxation of the people. So are baseball (the playing of it, not the mere watching of it), bowling, fishing, hunting, camping, etc. Americans work and play *en masse.* This is a powerful factor making for mass-consumption to match mass-production. And it renders the American scale of advertising and selling more fruitful.

Secondly, both sexes in American society are far more fashion-conscious than they are in Europe. Fashion moves *en masse,* too. In Europe there are fashions for every income-bracket or level of social status. European men do not change their hats on the same day of the year. Nor do they affect roughly the same kinds of style. Their styles reflect their more widely recognized differing degrees of social status. In America even women's fashions are themselves more matters of mass-production than in Europe.

Thirdly—and this is perhaps the most striking *social* dif-ference—American men tend to take their fashions, the driving force in their careers, and their social life, more from their women than most European men in all income brackets.

187

Women are far more the social and economic arbiters in America than they are in Europe.

This, too, stems in part from the comparative lack of any aristocratic tradition in America, and in part from the greater equality of the American co-educational system. In part, the American woman—like all other women—does not like her man to fall behind the level of achievement of 'the Joneses': which is the real and simple explanation of the phrase 'keeping up with the Joneses.' But in larger part, the Joneses in America (who are the average family in every income-bracket) are, anyway, setting and keeping up a high pace of material consumption because of other reasons mentioned elsewhere in this book:

In the competition for a higher standard it is the American woman who is the pacemaker. In striving for higher wages the American worker has unquestionably prepared himself unto the battle, and the trumpet, sounded by his wife, does not give an uncertain sound. On the contrary, viewed from the standpoint of industrial productivity, the influence of the American woman is distinctly valuable.[1]

This role of the American woman as economic arbiter is no new characteristic. It was noted as such by Shadwell half a century ago,[2] and by Muirhead and others before that.

The outcome of all these mass-adopted, mass-adapted influences is to make mass-production—'the three S's,' advertising and salesmanship—easier. But they also supply, in a fundamentally unaristocratic community, the incentives to reach differing degrees of 'social significance.' Thus what the medieval and aristocratic hang-overs of Europe provide in a non-economic sphere, American society provides in the economic sphere. It is an American paradox: the widest economic differentiation of incomes is found in the world's biggest democracy, where there are virtually no social classes.

(5) *As a result of all the foregoing influences there is far more competitiveness in all walks of American life.*

Very naturally, therefore—since business plays a relatively

[1] *Internal Combustion Engines* report, p. 7, para. 13.
[2] Shadwell, *op. cit.*, Vol. I, Ch. 1.

greater part in American society—there is more competition in business. We have seen[1] that this much greater degree of competitiveness in American business leads to a much higher average of productive efficiency, through a much higher degree of managerial competence. All the Teams noted that managements and trade unionists seemed 'more on their toes' to turn out the goods; and this was as true of an industry dominated by a few units (automobiles, chemicals, aluminium) as of an industry in which the productive units were smaller and more numerous (light engineering, clothing, food-processing).

The competitiveness of 'keeping up with the Joneses' in daily social life could be said to be transferred to business. 'The Joneses' of American business are the go-ahead firms who set the pace of technical and productive progress. They get the business. The others have to keep up if they are to get any. The price of high American productivity is also high. High wages, high standards of consumption, high output, all demand work of a high order. The work may be made physically lighter by machinery, but it demands a higher *quality* of work from the worker, in concentration, dexterity or keenness.

Material welfare may not be the sole aim of human life, the sole solution of human problems, or the sole criterion of human values. It may be that—in an ideal Utopia from which the State has 'withered away' and in which all men live as brothers—competitiveness could also wither away; that production by the incentive of altruism would replace that by the incentive of fear or family-interest; that *lower* standards of material living would prove acceptable to all men, because the standards of *non-material* living were so much higher than they are anywhere on earth today. It is, of course, possible that mankind in the West would be happier with lower material standards of consumption, more leisure, less anxiety, and far more simplicity. But few would dare to say so. And it remains true that if an industrialized nation acted on that hypothesis, it would rapidly face starvation. Industrialism must go forward to keep going at all. If it stops advancing, it goes into reverse, into decline.

Even in the favoured West, the desire of the overwhelming

[1] See pp. 164–5.

189

majority of adults seems to be for more material things, higher levels of personal consumption, and higher material standards of life—if necessary at the cost of some sacrifices of leisure, i.e. at the price of more or better work. If it be true of Western societies, how much more true is it of the world as a whole and of its overwhelming majority of people existing at sub-sistence level! Moreover, more and more capital goods are needed from the West, to raise the standards of life of that majority of the world's peoples who do not live in the West. The times in which men now live provide no justification for thinking that in America or Europe we are within sight of an era, or an organization of society, in which we could afford to prefer *non-material* gain to an increase of material output.

Having admitted that, however, one has not thereby sanctioned an over-concentration on material things, on the material components of a standard of life, and on the material criteria of success. The material successes afforded by the American productive system have their appropriate costs. The overstrain on American executives is proverbial. Their high pay reflects that strain and the casualties caused by it. (Perhaps that is why American trade unionists do not grudge them their high pay! 'The higher you go, the fewer.') Moreover, the equally high degrees of responsibility, concentration, and competitive-ness result in an almost necessary narrowing of outlook. Before the man who incurs them—and who takes 'the cash that goes therewith'—is aware of it, he finds himself, unless he is abnormally lucky or well-adjusted, very efficiently treading a mill, in blinkers. That is our contemporary human problem of specialization and sub-specialization.

These trends are being anxiously scrutinized by Americans themselves. The end of human life, 'the whole duty of man,' should not consist of consummate economic productivity to the exclusion of all human and non-economic values. Americans will contend that they do not produce all their material well-being for material ends, but to save work and get more leisure; that they are therefore no more materialistic than others. There is something in this—though not perhaps as much as Americans imagine before they study the uses to which most Americans put leisure! The point in the argument is surely that material welfare *is* 'a good thing'; that there is nothing to be ashamed of in emphasizing our need of a greater output of it: but also that it is not 'the whole duty of man.' In a book on material productivity it seems right to emphasize this.

We must therefore conclude that the assessment of Britain's (and Europe's) needs in terms of both greater material and non-material 'goods' is bound to be the result of a nice adjustment. Their needs at the moment are overwhelmingly and undeniably material. But, as we said about 'ten per cent crises,' the readjustment could come about more quickly than most Europeans realize, once material productivity was speedily and substantially raised. What is dangerous and damaging to Britain and Europe is the reversed order of things: the attempts to consume the greater amount of *non-material* 'goods' before the minimum of necessary material goods is being turned out.

To Europeans, Americans seem to err in placing undue emphasis upon the material goods, and insufficient upon the non-material 'goods.' To Americans, Europeans seem to err in putting too much emphasis upon non-material 'goods.' To economists each society seems to complain about not having enough of the 'goods' on which it places insufficient emphasis itself.

(6) *American education places more emphasis upon technology—techniques, skills, 'practical things,' 'the everyday business of life,' ways of making a good (or better) living—and less than European educational systems do on the humanities and cultural subjects.*

This is a delicate and contentious point, like 'materialism,' at which Americans are always likely to take umbrage. The A.A.C.P. Teams as a whole emphasized the more 'practical' and technical content of the American educational system, from infant school to universities and technical institutes. It may be incorrect (or even, to Americans, insulting) to say that their educational system is exclusively directed towards material success, productive achievements, technical prowess, practical efficiency, and money-making. But in their educational system the teachers of the humanities and the cultural subjects are on the whole less well-paid than teachers of more 'practical' subjects. That is the very opposite of the British and European

191

educational systems. The American teachers of more 'practical' subjects also dispose of the overwhelming bulk of all funds for research, equipment, buildings, books, etc. It may be that in time the extra leisure and higher material standard of life, made possible by such concentration on technology, will create a bigger demand for non-material training and 'goods.' There are signs that they are already doing so.

One Team rightly emphasized the general role in America of 'a basic foundation in the humanities.'[1] A few outstanding American technical institutions actually include courses in the humanities for their students of technology.[2] And the pundits of European history, archaeology, literature, arts, and the humanities all over the world must now acknowledge their debt to modern American scholarship in those fields. But it seems idle to deny that, in a society wherein the influences enumerated under (1) to (5) above are so potent, education in the humanities is, on the average, relatively less widespread, less intense, and less important than it is in Europe.

Obviously this educational ingredient of American productivity-mindedness is linked with that of mass-consciousness (section 4 above), of 'the three S's,' and of competitiveness (section 5). If American society places too little emphasis upon the humanities, cultural elements, and non-material 'goods,' it was the verdict of many A.A.C.P. Teams that British society placed too little upon technical education, education of skills and aptitudes, and technology. Oddly enough, it would seem that in both societies the requisite corrective should be the same; namely, no far-reaching change in their *systems* of education, but a change in the relative *contents* of 'practical' and 'less practical' subjects; or, to put it another way, an improvement in the relative status and rewards of the teachers of these things, in equipment, in buildings and other facilities.

In Britain this implies the provision of more facilities in schools, universities, and technical institutions, and much fuller use of existing facilities for technical training. That involves more capital investment in these things, and more teachers. In

---

[1] *Education for Management* report, Chapter 2, 'The American Educational Picture.'

[2] E.g. the Massachusetts and California Institutes of Technology.

America, on the other hand, it implies the provision of more facilities and the fuller use of existing facilities for the training of the mind in the humanities. The two countries', the two societies', educational advantages and disadvantages, their excellences and their deficiencies, are complementary.

Here, perhaps, a caution is necessary for British and European readers. There was, at one period after the war, some danger lest observers of the American scene and system should run away with the notion that all Britain (and Europe) needed was to transfer the weight of educational emphasis from the humanities to technology. There was danger of a new educational disequilibrium—this time on the opposite side. Happily that danger seems to have passed, just when Americans themselves have been debating their own need to de-specialize and de-technicalize their educational system, particularly in its upper reaches. Thus, both countries face educational problems as a result of their economic requirements.

There is no justification for the widespread belief that a young person trained in 'practical things' or techniques is more likely to make a better Big Business-man or public administrator than one trained until the age of, say, 16 or 18 in the classics, arts, literatures, and humanities. What really decides that issue is the kind of brain and of personality which emerges at the end of either kind of training. A general aptitude for *all* learning—for swift changes of concentration and thought, for the handling of human beings, for the marshalling of manifold recalcitrant and disparate factors—is rare and valuable. But this aptitude is not merely inculcated. To a very great extent it is, literally, 'educated' in the sense of being 'drawn out from' the right kind of person to begin with; and only then after considerable experience. That is why systems of education are so important. But it is rash to expect the finest system of education, whether its equipoise is endangered on the technological side or on that of the humanities, to turn geese into swans. After all, changes in education—in its manner and method, in its style and in content—can only work out their effects on a whole nation very slowly. And the effects of changes in technical and technological education are likely to be slower still, unless they are made on a striking scale.

193   N

(7) The legal and institutional framework of American society was partly devised to maintain, foster and secure competition in business.

Not only did it do so; but it still exists and operates to do so, despite the obvious trend in America over the past two generations to form bigger production units.

The greater competitiveness in American business has lasted longer than in European business. It is important to note the effectiveness of this factor in shaping Americans' productivity-mindedness. All the A.A.C.P. Teams noted its operation in one way or another:

> In the U.S., cartels, monopolies and price rings, after due trial, were outlawed, so that real and sharp competition developed between firms, and this, to a large extent, prevented any major rises in prices. The unions obtained a high wage level. Since selling prices could not be raised, the manufacturers' only recourse was to organize their factories to the highest possible degree of efficiency.[1]

We have seen that in America manufacturers can, at any rate, secure profits and new capital to 'organize their factories to the highest possible degree of efficiency'; that the unions actually help forward this process and in its execution; and that competitiveness still rules the roost, whether the competing units are few and huge or many and small.[2]

The secondary effect of this long-standing legal and institutional American insistence on competition is that *firms and unions must use methods and measurements of competitive efficiency much more widely, and apply the results more intensively to both machines and men.* The more open competition, freer pricing system, and freer markets of the American system allow of easier and more natural measurements, and of more valid comparisons of costs, efficiencies, etc. This is in a certain amount of contrast to the much more State-controlled, cartel-controlled, monopoly-controlled, or trade-association-controlled markets, the competition, and the pricing systems of Britain and of European countries. The ensuing degree of

[1] *Welding* report.
[2] But on the trend towards oligopoly and monopoly in America, see Galbraith, *op. cit.*, and Stein, *op. cit.*, and pp. 91–92 and 106 above.

American competitive business, of work, and of pace, may be unpalatable to Europeans; but it certainly 'pays off' in material productivity, rewards, and standards of living. On the other hand it must always be remembered that British firms trading *outside* Britain are keenly competitive one with another, and with all other comers too! This point is apt to be overlooked by Americans, who do not depend so much upon foreign trade.

The effects of the American 'anti-trust laws' are often misunderstood in Europe. More recently—since Mr. Thurman Arnold brought them into lively operation again after 1933—they seem to many observers to have been invoked as instruments of Federal policy to break up very big industrial complexes, deemed to be too powerful. But their origin between 1890 and the First World War was in the public and Congressional anxiety to maintain competition and free markets in the public interest. The actual size of firms or complexes of firms, by itself, did not originally inspire the public or Congress with fear, as long as real competition and really free markets persisted. More recently, doubts about the continued persistence of both in America have been widely expressed, as the trend toward bigger industrial units and the eclipse of 'small business' has proceeded.

That trend, observable throughout the industrialized world, continues in America—though we have shown that more recently there has been a new trend to break down huge concerns into looser complexes of *competing* units, using methods and measures of competitiveness and of high efficiency to a very great extent. Indeed, more recently the Federal Courts have required separate divisions of big concerns to become more competitive among themselves. This means that the large automobile concerns cannot fix their own prices for all models turned out by their separate productive divisions, but must allow those divisions themselves to fix the prices to cover costs, and abide by the result in open competition.

Thus, what the 'anti-trust laws' and the Department of Justice succeed in accomplishing—together with the force of a productivity-minded public opinion—is to maintain competitive efficiency. Whether they do so by fear of a court case, or of an adverse effect on public opinion (i.e. on consumers) is beside the point of the argument here. The result is to render competitiveness, and its methods and measures, more effective throughout American industry. And we may point out here that—as part of the American legal and institutional framework—the Anglo-Saxon common-law doctrine of 'restraint upon trade' still inspires American law and practice. It underlies the Courts' great power over business, and offers the possibility of invoking their aid to secure fair trading conditions. It no longer inspires the law and practice of the country of its birth.[1]

This is but one example—though a potent one—of the effects of the legal and institutional framework of business in America. These effects are almost completely different from those of the framework within which British business must operate. It is worth noting that many A.A.C.P. Teams remarked upon this one difference, which goes a long way to explain the higher degree of American productivity-mindedness.

(8) *There is a higher degree of American control over quality, hygiene, etc.*

The legal requirements in respect of advertised remedies, patent medicines and preparations, manufacturers' claims for their wares, and trade or other descriptions of goods and qualities, seem on the whole to be about the same as in Britain. But the controls over hygiene in restaurants, food shops, and public places are more drastic and more drastically enforced in most American cities than they are in Britain—though perhaps no more so than they are in Scandinavia or Switzerland. And, largely as a result of the use of more 'quality control' and other special machinery, American manufactures and their performances seem to keep to the standards set for them more uniformly.

These things keep manufacturers and traders 'on their toes.' They set and maintain qualities and standards; and they stop competitiveness from debasing them. They are an interesting example of the fact that American manufacturers do not object to State or other regulations in the consumers' interests, as long as they apply to all producers fairly and equitably. They are an aspect of the American manufacturers' doctrine that 'the cus-

[1] On all this, see Galbraith, *op. cit.*, Chapters 4 and 5.

196

tomer is always right'; and it is significant that American manufacturers must prove their efficiency in keen competition, but dare not sink the quality of their products, because of the discernment of the customers and of legal compulsions to maintain high quality.

In this respect American advertising—by press and radio—exercises an important effect on productivity-mindedness; for any lapses in quality, defective claims of performance by manufacturers, etc., quickly come to light. The outcome again is to put and to keep manufacturers 'on their toes.' As much can be said in the field of capital goods, too; for although legal requirements of quality, etc., do not apply there, the sanction of public opinion among customers and of the maintenance of advertised claims is just as strong, and the legal sanctions against fraud or false descriptions are extremely cogent.

(9) *Finally, the American systems of taxation permit greater real rewards and more private saving and investment.*

We have already had occasion to study one aspect of this. But other aspects of it must be considered here.

First, the general American 'climate of opinion'—and the American constitutional, legal, and institutional framework—favour 'profits,' private property, and the accumulation of private and corporate capital. They do not favour them as much as they once used to do; nor do they anywhere in the Western world. But they still favour these things far more than any other system in the Western world favours them. Moreover, private profits from private enterprise are not as widely viewed as morally unjustifiable as they are in Europe. Relatively, therefore, the premium upon the accumulation of 'profit,' capital, and private property is greater in America than anywhere else on earth.

It is significant that one of the most surprising economic developments in America in the last two years of record peace-time production is the insistence of Americans on saving 8% of the vast total of their money incomes. No personal saving of any kind—except in Switzerland, Germany, and Sweden—now occurs in Western Europe, on balance. Dis-saving either balances or surpasses personal saving. The only *real* national

197

savings are done by Budget surpluses (forcibly taken from taxpayers) or by corporate profits 'ploughed-back' into the businesses making them. Both together are insufficient.

The obvious corollaries to this in Britain (and Europe) are that the State, through Budget surpluses, must raise all the new capital required for State enterprises; or that private enterprise must 'load' its selling-prices with a higher ingredient of 'profit' than heretofore, wherewith to defray the ensuing higher taxation and still to leave enough over to finance *all* its needs of extra working and fixed capital. In an inflation, when tax yields rise with prices and profits, it is even doubtful if enough *real* new capital can thus be 'saved' at all. While self-financing of industry in this way was always part of the process of economic progress and industrial expansion in pre-war Britain, a large sphere was left open for private saving, private investment, and private initiative by new businesses. Today, on balance, *all* new capital for private enterprise has to be found by existing companies, and is insufficient.[1]

The American system—firmly supported, under the 'doctrine of the concurrent majority,' by both political parties—thus achieves two things which are difficult for British and West European systems: (*a*) the lowering of unit-prices by rapid technical progress; and simultaneously (*b*) the flow of adequate supplies of private savings to accelerate technical progress by the 'trial-and-error' of new processes or business ventures.

Secondly, most of the A.A.C.P. Teams noted that the *real* rewards for human work in America were much greater than in Britain or Europe. The higher levels of British taxation operated—and still operate—to increase the amount of human work required to buy a radio set, loaf of bread, a dozen eggs, a bicycle, washing-machine, car, refrigerator, etc., as compared with the amount of work required in America. This penalization of consumption in Britain is of course also due to Britain's post-war need to repay debts, to re-arm, to export more, to develop under-developed resources abroad, etc. etc. The perils of inflationary pressure in Britain (and Europe), due to attempts to discharge all these burdens at once, are greater than in

[1] See Table VI on p. 126 from Professor Paish's study of British Savings Post-War.

America, where they are nevertheless great. But the only real solution of this British and European dilemma is either to increase output per worker (i.e. increase productivity), or to give up carrying all the burdens (or *as much* of them all) at once.

The disincentive effect of the rapidly progressive British rates of taxation on individuals is aggravated by the comparative disappearance of the old differentials of pay for better skills, for craftsmen's status, etc. The levelling of all incomes has gone much farther in Britain—even among 'the workers' themselves. It is therefore easy to appreciate why young men in Britain seem less keen on apprenticeship, why unskilled work is relatively better remunerated, why the old 'wages lists' are so unpopular, and why a gulf exists in the British worker's mind between his awareness of the national need of higher productivity and of his own need of a higher real reward for his work. Some of these problems are also found in America—e.g. the decline in apprenticeship, the narrowing of 'differentials,' etc.—but in a system with such high productive efficiency, the effects are scarcely felt.

It is only fair to point out—as we did earlier—that British (and European) workpeople stand before a dilemma here. If they want the State to provide a large range of new or extended 'welfare services' for them (formerly supplied, if at all, out of their own pockets) they cannot—in the state of post-war Europe—expect not to pay for them in higher taxation, contributions, etc. There are not enough European sources of *current* wealth left to tax, in order to give these services free. Capital-consumption, and a diminution of managerial incentives, have already resulted in Britain from present levels of taxation on individuals, and would certainly become more widespread if there were further taxation of the higher incomes. The extent of social welfare is already so great that it is the masses of European workers who are already having to defray the bulk of its costs. The economic systems of European countries can therefore only provide *both* the present levels of social welfare *and* higher standards of private consumption if productivity is raised.

We have shown why a swift and appreciable rise in British

(and European) industrial productivity must depend on (*a*) greater utilization of existing capital equipment, or (*b*) more new capital equipment, or, indeed, on both at once. It is only fair, therefore, to remind readers that at this point of the argument we are begging our own questions. It is impossible to hold out the incentives for higher productivity to the mass of workpeople until the workpeople have helped to provide the extra goods for themselves as incentives. Alternatively, it is impossible to do so until Britain—which is mainly the British workpeople—has provided, set aside, and made the new capital equipment to reduce the need of human work. The only way to break this kind of viciously circular argument is at many points simultaneously.

This viciously circular argument does not apply in America. Despite their enormous needs—and output—of capital goods, armaments, and goods to be given to foreigners, Americans do not have to operate within such cramping and confining bonds. They do not have to engage in foreign trade before they can maintain merely a subsistence level as a people. As yet they have not had to bear the cost of rendering a high degree of public welfare services—and simultaneously of having to offer attractive material incentives in order to bear burdens of defence, re-equipment, development of resources abroad, and repayment of recently incurred foreign debt. They can still, therefore, offer individuals the incentives of bigger direct *real* rewards, and to companies the incentives of relatively larger profits to be retained as new capital. It is idle to deny that these *are* incentives to higher material productivity on both sides of industry. Most A.A.C.P. Team members found them to be so.

The American worker—high executive or trade unionist—realizes, senses, or is aware of a direct connection between the quality of work and the quality of his standard of living. The British worker—high executive or trade unionist—is no longer as aware as he used to be of any such connection. His real income is less linked to his personal skill or the quality of his work than ever before. He cannot increase his real income as much as he could before by his own efforts, whatever he does. His private, personal capital is threatened if he is well-to-do, so he takes care to consume some of it while he may. If he is not so well-off, he does not know, realize, or become aware of the amounts he pays—deducted from his pay-envelope, and concealed in the indirect taxes he and his family pay on almost everything—for 'State Welfare' and other services, which he accepts very largely as 'free.' Yet they cannot be literally free in an impoverished country, hard put to it to maintain and expand its capital equipment, and with crushing new burdens on its back.

The American economy is still—indeed, more than ever—dynamic. Whether it is dynamic because its people are, or the people are dynamic because it is so, we must leave as an open question. But the residuum of comparisons and contrasts between the post-war American economy and the post-war British economy is clear and simple. It is that the British economy cannot really be stabilized. It cannot remain static, merely carving-up and recarving the same annual income; for that income will not then remain the same. It will decline. The British economy, and the post-war kind of society reared upon it, must progress or decline.

Accordingly, if the high degree of 'State Welfare' is to be maintained in Britain by both political parties, any increase in *real* rewards and in *real* incomes of management and organized workers can only come from an increase in output. It can only come from an increase—*over and above* the simultaneously-shouldered burdens of re-equipment, defence, development of overseas resources, and repayment of debts. Within this setting arises the title which opens the final chapter.

9

Nations Live as They Deserve

Our argument so far has led us through many a byway, thicket, and cross-cut towards a broad highway of conclusions. That broad highway runs among more recognizable and familiar facts. One of the most obvious facts—yet the most obscure in its nature—is the psychological factor: the climate of opinion, the social environment and the morale of a people. Clearly this is a bigger factor than anything purely economic or technological—though it acts on the economic and technological and is acted on by them. Here emerges one sense to the phrase 'nations live as they deserve.'

In another sense, however, no people now living deserves its present standard of life. That standard arises from the work, thrift, and skill of former generations—or from their lack of work, their waste, and their lack of skill. The Americans of today could not live as they do if their forefathers had not broken a wilderness, lived in zero weather in three-sided open-faced camps, worked like Trojans in wooden shacks, toiled to raise towns, and saved to raise cities.

The Russians can build a jet-engine, a tank, a loom as good as any built by the West. But no one knows how much those things cost in man-hours, materials, fuel and power, wastage and spoilage, etc., or how intensively they are utilized. The Russian system gets proportionately more capital equipment from its workpeople in exchange for much less of a material standard of life; it gets more and longer work out of them than do the Americans or the British or the French out of their people. Again, the Russians, Czechs, Hungarians, Poles, and Eastern Germans are using roughly the same *kinds* of machinery and equipment in all their factories as we are in the West. Yet their way of life, social gradations and organization, standards of living, and qualities of finished goods and services are utterly different from those we can show in the West. Thus the same means reach utterly different ends. The same methods turn out utterly different qualities. The same principles issue into utterly different practices. The same capitalistic system of production fashions utterly different products.

If a people lacks education, technology, skills, stimulating ways of life, nutrition, and energy (physical and nervous), it will have to 'put up with' a low material standard of life. If it lacks effort, it will lack goods—but it may have lots of leisure in which to enjoy (or suffer) its lack of goods, i.e. a lower standard of life. On the other hand, if a people is educated, technologically equipped, skilled, constantly stimulated to 'better itself,' well-nourished and full of energy, it will constantly raise its material standards of life—*and* (this is important) it will also constantly increase its leisure in which to enjoy those rising standards. So at both extremes of the scale of the world's standards of life we find much leisure—in the poorest parts of Asia or Africa and in the richest parts of America. Only the standards of material consumption, accompanying the leisure, differ.

What sort of society do we—in Britain—want?

We can have, roughly, what sort we will. We have lost our best-paying investments abroad—the fruit of our forebears' thrift which they refused to consume—but we have inherited a very great deal of capital equipment inside our country. We are still maintaining it by making and installing new capital as the old wears out—though no longer by personal thrift, and though on balance we are not expanding all of it fast enough to match the recent growth of our industrial working force and our people's demands. We can turn out from our factories candy-bars like those of America, or sweets like those of Britain; British or American shoes; British or American motor-cars, tractors, textiles, furniture, bread, and ice cream.

But in the end, however we organize ourselves, we shall remain for at least another generation or two—cataclysms apart—a people of over 50 million souls penned in a small and vulnerable island off the Eurasian land-mass, able to feed from its own fields only half that number. The other half must live by trading with other nations. Which half is which? Who is to decide?

No one, if we are to remain a democracy. If we are to remain a democracy, the whole nation must sink or swim together. We cannot at any time say 'You must go hungry' and 'You must emigrate' to any given individual or minority, without becoming totalitarian. And whatever we decide to do, as a majority, we shall have to remember two inescapable facts: first, whatever we do will immediately have its effect on our competitiveness in a cold-hearted, trading world—even if it is only by making a minority of us dissatisfied and less productive; and secondly, whatever we do cannot solely be judged by its economic desirability, for there are many other desirabilities than the economic.

Let us develop the implications of these two thoughts.

First, the world does not owe Britain a living. We shall always—and in future more so—have to earn our British standard of life in competition. No one need love us. In-gratitude is a more general human characteristic than gratitude—as Americans can certainly testify from their experience in the past five years, and as the British can testify from theirs in the past hundred.

Secondly, everything we decide to do in our domestic affairs must inevitably have more of an effect upon our standard of life than would be the case in any other nation. We depend more on world trading than any other nation. Whatever we do inside our own boundaries will automatically affect the output of this or that group of British subjects engaged in their differing walks of life, all of which walks lead to world trade. A fall in the productivity of commercial clerks or bank managers in Britain would be as dangerous to our standard of life as a fall in the efficiency of coal-miners or dockers. A falling-off in the effective skill of factory managers, accountants, financial experts, and economists is as fatal to us as a decline in the output of textile operatives, fitters, and farmers. A poor and ineffective government would be as fatal to us as an incompetent master-mariner would be to the safety of one of our ships: the officers and the crew might perhaps 'carry' him in fair weather, but in foul he would probably cost them their lives and livelihood.

204

In some countries it is perhaps possible to say that one group of the nation is, or ought to be, independent of others. No one ought to say that in Britain. Just as Britain is more dependent for her material standard of life on world trade than any other nation, so are her own people more *interdependent* than the peoples of other nations. They are a more highly industrialized, more internationally trading people even than the Americans, who still have a larger percentage of people earning a living from farms and primary-producing occupations. So the British, more even than Americans, have the biggest material stake in raising the productivity of their industry.

That is a joint and several task, for in modern industry the parts are becoming more and more simplified, sub-divided, and specialized. The finished product is becoming more and more the result of assembly. For the British this means more—not less—interdependence. It means more—not less—co-operation, teamwork, and more of a flow in production. It means that in order to survive in the increasingly competitive world where they must trade—and in order to maintain (let alone to improve) their material standards of life—the British must continuously raise the fruitfulness, the efficiency of the work of machines and men: the work which they all do to turn out the exports, the equipment, the essential expert and other services, the education, the skills, and the goods themselves.

If they do not do this, they may still survive. But they will only then survive at a continuously falling standard of life, or (at best) at a stable standard of life while those of all other nations, East and West, are rising. That means two things. First, it means the end of the British kind of democracy. As economic hardships increase, successive governments (and forms of government) would be forced to impose more and more material equality, with worse and worse disincentive effects in a more and more competitive world. And all attempts at imposing material equality suddenly in history have been made by dictatorships. In the modern world—pulsating with dictatorships—the probability is crushing.

Secondly, because of Britain's peculiarly large dependence on world trade, all other nations' standards of efficiency and of living would rise faster than Britain's. That would tend to

205

freeze British goods out of world markets. The *terms* upon which Britain could continue to do business with them would then probably worsen, since British goods would have to be offered more cheaply to buy Britain's vital imports, in a world which needed them less. That means an aggravation, for Britain, of all the other unfavourable and disincentive factors.

If any reader thinks these implications fanciful, or drawn with the fearful pleasure of the Fat Boy in *Pickwick*, let him look back five years and follow the course of the recurrent 'ten per cent' economic crises in that time. They occurred despite devaluation of the pound, despite a nominally high rate of formation of total domestic 'capital,' and even despite rising productivity. Then let him look at the rate of recovery of Western Germany and Japan, at the rates of industrialization in primary-producing countries, and at the persistent tendency of Britain to import more and more without being able to pay for all the imports. Let him add the even greater British dependence upon the sterling area for trade; the dependence of that currency and that area upon Britain's own domestic economy for its reliability and its soundness; and the narrowness and delicacy of the links by which the more numerous sovereign nations in that area (all of them industrializing more than ever before) are held together. Then, finally, let him add the fact that none of the advantages of this system, by which Britain lives and survives, can be gained unless she goes on paying her new war-time and post-war debts, which have turned her for the first time in many centuries into a debtor country. Her own currency and credit, and that of the sterling area, depend on that.

When all these pieces are dovetailed, the picture which emerges is that of a tried and tested people, but a people still talented, faced with an urgent and inescapable task of recovery, reorganization, and re-equipment.

Hitherto, recovery from the unsurpassed effort and fatigue of war has taken place slowly, within a new and widely welcomed setting of social reform. But the speed with which reform has occurred has spread an impression over many British people that it has somehow been 'earned' on international account; that it can easily be maintained and expanded; that it is a matter purely and entirely of domestic conern. In the British economy, however, there is nothing 'of purely domestic concern.' Everything done in the domestic field affects output or availability for export, repayment of foreign debt, saving and the maintenance or formation of capital, and the relative dearness of Britain's wares. No Briton works, or absents himself from work, unto himself alone; nor even unto Britain alone; nor does a businessman 'milk' his business unto himself alone; nor a farmer his farm; nor a professional man his practice. Similarly, the domestic way of life which a majority of the British people decide to follow may seem to them 'of purely domestic concern'; to be defrayed by a purely domestic redistribution of incomes, or taxes, or contributions. Yet any and every domestic way of life followed by a majority of the British people will necessarily and inevitably react on their ability to compete in world trade, from which one-half of their number— or one-half of each of them separately—is nourished. It will react on their system of taxes, of costs, of selling prices; on their system of incentives for greater managerial and operative efficiency; on the degree of utilization of their machines and other productive capital equipment; and on the rates at which these machines are multiplied, written-off and replaced with newer ones.

All of this has emerged—from byway and thicket—as the pathway of our argument has cleared. All of it is implied in the A.A.C.P. reports: in the experiences of those members 'drawn from both sides of industry' who drafted and subscribed these reports, after they had put the straight-edge of their valuable experience against American methods and practices. Yet the validity of their reports—and of their experience—gains emphasis from the facts we have tried to establish in the course of our own argument:

(1) *That there is no peculiarly American 'secret' of high industrial productivity;*
(2) *that the principles and practices behind it are familiar, but are carried out in better ways;*
(3) *that they can be carried out just as productively in any other country with good management, good human*

work, and good equipment, but to produce finished goods which need not be like American goods; and

(4) *that the only real problem of productivity is that of securing the degree of 'goodness' of management, human work, and equipment.*

It is of some comfort to the British people to point out that the problem of productivity just mentioned is common to all countries engaged in maintaining and expanding their industries, or in industrializing themselves for the first time. It is by no means merely a question of getting and installing the appropriate machines. It is a question of getting these, and then using them to the best advantage by the most fruitful arrangement of human skills and the most economical use of materials and non-human energy. If British readers have the idea that their problems are peculiar *by nature and in principle*, they are wrong. They are only so *by degree*:

. . . there is a trend toward what might be called psychological engineering, and part of it touches the problem of incentives, for management as well as for workers. Wage rises alone have lost some of their glitter, partly through the corrosive effect of high taxes and partly because, in a period of full employment, there seems to be a limit beyond which higher wages mean merely that people can afford to take more time off to go fishing. . . . Incentives for management are even more subject to the law of diminishing returns when wage increases may be nullified by the next rise in taxation. There is a growing belief that new lures must be invented if the necessary number of university graduates are to submit each year to the rigorous discipline required to create a manager who can keep up with the speed and competition of modern industry.[1]

Those words were written by an American, of Americans today, and of the American system and its problems: of a country with 7% of the world's people, turning out 50% of the world's manufactures.

Indeed, the British are not peculiar in their problems. Americans face real and grave problems: economic as well as social, technological as well as diplomatic and strategic. The

[1] *The Economist*, American Survey, May 10, 1952, 'No Limits on Productivity?' p. 372.

first reports of the Materials Policy Commission set up by President Truman in January of 1951 repeatedly emphasized the rapidly growing dependence of the United States upon imported industrial materials: the country's rapidly growing dependence upon the material well-being of friendly nations; and the *rate* at which the country's productive system is swallowing up materials, fuel and power, and equipment of all kinds. The Commission flatly states that 'there is no such thing as a purely domestic policy towards materials that all the world must have; there are only world policies that have domestic aspects.'

The problems of the leading industrial countries of the world—all of them in the Western half of it—are far more similar than dissimilar. The greatest differences between those countries—even those between the American and British industrial systems—are but differences of degree, and not of principle. They face the same problems at different stages on a common time-table. Britain is at the stage where the problem of productivity is of the most extreme urgency. That is all.

There are, moreover, consolations which can be laid to the British bosom. They are comforts, not excuses; still less, reasons for complacency. Americans told the A.A.C.P. Team which reported on the manufacture of cakes and biscuits that Americans could probably learn more from the British— especially about quality—than the British from them. Ships, fine chinaware, fine textiles, motor-cars, the latest forms of electrical apparatus, plastics, glass, fine printing—these testify in the remaining open markets of the world to British quality, efficiency, and reliability. The nation in which ordinary folk produced the inventors of penicillin, radar, the jet-engine, the builders of the *Comet* and the gas-turbine automobile, need not fear for its brains or its ingenuity. It has only to fear for its power of application, its quality of work and organization, its methods, its administration, its teamwork. These are not the most difficult—they are the easiest—deficiencies to make good. The consensus of the A.A.C.P. Teams is that they can be made good fairly easily and quickly, and that over-all productivity can most quickly and substantially be raised by raising the *average* productivity of industry.

But how? And what has all these Teams' experience amounted to, in practice? Has any of it been put to the test of practical experiment since they have returned to Britain? And what results has it showed? These natural questions deserve a brief reply.

What Good Came of It?

The effects of the A.A.C.P. Teams' experiences in America were wholly beneficial; but they were beneficial in different ways. For example, we have already stressed the unanimity of the reports. That is in itself a notable achievement in bringing representatives of 'both sides of industry,' in so many differing industries, to one standpoint and one set of recommendations. But it would prove fruitless if the primary aim of the whole experience, of the whole vast international experiment, were not achieved as well. That primary aim was to study and report upon those methods in American industry which could most easily and swiftly be applied in British industry in order to raise its average level of productivity. What, then, has happened in Britain industry by industry since the reports have been studied and discussed by the men who have the responsibility of applying the new knowledge disclosed?

That there have been marked improvements in productivity is shown clearly in 'follow-up' reports prepared by the A.A.C.P. The A.A.C.P. never sought to claim that those improvements stemmed directly or even indirectly from the Teams' recommendations. It is difficult in a firm, an industry or a nation to say precisely how much of an improvement in productivity is due to specific measures: to redeployment or rearrangement of jobs or duties, to different methods or rates of remuneration, to better social or other conditions of work, to more or better use of mechanical equipment, or to better managerial skill. Similarly, it is impossible to discriminate clearly between action taken because of a productivity report and what has happened as a part of normal development in the post-war period. In any case, there is no need for discrimination. What matters is that productivity should increase. And, clearly, it is increasing in many firms—though, as yet, not nearly fast enough, and not sufficiently widely over industry as a whole—as new influences from America and elsewhere are infused into British thought, practice, and development.

One of the most striking examples of the A.A.C.P. Teams' contribution to the post-war raising of productivity is found in the *Cotton Spinning* and *Doubling* sections of the textile industry. The spinners and doublers each sent a Team to America. A special sub-committee set up by the Federation of Master Cotton Spinners' Associations to follow up the two reports was able to record, within two years' of their publication, such results as these:

(1) The original reports gave the required impetus to managements and unions to tackle together the problem of raising average productivity.

(2) The use and application of work-study has greatly expanded, the number of mills using it as a measurement having risen from 84 in 1949 to 141 in 1952 (30% of all mills).

(3) Increases in productivity reported from individual mills included one of 130% in output per man-hour in 'beaming,' and 50% in the 'ring-room,' due to new uses of machines; and of 30% in the card-room and ring-room (with a fall of 14% in carding costs and of 10% in spinning costs) due to the use and application of work-study.

(4) The Cotton Board and the various technical institutions in the cotton industry have co-operated in developing the principles and practice of work-study for the industry.

(5) Two British firms have begun to make 'travelling overhead cleaners' under licence from America since the Spinning Team drew attention to their advantages.

We have chosen this as our main example because it is an old, traditional industry, and because the developments in that industry clearly show how management and unions, working together, can successfully strike out new lines of thought and action.

A few other sketches will show the kind of result that can be achieved in a productivity-conscious firm or industry when new or better methods are introduced.

First we can take *Steel Founding*. Increased mechanization and use of conveyors in foundries making light castings, increased use of sandslingers in jobbing and heavy foundries, and closer attention to methods of servicing moulders, to handling, layout, and to getting a flow-line of work—all this has paid a handsome dividend in terms of higher output per man-hour and man-week. Some foundries have increased their productivity as a whole by as much as 30%. The figures for individual foundry operations are even more striking. The introduction of machine moulding, for example, has brought increases ranging up to 40%.

In the *Grey Ironfounding* industry, the work of the moulder and coremaker (on whom the level of output in the foundry depends) has been made more effective in several ways—by provision of mechanical aids, by simplifying jobs or methods, and by standardization of moulding boxes. One foundry has increased its output per moulder/coremaker a year from 42 tons to 70 tons, an increase in productivity of $66\frac{2}{3}\%$. Another has increased its output from 5 tons to 15 tons a week without increasing its direct labour. This represents an increase in the productivity of direct production workers of 87·5%

In *Drop Forging* the focal point of production is the drop-hammer. In general, the size of hammer teams has been increased, and forges have been able to report up to 80% utilization of hammer blows, and up to 40% increases in the output per man-hour of hammer-men as a result.

In the *Internal Combustion Engine* industry (which receives the finished products of drop forge and foundry as its raw material) one firm has quadrupled its output of connecting-rods and big-end bearings by setting up a special department and tooling-up a range of machines for machining them. The machining time for big-end bearings has been reduced by 42%, and for connecting-rod bolts by 50%. At another firm the output was 300 cylinders a week before the war, 100 immediately after the war, 800 in 1948, and has since reached 2,000.

Engine output has correspondingly expanded, with nothing like an equivalent increase in man-power.

The *Internal Combustion Engine* industry passes its products to, among others, the *Diesel Locomotive* builders. The recommendations in the Diesel report which created most impression are those on unit construction and welding. The industry is rapidly extending unit construction of gear boxes, frames, superstructures, auxiliary assemblies, cabs, and wheels; and several firms have reduced erection time to *a matter of a few hours*. Again, welding has saved time in manufacture as unit construction has saved time in erection.

A number of Teams representing consumer goods manufacture—*clothing, hosiery, footwear, furniture*—found their industries entering a recession in trade soon after their return to Britain. When firms cannot sell all the goods they are producing, the need to increase productivity is often lost on managements and workers (though in fact it is no less a need, and both for the firm's and the nation's interest it is generally greater). Yet at least one British furniture manufacturer has been thoroughly reorganizing his methods since the Furniture Team's visit. A company making shoes, although not adopting any specifically American ideas, has nevertheless been inspired to make a very large number of improvements in its manufacturing methods. A hosiery company has decided to specialize on women's fully-fashioned stockings, to equip itself with new machinery, and improve its production engineering and quality control. Several hosiery and clothing manufacturers have adopted one of the American flow methods of making up garments. One hosiery company has increased its output of certain underwear by 25% as a result. A company making men's clothing has increased the output of the whole factory by 10% since 1949 by improvements in methods and extension of piece-rate working which entailed no significant increase in employees.

Finally, the *Electricity Supply* industry. Power, as was emphasized in earlier chapters, is the foundation stone of increased productivity in industry. In Britain, inability to meet peak loads has been the main problem. In keeping with its Team's comments on selective development, the *Electricity*

213

Supply industry, aside from its basic task of building more power stations, has been investigating the effect of various kinds of consumption and of appliances on peak demand. This was to find out how far *control* of the load may be practicable, to avoid load-shedding and power-cuts. Encouraging consumers to buy one type of equipment or to use electricity for one purpose (e.g. lighting) and discouraging them from using electricity for another (e.g. cooking) is, of course, very indirect control; but it can be effective as a means of avoiding high peak loads at certain times.

Some of the foregoing may seem wreathed in technical mysticism; but not, surely, in statistical mysticism. Figures of higher output and productivity speak for themselves in the plainest of language. Behind those figures are certain supreme factors: better planning, better organization, better distribution of labour, better (and more) use of machines—in short, better management.

A further example can be quoted from an industry which did not send a Team to America. The brick-making industry in Britain has been short of labour for over ten years. In 1951 it reached a total output only five-sixths of its pre-war volume. But the London Brick Company—which is responsible for about 30% of the country's output of bricks—that year, on a number of days, managed to recapture its pre-war daily output with 800 fewer workers, and therefore with a gain of 17% in productivity over the 1938 figure. This was obtained by much more mechanization, especially of operations involving handling of bricks, which lightened the load of the labour employed. The increase in mechanization offset the reduction in human labour available.[1]

But one lesson of this advance in productivity was emphasized: 'the more highly a factory is mechanized, the more it is dependent upon having its full labour complement.'[2] This means that when there is a relatively smaller force of more specialized workers, the loss or absence of a very few of them, at a few key points, 'will reduce the output of a heavily mechanized plant by disastrous proportions.'[3] Thus two points

[1] The London Brick Co. Ltd., Annual Report, May 29, 1952.
[2] Chairman's Report, May 29, 1952.   [3] *Ibid.*

emerge from the greater mechanization and the redeployment of work and workers: (*a*) the resultant increase in productivity can be big enough to guarantee higher pay to the workpeople, lighter work, and steadier work of a more specialized kind; but (*b*) if these benefits are to be secured, either more capital is required, or the capital as a whole must be more fully and steadily utilized—i.e. by rearrangement of work, a shift system, or some other method. This is merely the practical expression of the principles we examined in earlier chapters.

Many such interim or progress reports could be made of other industries—fertilizers, farming, printing, pressed metals, food canning, pharmaceuticals, and so on. The various Teams' reports, summaries of them, conferences on them, and discussions about them—in which the Team members 'on both sides of industry' took part—spread the collective experiences of each Team through the industries concerned, and through related industries which had not sent Teams to America. Further, this experience was taken up as raw material by other bodies—by trade associations, trade unions, and the professional organizations of accountants, production engineers, personnel managers, industrial psychologists and others—in such a way that the technical implications for British industries and firms were (and indeed are still being) thrashed out, from all angles and standpoints.

This is as true of the specialist reports—which deal with subjects common to industry as a whole, such as Materials Handling, Management Accounting, Simplification and Training—as it is of the productivity reports which refer to specific industries. The number of discussions which have been held across the length and breadth of the country on the *Materials Handling* and *Management Accounting* reports, two of the best-sellers in the A.A.C.P. series, has been exceptional. This was partly due to the pioneering work of the Team members themselves, but it is also indicative of industry's awakened interest in (*a*) the extent to which efficient handling of materials can save effort, time, and money, and (*b*) the importance of costing and accounting methods as tools for day-to-day control of operations, as well as for the fixing of targets.

The leaven has quickly begun to work in the lump. No one

215

whose everyday business takes him into all these industries and professional circles can escape the sense of its working. But difficulties and obstacles remain. Most of them are mentioned in this book. To be fair we will mention others in the setting of the cotton spinning and doubling sections of the textile industry, of which we cited some very favourable interim results on page 211.

First, then, despite a governmental subsidy of 25% for capital re-equipment in that industry, it has been economically impossible for some firms to re-equip owing to difficulties raised by some of the workers about the proposed rearrangement of work. The ignorance of such workers about the effects of the economies involved in redeployment is unfortunately often matched by ignorance of managements about costing and other managerial techniques. As in so many sub-average cases, there are faults on 'both sides.' Neither side makes clear to the other what its chief concern and its aims are; and a good case goes by default in bad preparation or presentation. Here is what the cotton spinning and doubling progress report said:

since very many of these improvements to spinning and doubling machines result in reducing work performed while the machines are running, the full gain is not obtained unless the operative minds more machines than before.

The Times, commenting upon this, put the problem in a nutshell:

It is almost fair to say that at this stage re-equipment and improvement of machinery are not primarily technical problems. They depend first on training in proper methods of work-study, secondly, on applying these in such a way as to break down the worker's psychological abhorrence of the man with the stop-watch, and thirdly, on negotiating the redistribution of workers—which may mean anything from another machine a man to a second shift. . . . At every level success or failure in winning labour's confidence are [*sic*] paramount; and they [*sic*] seem to vary widely.[1]

Secondly, some firms can succeed in one of their factories and fail in another—probably for the human reasons just mentioned. (One anonymous firm cites that very experience in

[1] *The Times*, June 23, 1952.

the cotton progress report.) Lever Brothers and Courtaulds—two of the biggest British concerns—had the same experience, when comparing productivity figures for different factories making the same things. It was not *necessarily* the factory with the newest machinery which showed the best result.[1] Machines are but one vital factor in the productivity equation; men are just as vital; and the most efficient combination of the two is the most vital factor of all. This has a notable bearing upon the question 'What sort of society do we want?'

The condition—one can call it the cost—of a rise in the average of British industrial productivity must be an increase in mobility, in adaptability, in fluidity, in flexibility: the more so because of the far greater British dependence upon world trade, and of the far greater interdependence of British industries themselves in consequence.[2] The old British hangovers of rigidity, immobility, and guaranteed stability stem from a time when British society could afford waste and leakages at the seams and joints. It cannot afford waste today. We showed in Chapter 1 what an over-all moderate rise in British productivity would contribute to solve Britain's postwar problems: problems of defence, the maintenance and extension of State welfare, more incentives to 'both sides of industry,' development of overseas resources, repayment of new debts, and re-equipment of British industries and services.

The A.A.C.P. Teams believe, industry by industry, that an over-all rise in industrial productivity of the magnitude required is possible, without increasing human stress and strain. Now, in the attempt to gauge what sort of society we can have, we must examine the task of raising that average of productivity against the back-cloth of Britain's post-war limitations.

[1] For Lever Brothers, see Sir Geoffrey Heyworth's annual address, July 27, 1950, *Productivity*, published as a booklet by the Company. For Courtaulds, see *Productivity Measurement in British Industry* report, A.A.C.P., pp. 10–17.

[2] Economists, statisticians and other technicians will find this aspect analysed in something of a *tour de force* in the Royal Statistical Society's *Journal*, Vol. CXV, Part I, 1952, by Mr. Tibor Barna, entitled 'The Interdependence of the British Economy,' on p. 29.

Limits and Possibilities in Post-War Britain

The repetitive 'ten-per-cent crises' in post-war Britain have all been crises of inflation. These acute attacks of inflation in turn have been due to simultaneous claims on the British productive system (from abroad and at home) to supply more than it was turning out. So prices rose, the balance of payments went awry, and economic disruptions occurred. It is easier to assess the possibilities and limits of raising British productivity by proceeding from one aspect to another of these 'ten-per-cent crises.'

(1) *Britain's economic crises must always manifest themselves at their worst in her balance of payments: her international accounts.*

Hitherto, in each crisis government after government has had to cut imports or stocks, and therewith (or thereafter) to cut the capital programmes of British industry. Hitherto, therefore, the chief recurrent problem has been to lower British unit-costs; to expand output; to transfer men, machine-capacity, and materials from home-market lines to export lines, or from consumption-goods industries to capital-goods industries (including rearmament). This transfer problem is essentially one of redeployment, flexibility, adaptability, and social mobility. It is a problem imposed on Britain from without. It implies that Britain is not adapting fast enough. The signposts of world trade point to the same conclusion. Happily it has become clearer in 1952–53 that the initial post-war era of sellers' markets has ended, and that British (and European) industry must be adapted to different needs.

Accordingly, no recommendations to raise industrial productivity can proceed far—in any practical sense—without recognizing that the task, like the problem, is both general and particular, both national and peculiar to every single firm or industry, whether working for the home market, or foreign markets, or both at once. It is both of a short-run and long-run nature. In the long run, Britain will only survive if she solves this problem. Her dependence on foreign trade, and on a sound currency for the sterling area, will see to that. In the short run, this or that industry can be helping to achieve all this—and all of them can be helping together.

(2) *The British inflation, caused by overburdening of the productive system, can only be solved by lightening the burdens or by increasing the productivity of the system.*

If it is to be solved by lightening the burdens, where do we begin? By what process do we allot the tasks or the sacrifices? By cutting rearmament; or cutting our domestic standards of living; or refusing to repay so much of our debts; or cutting re-equipment of our own productive system; or refusing to develop resources overseas? Differing politicians, social philosophers and ideologists have advocated differing cuts. Differing governments have made both different and the same cuts. Yet the crises recur.

There are many and great dangers to Britain's survival in all cuts. The only sound and safe solution is by increasing productivity all round.

There was, early in 1953, still 'full employment' in Britain, still more vacancies than applicants to fill them—though there was also a good deal of 'hoarding of labour' which prevents its mobility. The sound and steady maintenance of full employment, at a better standard of life, could be made more safe by an expansion of output and a lowering of unit-costs and prices. Normally, increased investment in new equipment would have offset the man-power problems, and raised productivity. But the cuts have already thrice fallen upon the re-equipment programmes of British industry. The fullest possible utilization of both man-power and machine-power is therefore more imperative in Britain today than ever. It is an odd productive system which has to depend for rearmament upon a heavy import programme of new machine-tools, when its international accounts are already unbalanced, and its re-equipment programme for domestic industry is cut.

(3) *The effectiveness of British work can be substantially raised, swiftly, without increasing strain or stress on workpeople, and with a modest re-equipment programme, mainly by better managerial and trade-union methods.*

This is the overwhelming—the unanimous—conclusion of all the A.A.C.P. Teams, and of all work-study experts, cost-accountants, and economists.

Before the war, Britain never had less than an average yearly figure of 1,250,000 unemployed. The post-war average figure was under 400,000 (after eliminating demobilized members of the armed forces). Today there are 2,000,000 more 'fully-employed' persons (after offsetting the increase in the armed forces) than before the war: an increase of about 10% in the civilian working force.

Thus, before the war, the British productive system 'carried' at least 1,250,000 'passengers on the ship,' as unemployed, at specially low rates of income and standards of living. Today, apart from the increase in the armed forces, the 'passengers on the ship' have been reduced to 400,000, at much higher standards of living.

But simultaneously Britain has increased the numbers of 'officers' on that ship—in the guise of administrators, public officials, and private clerical staffs—by some 1,000,000 or so; and the armed forces have been more than doubled.[1] So in the place of poorer passengers before the war there are now at least 1,250,000 more 'officers,' living at far better standards of life than the pre-war unemployed, which means bigger demands upon the ship's commissariat. (This is not to prejudge the necessity of these workers; it is only to assess the cost of them.) There is no way of increasing the number of the crew beyond its present size. Yet the ship must now do more voyages, turn round faster, carry more cargo, earn more—in order to discharge a whole lot of new liabilities to new creditors, and to cover greatly increased costs.

The only feasible conclusion is the same as that implied for the shipping industry of Western countries: to raise the effective quality of the work done by the crew and officers, by the dockers who turn ships round, and by all who use the ship in any way. In time—both in a short and a long time—the ship's equipment can be maintained, overhauled, replaced, and finally an entirely new ship built. But for the moment the more effective *manning* of the ship and its machinery is the obvious solution to the problem.

[1] The figures show 650,000 more in central and local government clerical and executive occupations alone. To these must be added extra staffs for new public boards and for new clerical work (P.A.Y.E. and social service cards, etc.) in both public and private enterprise.

(4) *British consumers can live in any way they want to support. There is no sacrosanct way of organizing work, industry, commerce, or the State itself. But rising standards mean raising productivity.*

There are more retail shops per head of population in Britain than in America: almost twice as many for most categories. That raises the distributive costs of consumption goods in Britain. British housewives persist in preferring to buy smaller packets of detergents; American and Continental housewives will buy much bigger packets, and so the cost of a given quantity of detergent in those countries is cheaper than in Britain. Is this 'the sort of society we want,' at a higher cost and a lower material standard of life? It may well be so. But no one has ever really found out, because no one has ever put the question to the British people that way.[1]

It is important that political '-isms,' slogans, loyalties, and beliefs should not be allowed to obscure one fact. *The peculiarly British nature of the problem of raising the average level of productivity is fundamental to all conceivable '-isms' in British public life.* (Above all is it so to Communism and all extreme Left-wing '-isms.' It should be noted that, since war ended, the most threatening admonitions to workpeople and managements to raise industrial productivity have occurred in Communist countries.) No British '-ism' can hope to succeed or endure, even by establishing a dictatorship, unless it helps to secure and maintain a rise in productivity.

Many people doubt whether the great mass of the British people—organized in their various political parties—have yet realized all this, or have yet been helped to realize it.[2] Others believe they realize it, but that the difficulty is over the next step after its realization. Yet one thing is clear: the British people cannot get 'the sort of society' they want merely by trying to stabilize the size of the national output; by carving it up and recarving it from time to time to suit this or that sectional interest among them; or even by a bi-partisan and pious resolution to 'leave well alone.' The world will not leave a more dependent, more vulnerable Britain well alone.

[1] See *Retailing* report, one of the most illuminating on national differences.
[2] See speech by Lord Kirkwood, p. 180.

(5) *The rise in industrial productivity required to solve Britain's chief social and economic problems is of about 10% to 15%, to be achieved within two to three years.*

If this rise *were* so achieved, all the ingredients of that 'recipe for the millennium' set out in our first chapter could be met. After greater productive investment at home and abroad, the standards of living in Britain could also be raised substantially—though, on the assumption of the A.A.C.P. Teams and of this book, the rise would come more in private purchasing-power than in publicly transferred welfare (the 'incentives' argument).[1] It could then be spent or (better) increase personal saving. Of course, the rise should continue, if progress is not to turn to regress; but its continuation would then be easier. There would be more productive capital, for one thing.

An over-all increase of 10% to 15% in productivity, achieved in two to three years, in the light of improved techniques, may be considered more feasible in Britain today than in America. The American economy is already at a far higher level of productive efficiency than the British; therefore technically it has less *potential* expansion in it, because it has already shown far more *actual* expansion in the past decade. Further expansion can come only from more capital investment. In short, an increase in productivity of this magnitude in Britain is more immediately possible merely—and mainly—by reorganization, better management, better methods, and better quality of work. In American industry those improvements of reorganization, management, and work-methods are already 'bumping against the top'; and in America—though some improvements under these heads are still (and always) possible—the bigger and swifter rises in productivity which have been planned[2] must now come mainly from heavier investments in new capital equipment. New capital equipment is also an urgent—the most urgent—need of British industry; but in default of being able to save for it and make and install it, the 15% rise in productivity can still be achieved by reorganization of work.

[1] The distribution of the 15% rise, as between exports and home trade, British income-groups, armaments and civilian goods, etc., depends on domestic and foreign politics; but unless the rise occurs, every one of Britain's strategic, political, and economic problems must become more intractable.
[2] See p. 182.

(6) *Such an increase in British productivity cannot occur without the maximum of joint, co-operative consultation between management and organized labour.*

Every Team has emphasized this, within its own terms of reference. It is true of every single firm and industry. But it is more forcibly true of the national problem as a whole. There is a potential British advantage in having industry and labour more centrally organized than in America: the more swiftly and widely a general campaign for reorganization can be carried out to raise productivity, both by management and by trade unions, the more quickly will it 'pay-off' to the persons concerned and to the nation as a whole. The added advantage, already mentioned, of better industrial relations *at the top* than for perhaps generations past, also needs to be widened and generalized *down to the shop-floor*, if the vitally necessary rise in productivity is to take place within the short time available.

But it is idle to pronounce upon all this without re-emphasizing the necessary changes and adjustments; the increased flexibilities and adaptabilities required; the re-alignments, transfers, and rearrangements which are so badly needed—in the national economy as much as in whole industries and in the firms composing them. Accordingly, with so vast and general a national problem, the nation as a whole must be made aware of it, as a matter of immediate personal responsibility. To that extent, the government of the day must bear a special responsibility. It must do so for ensuring the smoothest transfers and transitions, for facilitating special supplies of equipment or materials, and for making both the necessary industrial readjustments (and the financing of them) as easy is possible. What touches the general welfare should receive the widest measure of personal and institutional support, and the greatest possible aid from all public authorities.

Beyond emphasizing this we cannot go, without entering into politics. But it is right to observe that if the so-well-organized partners in British industry—labour and management—cannot ensure this degree of help from citizens in all walks of life, and from the government and other public authorities of the day, then Britain's prospects are grim.

The Conclusion of the Whole Matter

It is of help to distinguish between the immediate short-run possibilities of raising industrial productivity in Britain, and the more remote longer-run aims.

The longer-run aims are easier to define and discuss. The main aim is to increase productive capital equipment per worker in British industry to a pitch comparable—though not necessarily equal—to the ratio found in American industry. That involves the redeployment of workpeople and rearrangement of their jobs, between parts of the same firm or industry and between all industries, in order to secure from British exports of manufactures the essential degree of buying power, in order to cover British needs of foodstuffs and industrial raw materials, to discharge debt, to develop overseas resources, etc. It is linked to economy of human work by the more intense use of better machines. None of this can occur without greatly increased flows of technicians, specialists, and managers, who have been better trained. All these improvements should result in a better flow of properly pre-planned work through factories.

But one cannot define and discuss such longer-term aims of industrial policy without taking note of any time-table. In what order should one proceed at once? Which is immediately the more practicable path to higher productivity, the more profitable way, in the sense of being more economical of effort and of the other resources of the country? The course of economic events in the world, and therefore in Britain, between 1951 and 1953 is a pointer to the distinction between short-term and longer-term aims.

During 1952, industrial production declined in Britain; unemployment rose very little; and productivity fell for the first time since the gradual British economic recovery from the dislocation of war began (with aid from America, Canada, and other countries) in 1947.[1] In the same period the capital programme of private enterprise (and of some State enterprises) had to be reduced; profitability of industry fell; and therewith the one

[1] The decline in 1952 ranged from 5% for all production to 7½% for manufacturing. Unemployment was on the twelve months' average below 2%, as in 1949–51.

224

remaining source of new finance for future capital programmes was endangered. The 'hoarding of labour' by employers in many lines of industry continued; whereas from those lines, in terms of strict economic need, labour ought to have moved into industries better placed to maintain or increase exports.

In this third version of Britain's post-war economic crisis, therefore, the short-run measures for improving productivity were bound to revolve, in the main, about organizational improvements and the more intensive use of labour and existing machinery. At such a time it is no use concentrating upon new capital equipment, re-equipment of factories, and rapid or large-scale mechanization of operations formerly done by human beings; for these are long-term (though, to Britain, overdue and vital) improvements.

Immediately available are what can be termed the administrative, organizational, and functional improvements to productivity. These are the rearrangement of work, from drawing-offices and clerical staffs to the shop-floor; the improvements in pre-planning of the various flows of production; the economy of fuel and power, materials and transport; the rapid furtherance of the 'three S's,' from designs and ranges of products to component parts; the overhauling of sales and advertising; and the preparatory discussion and elaboration of methods with the trade unions concerned for the introduction of the longer-term improvements, like more intense use of existing machinery, or incentive schemes of payment for work, or the training of supervisors, and so on.

It is natural that a recession of trade should lead many businessmen, being human, to draw in their horns; to abjure experiment, initiative, and rearrangement. By the same token, at such a time, trade unionists naturally listen with less enthusiasm and more scepticism to proposals for regrading, redeployment of labour, and rearrangement of work. Defensive moods possess both sides of industry. Cautiousness easily leads to attitudes of 'wait and see,' or 'we'll sit this one out,' or 'leave well alone.'

Yet the time of recession is really the time of preparation for revival; and when a revival of trade comes, it nearly always finds manufacturers surprisingly short of resources—from key men to materials and machine-capacity—and unable to quote quick delivery dates. And so it is with a whole industrial country. With Britain in her present economic predicament, there is everything to be said for as extensive a short-run preparatory campaign as possible, in order to 'clear the decks' in industry. That short-run campaign would necessarily have to partake more of what we have just termed the administrative, organizational, and functional improvements set out earlier in this book; those comprising training schemes, rearrangements of work of both men and machines, reorganizations of the lay-outs of the production process, and reforms or overhauls of various functional departments from drawing-offices to adver-tising and from clerical staffs to storekeeping.

Nothing said so far should be taken as implying that the normal expenditures of British firms on the maintenance of equipment, and its due replacement with new machinery, must be cut down. On the contrary: a strong case can be made out for acceleration of this *maintenance and replacement* process, in order to offset the cut in the capital programme of industry as a whole. If the productive apparatus of British industry is both run down (by slower maintenance and replacement) and stopped from expanding in total volume (and normally it must expand in a progressive industrial nation), the economic apparatus of Britain will fast become out of date, inefficient, and non-competitive. As it does so, the pressure will rapidly increase to make the workpeople offset the running-down of the capital-apparatus by more and better human work—either that, or their standards of life will have to run down with equal rapidity, or some of both will occur. So even if the long-run expansion in the volume of productive apparatus per worker is temporarily stopped—in order to tide over a short crisis—the short-run maintenance and replacement of the existing pro-ductive equipment ought to be correspondingly accelerated. This accelerated maintenance and replacement of capital equipment should be added to the other short-run improvements of an organizational kind just mentioned. In that way, these short-run organizational improvements are likely to prove more productive: to raise workpeople's productivity more rapidly (and less expensively) than by the long-run programme of expansion in the total volume of productive equipment per worker. But they will not, of course, raise productivity enough to discharge all our commitments.

In brief: the distinction between the more immediately practicable, cheaper, short-run improvements to productivity on the one hand, and the more expensive, long-run improvements demanding much more new capital equipment on the other hand, is very useful in an economically critical period. The entire post-war period—quite apart from its three crises—has been, and still is, such a period for British industry. Accordingly—though this book must eschew politics, prophecy, and programmes—a time-table for measures to raise British industrial productivity could tentatively be made out as follows.

The year 1970 is a useful deadline, as until then Britain is bound to operate with an ageing labour force: even if the birth-rate rises from now onwards, the working population cannot rise before 1970.

(1) *Short-run, i.e. up to* 1956: organizational measures to improve planning, flow, and arrangement of work and training of personnel, coupled with acceleration of maintenance and replacement; and

(2) *Long-run, i.e.* 1956–70: development of the longer-run organizational measures in (1) above—e.g. flow of trained personnel, redeployment of labour, etc.—as more integrated parts of a programme for the substantial expansion of productive capital apparatus per worker.

One can summarize this brief sketch of a possible productivity programme for Britain by saying that before 1957 most of the immediately practicable short-run improvements to productivity could be carried out in a three-year programme: a necessary piece of pre-planning before the longer-run (mainly capital-expansion) programme could be begun. Such a division of a long-term productivity programme into short-run and long-run sections has the advantages of (*a*) preparing the ground properly in an immediate and less costly preliminary programme; (*b*) adjusting the greater, longer-term burden of capital-creation to the nation's greater productivity and resources, after the

227

preliminary programme has proved successful; (c) facilitating the development of certain longer-term improvements, out of the preliminary stage into the later stage (e.g. training of managers and other key-men, solution of 'redundancy' due to more intense utilization of machinery, etc.); and (d) allowing enough flexibility in the programmes to favour particular expanding industries.

In the successful working-out of both the short-run and longer-run sections of some such productivity programme for the country, every one of the means to higher productivity examined in this book must find its due place. The results of such steady and planned improvements to productivity would, by their very nature, be cumulative and accelerating.

Not one of these objectives is theoretically or practically impossible of achievement in Britain today. Not one would fail rapidly to improve the British people's lot. Not one need impair social security, State welfare, or the fortunes of an industry, a firm, a trade union, or a person—beyond a period of weeks or, at most, months. Not one need impose any extra strain upon Britain's resources—human and non-human. The attainment of every one of these objectives can be reduced to a problem—and not too complex a problem—of human organization, of methods, and of means. The ends they would serve need not be other than 100% British and determined by the British people themselves.

The Good and the Goods

What are the ends before human society? For what ends are nations organized? By what standards are those ends to be judged? In what dim 'middle mist' do politics, economics, and ethics merge? Is the raising of productivity—the production of more material welfare at less human and material cost—to be judged merely as a material problem? Or is it also assessable as a help in achieving *non*-material ends; to ethical, social, or even spiritual ends?

The task of economists, production engineers, industrial relations experts and psychologists—indeed, of managements and trade-union leaders 'on both sides of industry'—is often

228

misunderstood. They are thought always to be concerned with 'merely' material things, material welfare, material production, and the output of goods. They are not generally thought to be concerned with 'the Good' in itself, or with the Good Society.

Yet all these experts are forced by their everyday work to realize—far better than most students of the so-called 'humanities'—the limitations of humanity. The 'everyday business of life' of economists, trade-union leaders, managements, production engineers, etc., is concerned after all with human behaviour. Their business is limited in every direction by the intervention of non-economic, non-technical, ethical, emotional, and other very right and proper human factors. There is everything to be said against the misconception that trade-union leaders and businessmen, managers and production engineers, economists and other technicians of productivity are 'merely' concerned with material output, material things, and material welfare. They are concerned with the means to almost everything.

For one thing, they are more concerned than any others—and far more professionally concerned than the general public of consumers and producers—with the day-to-day effects of emotional, ethical, non-materialistic decisions and behaviour of great masses of men and women. These masses may be organized or unorganized, trade unionists or consumers, taxpayers or non-taxpayers, compatriots or foreigners, members of one political party or another. But their decisions and behaviour—decided by both material and non-material considerations—will have both immediate and long-run effects in the economic field, the field of material welfare and material production. Their behaviour, as a result of their decision and their impulses, will tug the economic and material resources of their society different ways. The outcome of these innumerable tugs-of-war, continuously going on, emerges as the material welfare of the society and its members. The level, and the progress, of that material welfare depend on both material and non-material considerations, on human decisions and impulses, and on both economic and non-economic factors. In short, material welfare is the result of more than 'merely' material causes.

229

Today, throughout the Western half of the world, society is in ferment; and it is probably just as much so in the Russian half of the world. The pace at which technology is developing in the West is already many times that at which it was developing a mere generation ago, when the Great Depression began. It is not just something vague and platitudinous—like 'science' outpacing the wits of men to cope with it. It is rather a question today of old-fashioned, emotional, traditional, understandable, likeable human beings—East and West, developed or under-developed, industrialized or not—standing on the threshold of developments which demand, for their fulfilment, the abandon-ment of many familiar and understandable ways of thinking and acting.

Will their society be a Good Society if they take the step forward, and abandon traditional and comfortable thought and practice?

Clearly, it can be—for the technological portents already show that a real alleviation of the curse on Adam's sweating brow is nearer accomplishment than ever before in the history of humanity. But that, by itself, is not enough. Man's brow might sweat less; but it might also wear the brand of Cain. Ease, material welfare, more leisure—these 'goods,' both material and non-material, do not make a Good Society. They only make the foundations for it. On the same foundations an Evil Society can also be reared. In the ferment of our time, we of the West have not paused to ponder the ends before us, the ways we are going, the perils of over-concentration upon means alone.

The raising of the level of a nation's productivity is but one of those means. It is not an end in itself. At any rate no economist would ever view it as one, for the reasons just mentioned. The raising of a nation's productivity could serve Com-munism as much as Capitalism, Socialism as much as Con-servatism, atheists as much as believers, ascetics as much as sybarites, and vegetarians as much as carnivores. There is no goal, aim or end before a Good Society which the raising of that society's material productivity cannot render easier of achievement: material or non-material aims, leisure for ascetic contemplation or leisure for sybaritic luxury, greater equality

230

with a higher level of consumption all round, or with more leisure, or with both at once. If humanity is capable at all of creating a Good Society, humanity will create it more quickly and easily on a higher level of material productivity than on a lower level. On that score alone the Communist insistence in their own countries—though not in other countries—upon higher productivity (to the point of the death penalty) is logical, understandable, and 'correct' as long as Communism is to be reckoned a Good Society. Granted the goodness of the end, the correctness of raising productivity to achieve it more quickly is beyond question.

There is no human society today—on either side of the Iron Curtain—able to contract-out of the problems and dilemma posed by the technological revolution of our era. There is none able to contract-out of the ferment of our time. Even America, a land of agrarian pioneers three generations ago, is now (according to the 1950 Census) a land in which urban dwellers outnumber rural dwellers by two to one. No country today can hope to stop the hands of the technological, industrial, urban clock—let alone turn them back. The only thing which can—and may—do that is such a cataclysm that lays waste humanity's cities, and leaves the grass to grow over them, as it did over those of the Roman Empire, and over those of Macaulay's and H. G. Wells's imagination.

To this extent alone, perhaps, is Britain bound to accept what is wrongly called standardization as her way of life. She is only bound to accept it because technological progress spells something like it. It does not have to be Americanization—any more than it need be Russianization—of the British way of life. The technological means, the raised level of productivity, the improvements set forth in our argument, are all capable of producing peculiarly British 'goods' for a peculiarly British Good Society, living under any kind of social system a majority of the British people wish to adopt. But those means, that productivity, those improvements *do* necessitate a greater degree of simplification and standardization of all the *methods and apparatus* by which the British way of life in the future is to be secured and served. That is all. But it is a big 'all.'

'The greatest obstacles to increased productivity are psycho-

231

logical rather than technical.'[1] We have to deal first and foremost with men, not machines: men 'on both sides of industry': men capable of achieving big improvements in their joint output of material welfare, quite quickly, provided they co-operate in making new methods work: men not needing to undergo stresses or strains to do so. They are ordinary people; the common folk of the nation. It is useless to rail at the few leaders of management, or the few leaders of trade unions, if the rank-and-file of the nation constitute the problem at which remedial measures must be directed. A better general 'climate of opinion' can help, but it cannot be the remedy.

To create the healthy social climate in which productivity flourishes—competition, labour co-operation, investment—requires the kind of revolutions that were [sic] forced on American business fifty and fifteen years ago.[2]

Fifty years ago American had Theodore Roosevelt's 'square deal.' Fifteen years ago it had Franklin Roosevelt's 'new deal.' Since the war Britain has had a more thoroughgoing 'new deal' than America: so thoroughgoing as to scare many Americans. Yet it has been but a framework of new national and industrial influences around organized British labour, around the new British society:

However important these national and industrial influences may be, it is those at works level and in the workers' social conditions which really determine whether productivity can be raised. The 'climate of industry' is a misleading phrase, for it implies that a single attitude can exist in workers' minds throughout an industry or even the country as a whole in such a way as to affect local productivity directly. . . . It is a truism that 'work satisfaction' encourages higher productivity, but it is not always appreciated that it also makes it easier for management to introduce changes to secure higher productivity still. Research workers have found—and this is the key to the whole problem—that operatives, shop stewards, and local union officials alike will accept time and motion study, relax rules limiting the number of machines to a worker,

---

[1] *Productivity Measurement in British Industry* report, p. 24.
[2] *The Reporter* (New York), October 30, 1951, p. 15, 'New Productivity for the West,' by Theodore White.

allow redeployment of labour, welcome mechanical aids, agree to upgrading of unskilled employees to semi-skilled operations—in short, abandon to some extent all restrictive practices, in spite of traditions or union policy, in a 'good' factory or workplace. In a 'bad' one their attitude can be quite the reverse. . . .[1]

What sort of society do we want? What sort of factories and workplaces do we want? Who are 'we'?

The answer—the conclusion of our argument and of this book—is neither secret nor self-evident, neither esoteric nor epoch-making, neither superhuman nor sub-human. 'We,' and the sort of society we want, are the British people—all of them, old and young, producers and consumers, engaged 'on both sides of industry' or not in industry at all. We want our society to be Good, to be better, both in material goods and in non-material ways. We differ in our conceptions of that Good; of how to achieve it; of one another's merit, or contributive worth, in achieving it. We must so differ if we are to remain both democratic and progressive. But just as it takes two to make a marriage, so it takes 'both sides of industry' to raise productivity, to make 'a "good" factory or workplace,' and to lay the better material foundations for a better society.

The social ferment of our time faces Britain with graver problems and greater challenges than any other land. Five years ago she took up, as the foremost challenge, and as her problem of No. 1 priority, the task of raising industrial productivity. She took it up under the economic leadership at that time of a great Englishman whose almost solitary voice before war ended warned the nation that its way after the war would be hard, and whose effort to bring the economic facts of life home to Britain's people achieved so much in preparing the ground for the raising of productivity. Sir Stafford Cripps sowed that others might reap.

Thanks to unstinted aid since then from other busy men 'on both sides of industry' and on both sides of the Atlantic, Britain has acquired, in a short time, a fund of experience unparalleled in her own or in any other country's history. It is embodied in a set of documents the like of which, on such a scale and of

[1] 'Workers' Attitude to Productivity,' *The Times Review of Industry*, May 1952, p. 11.

such practical value, has never been seen in the history of international and cultural borrowing. It has been established by British folk of one mind, for British folk of many minds. It has launched a great experiment, out of the experience of many experts.

That experiment is a manifold challenge in itself: to all those who prefer the comfort of familiarity and the traditionalism of the sub-average; to the timid, the ventureless, the despairing, the apathetic, and the mentally and physically lazy; to the people who dare not hope for the future—for any future—in Britain, and to those who dare hope, but dare not do anything to realize their hopes; to those in all classes, all income-groups, all political parties, and 'on both sides of industry' who 'couldn't care less'; and to all those, too, who care only for the present, come what may. All these folk, too, are the British people. All of them make the Good Society harder of achievement. All of them are being 'carried' by those who have accepted the challenge, who are making the experiment.

Those who have accepted the challenge, who are making the experiment to raise British productivity, believe that there is much hope, much promise, before the British people. But from now onwards, the foremost challenge to the British people is no longer the conversion of its leadership but of its followership 'on both sides of industry.' That means it is the problem of the whole nation and of particular workplaces; of the Grand Army, and of 'the little platoon.'

The task of the nation's leaders on both sides of industry is clear. The experiment drawn from the experience of experts has made that task in Britain manifest. But the moment has come when the entire nation in all its walks of life must realize that what is at stake is not the way of life of a few leaders. It is the way of life of all of us, the whole people, a family folk. In this problem of productivity, nothing less is at stake. And in that knowledge the alternative to success need only be considered to be instantly rejected. No one in Britain today can afford failure.

APPENDIX A

Broad comparisons of *productivity of labour* in manufacturing industry pre-war and post-war in Britain and America, appear as follows:

	Pre-war average (U.S. '38–'40) (U.K. 1938)	1946	1947–50	1951	1952*
U.S.	100	118	123	134	140
U.K.	100	95	110	116	112

The volume of industrial production in the U.S. and U.K. moved as follows:

	Pre-war average (U.S. '38–'40) (U.K. '35–'38)	1946	1947–50	1951	1952*
U.S. ('35–'39 = 100)	100	170	190	220	213
U.K.	100	96	115	132	128

Over the same period, average *earnings* (not wage rates) of workers in manufacturing moved as follows:

	Pre-war average (U.S. '38–'40) (U.K. '35–'38)	1946	1947–50	1951	1952
U.S.	100	201	220	229	235
U.K.	100	185	221	260	275

The series are not, of course, strictly comparable: identical industries or classes of operatives are not covered by the available statistics. But much more overtime was worked in the U.K. than in the U.S., thus raising earnings as opposed to wage *rates*, which moved roughly as follows:

	Pre-war average (U.S. '38–'40) (U.K. '35–'38)	1946	1947–50	1951	1952
U.S.	100	200	219	227	230
U.K.	100	155	175	194	200

* Estimated on eleven months for full year.

235

Over the same period retail prices (prices to consumers, including both indirect taxes and subsidies) moved as follows:

	Pre-war average (U.S. '38–'40) (U.K. '35–'38)	1946	1947–50	1951	1952*
U.S. ('35–'39 = 100)	100	139	169	186	189
U.K.	100	156	181	204	218

And wholesale prices (prices to and for manufacturers including both indirect taxes and subsidies) as follows:

	Pre-war average (U.S. '38–'40) (U.K. '35–'38)	1946	1947–50	1951	1952*
U.S. ('35–'39 = 100)	100	135	179	203	200
U.K.	100	180	230	315	320

These comparisons give a broad impression of output, productivity, value of·money and efficiency of enterprise and work during the period.

In each case, the figures have been calculated by the author from the respective sources, which are: for the U.S., the Department of Labor, Federal Reserve Board, and Statistical Abstract of the U.S. (the U.S. figures are regularly set out in the London and Cambridge Economic Service); and, for the U.K., the *Ministry of Labour Gazette* (wages and earnings), Professor Sir Arthur Bowley's figures in the L. & C. Ec. Service, the L. & C. Ec. Service and official indices of industrial production, the L. & C. Ec. Service index of retail prices based on the official National Income White Papers, the Board of Trade index of wholesale prices, and the post-war *Annual Abstracts* of Statistics.

These figures should not be used as absolutes, but over so long a period they do represent the only reliable measure of probable and proportionate trends.

The figures of industrial production slightly *underestimate* American performance, and therefore *overestimate* the British, in any comparison, because the American figure includes mining and extractive industries (which do not make as good

* Estimated on ten months for full year.

236

a separate showing as manufacturing) while they are excluded from the British figure (which they would substantially have pulled down).

The comparisons of prices will be misleading if no account is taken of the inflationary effect of the British devaluation of sterling in September 1949.

APPENDIX B

Statistics are deficient for 'capital employed in industry.' The inquiring economist can only use the rough-and-ready figures of new investment in leading industries between the wars, and the more adequate figures after the war from the National Income White Papers (particularly *National Income and Expenditure 1946–51*), corrected by indices compiled from the relative prices of typical pieces of machinery, equipment, building, etc., before and since the war. Further corrections should be made for the much greater post-war 'investment' in defence services' equipment, defence industries, etc. (since such investment does not result in trading); for the long post-war effort to make good the terrible running-down of British industrial capital equipment between 1939 and 1946; for the $5\frac{1}{2}\%$ increase in population (and a $2\frac{1}{2}$ million or $12\frac{1}{2}\%$ increase in working population) from 1939 to 1953; for the necessarily greater degree of maintenance and obsolescence; and for the readily observable—but unmeasurable—trend towards greater 'investment' in less directly productive equipment (e.g. office machinery, canteens, other amenities). While some industries (e.g. the automotive and coal-mines) have vastly modernized and increased their productive equipment, others (e.g. the railways, the highways used by motors, and shipping) have actually run down theirs, or (much the same thing) let it grow older. Professor Austin Robinson (L. & C. Ec. Service *Quarterly Bulletin*, May 1950) estimated that, if all other things remained equal, British industry would get back to the *capital equipment per worker employed in 1938* by the end of 1952. As we know, other things did not remain equal, industry's and the nationalized undertakings' capital programmes being once more cut back in 1951 and 1952.

The author concludes that by the end of 1952, if manufacturing industry and the basic (mainly nationalized) industries and services are taken together, there was about the same productive equipment available per worker employed as in 1938.

There is a discomfiting cross-check available on all this. In the L. & C. Ec. Service in *The Times Review of Industry*,

September 1952, p. iii, Messrs. A. A. Adams and W. B. Reddaway reach this conclusion about the real product of the U.K. before and after the war:

The comparison between 1951 and 1937 shows that the total product of the United Kingdom rose in real terms by about 20%; at the other extreme, however, the amount of real national expenditure available for purposes other than defence, when expressed per head of the population, was approximately unchanged. The rise in production [*Author's note:* not productivity] was needed in very broadly equal amounts to offset, first, the loss through the deterioration in the terms of trade and the reduction in the real value of the country's net income from abroad; secondly, the increase in the real value of defence expenditure; and, thirdly, the increase in population. The amount available for civilian purposes would show a significant fall if divided by the number of people actually at work.

As U.K. population rose by about $5\frac{1}{2}\%$ in that period, the rise in production of about 20% suggests a rise in *over-all* productivity of about $12\frac{1}{2}\%$. (This is an overestimate, since more than $5\frac{1}{2}\%$ more people were in work after the war—nearer 10%; and in any case there was an even greater increase in workers in *manufacturing*—nearer 14%.) Over those same years (1937–51) American production in real terms has more than doubled, and industrial productivity would seem to have risen by some 45%. Clearly in so big and quick a rise there is much room both for raising American consumption by 70% and increasing and accelerating investment in new capital equipment, which in turn leads to further increases and acceleration.

In the U.K., on the other hand, the annual service on the new post-war foreign debts, change in terms of trade compared with pre-war times, doubled defence burden, and loss of overseas income have left too little of total production available at home to maintain both a fairly high standard of consumption (equal *in toto* only to that before the war) and to renew and expand domestic productive capital equipment as fast as was necessary.

The above-mentioned authors go on to suggest, very approximately, that since so much more was taken from the remaining domestic U.K. production for defence purposes in 1951 (and of course later), and consumption was maintained *and even increased in 1951* compared with pre-war and post-war years, capital formation at home had to suffer. This agrees with common observation, the calculations referred to earlier, and the official and other figures (shorn of their inflationary content).

APPENDIX C

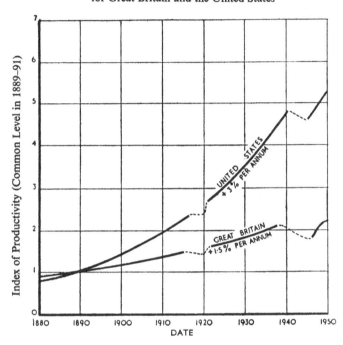

It is not claimed that the above curves are accurate in detail. However, the differences which are indicated between the two countries are so large that the broad lessons to be deduced from the curves are not affected by any changes which might be made within the range of uncertainty associated with any part of either curve.

(1) These indices represent

$$\frac{\text{Volume of total industrial output per year}}{\text{Total numbers employed in industry per year}}$$

relative to 1889 as the base year. The volume figures are mainly derived from the monetary total of industrial output corrected for changes in currency values.

241   Q

(2) The data have been derived from many sources, such as the British and American *Censuses of Production*; British *Annual Abstract of Statistics*; the *Economist*; papers by L. Ord and L. Rostas, etc. Where such data refer to hourly output, suitable corrections have been made to allow for the reduction in hours of work since the earlier years of the study. Information with regard to the first forty years covered is very sparse, but there is considerable general evidence that the trends shown by the curves are in broad agreement with the facts. The Paley Report (Report to the U.S. President by the Materials Policy Committee), Vol. 1, gives general support to the figure of 3% as the approximate rate of growth of manufacturing productivity in the U.S.A. over the past fifty years.

(3) The curves do not include agriculture, or non-producing industry such as transport. If these activities are also taken into account, and if allowance is made for the different proportion of the total population who are employed in the two countries, the industrial productivity figures are in close accord with the over-all average income per head of population worked out on current exchange rates. The figures published more recently by Mr. Colin Clark in *The Review of Economic Progress*, 1951, show smaller average rates of increase in productivity in both countries, but are in agreement that from 1889–1949 the American rate of increase (at compound interest) was almost exactly twice the British rate.

(4) These indices were constructed by Dr. R. Beeching, and were first published in a paper read to the British Institute of Management (Winter Proceedings 1948–49, No. 4), by Sir Ewart Smith and Dr. R. Beeching. I am indebted to them for permission to reproduce them here.

APPENDIX D

Altogether forty-seven industry teams and twenty-one specialist teams or expert groups have visited the United States. In addition, three U.S. teams have visited this country. The Reports so far published are as follows:

Productivity Teams
Building
Cotton Spinning
Cotton Weaving
Men's Clothing
Footwear
Pressed Metal
Grey Ironfounding
Brassfoundry
Non-Ferrous Metals
Zinc and Aluminium Die Casting
Valves (Steel, Iron and Non-Ferrous)
Iron and Steel
Steel Construction
Coal
Diesel Locomotives
Woodworking Machinery
Metalworking Machine Tools
Electricity Supply
Meat Packaging and Processing
Packet Foods
Cakes and Biscuits
Food Canning
Fruit and Vegetable Utilisation
Productivity in Farming
Hop Industry
Letterpress Printing
Lithographic Printing
Provincial Press
Rigid Boxes and Cartons
Brushes

Productivity Teams (contd.)
Pharmaceuticals
Heavy Chemicals
Furniture
Retailing
Plastics Moulding
Gas

Final Report
Final Report of the Anglo-American Council on Productivity

U.S. Teams
The British Cotton Industry
The British Electricity System

Specialist Teams
Saving Scarce Materials
Packaging
Freight Handling
Materials Handling in Industry
Materials Handling in Industry (pamphlet)
Productivity Measurement in British Industry
Simplification in Industry
Simplification in British Industry
Management Accounting
Metal Finishing
Hot Dip Galvanizing

Specialist Teams (*contd.*)
Welding
Training of Operatives
Training of Supervisors
Universities and Industry
Education for Management
Plant Maintenance
Fruit and Vegetable Storage and
    Pre-packaging
Inspection in Industry

Reports Forthcoming
Milk utilisation
Conservation of Fuel, Heat and
    Energy
Design for Production
Production Control

Reports Forthcoming (*contd.*)
Ammunition
Industrial Engineering
Maintenance of Automatic
    Telephone Exchanges
The British Pressed Metal
    Industry (U.S. Team)

Reports out of Print
Steel Founding
Rayon Weaving
Hosiery and Knitwear
Drop Forging
Internal Combustion Engines
Fertilizers
Electric Motor Control Gear
Cotton Doubling

The Reports are obtainable from the British Productivity Council, 21 Tothill Street, London, S.W.1 (WHItehall 1671).

Index